Great Displays for Your Library
Step by Step

Great Displays for Your Library Step by Step

SUSAN P. PHILLIPS

McFarland & Company, Inc., Publishers

Jefferson, North Carolina, and London

LIBRARY OF CONGRESS CATALOGUING-IN-PUBLICATION DATA

Phillips, Susan P., 1945–
Great displays for your library step by step /
Susan P. Phillips.
p.   cm.
Includes bibliographical references and index.

ISBN 978-0-7864-3164-9
softcover: 50# alkaline paper ∞

1. Library exhibits—Handbooks, manuals, etc.   I. Title.
Z717.P48   2008
021.7—dc22   2007047450

British Library cataloguing data are available

On the cover: Three "...in Books" displays: American Folk Art,
Jazz, and Flowers

Manufactured in the United States of America

McFarland & Company, Inc., Publishers
Box 611, Jefferson, North Carolina 28640
www.mcfarlandpub.com

To the memory of my father

Charles Plunkett

who embodied goodness
and cherished his daughters ... all four.

Acknowledgments

This book would not have been possible without my staff of student assistants at Cressman Library, Cedar Crest College, Allentown, Pennsylvania.

Karen Babson, '05, provided daily assistance and a critical eye which were invaluable. Her efforts to manipulate the original photographs used in the book proposal were key to obtaining the contract. Karen can also be credited with the swords for Whodunit, cranes and their arrangement in One Thousand Cranes, the saxophone in All That Jazz, the helmet, rifle and SHAEF patch in D-Day Remembered, the paws and their arrangement in Nine Lives or More, the arrangement of Lewis Carroll and Alice, the timeline in The Awesome 80s, as well as the parrot in The Mystery of Blackbeard.

Thanks to Patti Cilwik, '05, whose contributions included the Mad Hatter's hat in Lewis Carrol and Alice, palm trees for Hot Nights, Cool Reads and The Art of Ponder Goembel, cranes in One Thousand Cranes, and original tile prints featured in Day of the Dead.

Special thanks to Stephanie Nowotarski, '06, who was responsible for the ball in Baseball as America, the title signage in From Page to Screen, In the Garden and Women Worldwide, and the portico for Sage of Monticello. Stephanie also contributed to the overall layout for Celebrate the New Year, Tales of Horror, Wild, Wild West, Italia, Jewish-American Authors and The Awesome 80s. She was responsible for the photography of Manet by the Sea, Wild, Wild West and Day of the Dead.

Hats off to Chelsea Lobdell, '06, for her photographs of Skyscrapers of Manhattan and On Seeing, cranes for One Thousand Cranes, the 3-D bomb in D-Day Remembered, and her original drawings of mice for Nine Lives or More. Chelsea's mastery of Photoshop accounted for a clear image of the featured illustrations in Art by Ponder Goembel. Chelsea's antique camera collection was featured in Exposed. Her Power-Point creations were featured in Mood and Madness, The Life and Times of Bram Stoker and Paris, City of Lights.

Linda Misiura, '07, gets credit as editor for the overall contents of the book, and photographer for Chinese Calligraphy, Santa Blue, Whodunit?, Lewis Carroll and Alice, Baseball as America, Flowers in Books and Drawings, Italia, John Muir, Michener at 100, All That Jazz, Indian Arts, Tribal Treasures, From Page to Screen, Sailors' Tales, The Awesome 80s, Dreams, Sage of Monticello, Hold 'Em, Fold 'Em, Women Worldwide, Jewish-American Authors and American Folk. Linda's talents are legend!

Laura Cole, class of '08, stepped up during the summer of 2006 to photograph In the Garden, Citizen Ben, Star Bright, Exposed, Mind and Madness, Paris, City of Lights, Dying to Be Thin, The Life and Times of Bram Stoker, Ten Days That Unexpectedly Changed America, C.S. Lewis: Into the Wardrobe and Art by Ponder Goembel. Laura did much research for the fonts used in these displays. Her work is seen in the ocean waves in Art by Ponder Goembel, the pastel application in Mood and Madness, and the Eiffel Tower and balloon in Paris, City of Lights. Her original photographs were featured in Exposed. Laura also assisted with the layout for Ten Days That Unexpectedly Changed America.

Special thanks to

- Amie Fox, Kristina Dennis and Nusrat Fatima and Lisa Fitz.
- Marie Nguyen and family for items featured in Chinese Calligraphy.
- artist Russ Famulary for the John Wayne portrait featured in Wild, Wild West. He also lent his WW II photographs for D-Day Remembered, and the *Encyclopedia of Jazz* in All That Jazz.
- Thomas Patrick Hanlon for use of his print *Soft Rain*, featured in C.S. Lewis: Into the Wardrobe.
- Mark Kirlin for use of his photographs of Bethlehem Steel, Hopewell Village and Gettysburg, featured in Exposed.
- Frank Amico for the rubber chicken and glasses/eyebrows/nose combination in No Pun Intended.
- Christine Koerbler for the steer's skull, rope, blanket and cacti featured in Wild, Wild West.
- Amy Sittler for the harness racing whip in The Life and Times of Bram Stoker.
- the Theatre Department at Cedar Crest College for the feather boa in All That Jazz.
- Marilyn J. Fox, Penn State–Berks, for the loan of the skeletons, flowers, and skulls in Day of the Dead.
- Birgitta N. Bond, librarian of the James A. Michener Art Museum Library, for her cooperation in the loan of two photographs by Bob Gross, the drawing by C.P. Vaughn, an album cover, and the book *Michener and Me: A Memoir* by Herman Silverman from the library's collection.
- Ponder Goembel for taking the time to share her artistic process and for lending her beautiful illustrations from *Castaway Cats* featured in Art by Ponder Goembel.

- Warren Kimble for permission to use his illustration of the Horseshoe Inn on the book's cover.
- Mary Beth Freeh, library director, Cedar Crest College for her support of this project and for the use of the family jewels featured in The Legend of Blackbeard.
- Jim Marstellar and his excellent crew for numerous acts of support.
- JoEllen Christensen for her fine editing, critical eye and constant encouragement. Special thanks for the loan of the Cabbage Patch dolls in The Awesome 80s. Thanks, too, for the use of the walking stick in John Muir, the balancing toy in American Folk and carved primitive figure featured in C.S. Lewis: Into the Wardrobe. Both of the carved items were crafted by her father, New York artist Joseph Scasny (1920–1994).
- my sisters: Barbara Famulary, Eileen Griffin and Mary Ellen Palmieri for their sustained interest and vote of confidence.
- my friend Joan Allen, who has simply always been there.
- Brian[2], Jeff, and Dennis for being my guys, and to Teresa, Mary, Amy and Chloe, who complete my family. And to the next generation—Gage and Callie.
- And finally, to my husband, Dennis whose worldly possessions are on display throughout this book. I am grateful for his advice, hours of edits, many photographs (especially of Florence and Rome, featured in Italia), and who, apart from his other talents, had all the right connections! He was responsible for the photography in the following displays: No Pun Intended, The Legend of Blackbeard, D-Day Remembered, One Thousand Cranes, Hot Nights, Cool Reads, From Page to Screen, Nine Lives or More, Tales of Horror, Paris, City of Lights and Celebrate the New Year.

It took a village!

Table of Contents

Preface

This book is about creating effective displays for libraries. As the person responsible for filling display spaces, I researched the literature on this topic in an attempt to find a usable resource that contained multiple ideas. However, of the over 200 displays that I have created over the years, none were inspired by a display book! Many of the books on the subject of displays were published before the Internet and the technology available to librarians today. Desktop publishing has changed the game, permitting much more professional results.

It is my hope that this book will serve as an effective tool for those searching for innovative ideas that will stimulate interest in the library collection and accompanying programs. Positive PR is something to which librarians aspire. We realize that creating an inviting environment where people choose to gather may make a difference when decisions for funding are made and community support is required.

I wanted to share my process for gathering ideas. Each of the 46 displays featured in this book includes an introduction to the subject, gives the genesis of the idea, offers specifics as to the information included and its source, and provides ideas on how to expand and/or alter the concept for your specific exhibit space. Seventy seven additional display ideas are offered in the Resource pages of this book.

The cost of creating these displays was negligible. In most cases the total outlay was a matter of a few dollars. The materials used were readily available and easily manipulated. The most effective displays included items lent to me at no charge for the length of the installation.

Much research went into crafting each of these displays. This is reflected in the extensive bibliography, which includes over 200 references in addition to dozens of online sources. Ideas for displays evolved from simple excursions through area attractions to an amazing venture to a European capital. I endeavored to include a wide range of subjects, from pop culture to world cultures, from prolific writers to wanton pirates, from tribal artifacts to treasured traditions, and from weekend hobbies to lifetime passions.

It is my hope that this source enlightens and inspires you, and eases the task of creating that next display. I am confident that it will help to make you aware of the treasures in your midst that can ultimately find their way into a space in your library where they can be admired and appreciated.

Getting Ready

Crafting library displays is really all about gathering ideas: where to find them, how to get them, and finally making them materialize. Those of us charged with creativity in the workplace are constantly in search of ways in which to make effective visual statements. We attempt to highlight selected areas of the library collection, feature important authors, promote upcoming political elections, support campus and community events, celebrate holidays and commemorate birthdays, publicize local history, and tie into publicity surrounding upcoming TV and film productions of note.

In Jack Foster's book *How to Get Ideas*, he tells of one important factor necessary for those seeking to enhance their creative abilities: conditioning your mind. This is a critical step that will permit you to actually extract the ideas of which you are capable. Foster warns that this conditioning is an ongoing exercise, a task you will not finish and a goal that will never be reached.

The average person has numerous ideas each day. They respond to challenges at home and in the workplace with new and different solutions. They find new answers to old problems. These people create ideas by combining known concepts. Granted, some people are more idea prone than others, but that can change. It's all about conditioning.

How, then, do we condition the mind? All of the authorities on the subject say, first of all, learn to have some fun. If you are able to laugh and enjoy life, you will be more receptive to seeing the possibilities. Humor begets creativity.

> If it isn't fun, why do it?
> —Jerry Greenfield of Ben & Jerry's Ice Cream

Tune into ideas. For every problem which exists there are multiple solutions. Revisit the problem. Rethink your thinking.

Believe in yourself. You will absolutely need to have this conviction in order to succeed.

Remember the child within. In his most recent book, *Ideaship: How to Get Ideas Flowing in the Workplace,* Jack Foster reminds us to learn to trust our child-like natures. He urges us to become idea prone, just as we were during those early carefree years. At the outset, try to keep your expectations reasonable. Consider the fact that all you can hope for with the initial idea is that it has growth potential.

> An idea is nothing more nor less than a new combination of old elements.
>
> —James Webb Young

Remember that good ideas are precious. They are hard to come by, fragile at their inception, but powerful when established. Ideas frequently come in unexpected places, such as the bathroom—when showering or shaving. Archimedes discovered the concept of buoyancy while in the bathtub!

The Creative Process

The creative process involves a minimum of three main phases or functions:

1. Concentration—Immerse yourself in problem solving.
2. Incubation—After a period of consideration, put the problem aside.
3. Inspiration—Occurs when your subconscious mind finishes deliberating the problem, and informs the conscious.

Some experts expand the number of phases to five and include saturation as step #2, and verification as the final additional step. Creativity involves the combination of existing elements. It reveals, selects, rethinks, joins, and finally merges already existing facts, skills and ideas. Creativity implies a certain amount of risk and a tolerance for error.

In *How to Advertise*, authors Kenneth Roman and Jane Maas give examples of the successful merging of concepts that resulted in creating something new:

- Ben Franklin found using two pairs of glasses bothersome. So, he developed bifocals.
- eBay combined the appeal of the flea market with the convenience of surfing the Internet to create their successful online auction site.
- Sony Walkman added a headset to a tape player to create mobile music.
- Heineken distinguished itself by marketing their product in unique green bottles, rather than the standard brown and gained international recognition for their product.

Award winning choreographer Twyla Tharp suggests that in order to be creative you have to know how to prepare to be creative. In her 2003 publication, *The Creative Habit: Learn It and Use It for Life*, Tharp tells the story of young Wolfgang Amadeus Mozart. Amadeus had been exposed to philosophy, religion and music by his father, Leopold, who was viewed as both a composer and a pedagogue. The elder Mozart had a profound influence on his son and was careful to expose Amadeus to the world of composition, counterpoint and harmony. Although no one would argue that the younger Mozart was a brilliant and gifted musician, his early exposure, discipline and work ethic permitted him to apply and focus all that he had learned. Despite a lifespan of only 35 years, Mozart was able to achieve his maximum potential.

Most of us weren't nurtured and influenced in the way that young Mozart was, but we are still capable of developing the creative habit. When Tharp is in need of new ideas, she "scratches." This term can encompass any number of activities, such as reading, which is Tharp's first line of attack when searching for inspiration to design creative dance combinations. Tharp also suggests listening to everyday conversation, which can be of great benefit for all types of writers. Perusing people's handwork in a museum or exhibition may serve as an inspiration. Looking to your mentors and heroes for starting points can be most helpful. And finally, returning to nature for visual or auditory stimulation can be a highly effective avenue for gathering ideas.

My personal method of "scratching" for ideas always begins with research. It frequently includes a visit to the local bookstore, where I observe book jackets and popular literary themes, fonts, signage and posters. I jot down titles when identifying a book which I think will serve as the nucleus for a future display. When researching a lighter topic, I'll scan the aisles of a craft or party store. Scrapbooking materials and techniques can frequently be adapted for a larger space and incorporated into library displays. Museums are a must, of course, and always inspire. Inevitably travel sparks at least one idea for a display.

I carry a small tablet and frequently sketch interesting graphics or design arrangements from billboards or advertisements. I note unique color combinations when shopping. I look for decorative items or collections in people's homes and make a note of them for inclusion in upcoming displays. Over three dozen of the displays in this book include items from my own home. I take advantage of talented individuals whom I meet and inquire about the possibility of designing a display featuring their work. I have asked merchants about the possibility of recycling effective three dimensional displays at the close of their marketing campaign.

Consider a library display exchange. If your spaces are similar, this would give each display a lot more exposure and make your efforts worth their while.

I frequently do online image searches when formulating a display design. These photographs and illustrations often provide excellent direction. Almost every display within this book includes images found in this manner.

Perhaps the greatest asset available to me in my job is my staff of talented students who are willing and able to make contributions to these displays. I savor their enthusiasm and the interest that they have sustained throughout this project. As ideas take form, I have learned to listen to and respect their opinions. I have sometimes used themes they have suggested, and featured their artwork and collections whenever appropriate. Of course, I pull rank when necessary. For online information on how to get ideas, visit http://www.writerswrite.com/journal/feb00/holtz.htm

Design

The Library Displays Handbook by Mark Schaeffer gives good suggestions on skills as well as ideas. Schaeffer identifies elements of design that are necessary in order to create effective library displays. He emphasizes and defines these aspects of the creative process:

Design—The process of forming a plan.
Production—The process of implementing the plan.
Line—This indicates order and gives the eye direction as to where to look.
Shape- Shape represents substance and is the visual core of any design.
Space—Correct spacing permits the eye to read textual material comfortably.
Color—Allows objects to stand out from their surroundings.

Other considerations when arranging a display are balance, emphasis, simplicity, variety and unity.

Lettering is a critical part of each display you craft. It conveys your message and sets the tone for the exhibit. The size, style and hues selected for lettering are as important as the title chosen. The number of fonts available today in Microsoft Word, and others which can be downloaded for no cost online, is phenomenal. I have included many sites in the body of this book.

Take advantage of the copyright free images that are available online and in print form. The bibliography in this book lists four collections edited by Jim Harter.

Advertising

Look to advertising for some excellent pointers that would help in the creation of effective library displays. Advertisers recommend that you identify your audience. In *How to Advertise,* the authors warn that if you are attempting to talk to everybody, you probably aren't talking to anybody. Also, know your objective. What is it that you want to convey? What is the core idea of your display?

Advertising is about ideas and how to attract attention. This may be effectively accomplished through humor and eye-catching graphics. Advertising must be accountable and is judged on the merits of the bottom line.

One of the more challenging tasks in an advertising campaign is formulating ideas for billboards. The bold, framed and freestanding billboard is an American invention. In James Fraser's book *The American Billboard: 100 Years*, the simplicity of design and the brief message conveyed through billboard art is explored. The words and phrases used are meant to grab your attention quickly in order to get the point across to drivers in a matter of seconds. There are many ideas for billboard signage that would also work in your display space. Here are a few examples:

Miro, Miro on the Wall—used to promote an exhibition of Joan Miro at the Minneapolis Institute of Art.

When Mr. Right Starts Throwing Lefts—promoting help for battered women.

Friday, November 22, 1963—remembering the assassination of President John Fitzgerald Kennedy.

Everybody Loves a Good Egg—Fabergé egg exhibit at the New Orleans Museum of Art.

Marketing the Library

In *Marketing for Dummies* by Alexander Hiam, the author quotes management guru Peter Drucker who defines marketing as "the whole firm, taken from the customer's point of view." This definition is applicable to libraries as well. Remember that your view of the organization is likely quite different from that of a patron. The patron's interaction with the staff, introduction to the facility and the collection, exposure to technology and the products offered combine to create their point of view. The patron's perception of the library and what it has to offer is what matters. Market the library in a manner which assures that this view will be positive and patrons will want to return to the facility.

If you are promoting a school or community event through a library display, offer brochures with information about the event. Although patrons may take pleasure in viewing a display, people still enjoy reading through a brochure at their leisure. Include bibliographies and URLs in the pamphlet. Remember when using graphics that one large illustration is more captivating than several smaller images. Caption any photographs featured and use familiar images when possible. A postcard of the display could also serve as an announcement which includes the dates of the installation, or as an invitation to a reception acknowledging the artist involved.

When creating a display that commemorates the anniversary of your library, or one celebrating books and libraries, feature amnesty tickets that patrons can use to waive their fines, or a portion of their debt. This gesture, which you may want to include on an annual basis, creates positive feedback, assures that material will be returned, and is certain to generate buzz around campus or town.

Make sure that your academic library is included in fall orientation. Have handouts which include facility floor plans, access policies, a library newsletter and schedules of upcoming library instruction and programs. Giveaways could include pencils, pens, mugs, tablets, tote bags and bookmarks imprinted with the library name. Hang balloons, fill candy jars, and advertise times of the library tours. Have a contest. Perhaps it could be to guess the number of books in the collection. The prize could be a gift certificate to the college or community bookstore. Have the display case feature photographs of your senior and student staff and a brief summary of their responsibilities. Promote the special features of your library or collection. Make the experience positive and it will be memorable!

For me, creating displays is a form of continuing education. I love the discovery process and the research involved in the formation of each display. During this process, I gain new insights and valuable information. I have learned to be wary of online sources that are not reliable. I check the facts against valid print sources.

Tap into your community's talent. Find the artists, craftsmen, writers, photographers and collectors who live among you and feature them in a display or program. Make sure that after installing the display you promote it through e-mail, a public service announcement on the local radio station, or in a newsletter or community publication, so that the artist or patron involved feels that the effort put forth was worth it for the exposure he or she received.

Oh, and have some fun!

Authors

THE LIFE AND TIMES OF BRAM STOKER

> Then a dog began to howl somewhere in a farmhouse far down the road, a long, agonized wailing, as if from fear. The sound was taken up by another dog, and then another and another, till, borne on the wind which now sighed softly through the Pass, a wild howling began, which seemed to come from all over the country, as far as the imagination could grasp it through the gloom of the night.
>
> —*Dracula* by Bram Stoker

Abraham Stoker was born November 8, 1847, at Clontarf in Ireland, a coastal town just three miles north of Dublin. Nicknamed Bram, he was the middle child of a brood of seven born to Abraham Stoker and Charlotte Mathilda Blake Thornley. Even though his parents were Protestants, which suggested social prominence and a certain level of wealth, they had neither.

Bram was unable to stand or walk until the age of seven. His mother, a charity worker and writer, helped to pass the time with her bedridden son by telling scores of stories, many of them tales of horror. Despite years of recurring illness, Stoker eventually was able to overcome his early frailty. By the time of his adolescence, he had developed into an exceptional athlete.

Bram was considered an outstanding football player and scholar during his years at Trinity College in Dublin. It was there that he was awarded the title of University Athlete. His childhood illness, however, remained a traumatic experience which permeated the themes of his adult literary work. Everlasting sleep and eventual resurrection from the dead were of great importance to him.

Stoker graduated with honors in mathematics from Trinity College, and despite his desire to write, succumbed to paternal pressure and secured a position as a civil servant at Dublin Castle. While in this position, Bram wrote his first work, titled *Duties of Clerks of Petty Sessions in Ireland: Collected Works of Bram Stoker.* It was not published, however, until 1879, well after he had become famous. Bram began contributing stories to magazines while at Dublin Castle. During his tenure there, he also worked as an unpaid theatre critic for Dublin's *Evening Mail,* and as editor of the publication *The Irish Echo.*

Bram Stoker married a classic beauty and aspiring actress, Florence Balcome, in

The Life and Times of Bram Stocker—This stylized silhouette of Count Dracula is equipped with a rider's crop for nocturnal activities.

1878. Prior to their engagement, she had been romantically linked to Oscar Wilde. It has been said that her decision to marry broke Wilde's heart and caused him to leave the country. After their wedding, the Stokers left Dublin and moved to England. Bram had accepted a position as business manager for the charismatic Sir Henry Irving, who ran the Lyceum Theatre in London. This was a position he held for 27 years.

Sir Henry Irving was considered the most significant actor on the English stage in the last decades of the nineteenth century, and was the first member of the acting profession to be knighted (1895). Irving's association with Stoker would endure throughout their lives and have a profound affect on them both.

In the first year of their marriage, Florence gave birth to their only child, son Noel. The literature suggests that Stoker and his wife continued to keep up respectable appearances, but, in actuality, had become estranged. Bram was more at home in the company of gentlemen athletes and intellectuals, which was not an uncommon situation in sexually divided Victorian and Edwardian London. In Stoker's 1906 biography, *Personal Reminiscences of Henry Irving,* he described a masculine world of theatre management, after-dinner speaking, gentlemen's clubs and an intimate male brotherhood.

Despite the responsibilities of his position at the Lyceum, Stoker somehow found time to write fiction. His first book, *Under the Sunset* (1882), was comprised of eight hair-raising fairy tales designed for a juvenile audience. A full-length novel, *The Snake's Pass*, followed in 1890. That same year marks the genesis of Stoker's research for his literary masterpiece, *Dracula*. This tale of vampires would be published in 1897 to immediate, international acclaim and notoriety. Stoker's place in literary history was assured. Some say that Stoker based his "hero" on a fifteenth century Romanian prince. The historical Dracula was known to have been appallingly cruel and had been nicknamed "Vlad the Impaler." There is no evidence that linked the prince to vampirism.

The Victorian mores of Stoker's time would have found the unleashed female sexuality apparent in *Dracula* quite shocking. Vampires, however, had been the central subject of books on mythology and legend for hundreds of years worldwide. With violence, fear and fascination at the core, there were always plentiful readers for books of this genre. The Slavic people, including most eastern Europeans from Russia to Bulgaria, and Serbia to Poland, have the richest vampire folklore and legends in the world. The mythology suggested that vampires could be destroyed in any of the following manners: staking, decapitation, burning, repeating the funeral service, holy water on the grave or exorcism.

The idea of the "undead," who attempt to drink the blood of the living, has been around for centuries. One possible explanation is that in the days before modern medical technology, such as brain scans and heart monitors, was developed, some comatose patients who appeared to be dead were buried alive. Occasionally, these coffins were reopened, exposing the horror of a corpse with blood about its face and hands. The unknowing victim had clawed and bitten in an effort to escape its untimely burial. It is interesting to note that Stoker's working title for *Dracula* was actually *The Undead*.

In 1905, Sir Henry Irving died. The shock of his death caused Stoker to have a stroke. Despite this traumatic event, he continued to write and publish several other books, including *Personal Reminiscences of Henry Irving* (1906) and *The Lair of the White Worm* (1911).

Bram Stoker continued to write and produced an extensive body of work which included novels, short stories and essays, until his death on April 20, 1912. To Stoker's credit, *Dracula* remains in print today, well over 100 years after its original publication. For more biographical information about the life and times of Bram Stoker, visit http://www.online-literature.com/stoker/

CREDITS

My husband and I attended the American Library Association conference in Manhattan in the late '90s. A reception was held for ALA members at the New York Public Library. After the festivities, many of us toured the special exhibit that was featured.

In a roundabout way, my visit to the New York Public Library to view the display on the 200th anniversary of the death and birth, respectively, of Mary Wollstonecraft, and her daughter, Mary Shelley, served as a catalyst for this display on Bram Stoker. Although the exhibit, *Visionary Daughters of Albion: A Bicentenary Celebration of Mary Wollstonecraft and Mary Shelley,* was mounted in the spring of 1997, the visual impact of the more than 350 items, which included manuscripts, correspondence, portraits and prints, remains with me today. Clearly we can recognize the strides these women made in attempting to overcome the sexual oppression and the possessive morality of their time.

As a result of this experience at New York Public, I mounted a small scale display on the Wollstonecrafts for our library—minus the first editions and primary sources of course! While researching Mary Shelley and her fascinating life as an expatriate with her husband, the poet Percy Bysshe Shelley, I began to read some biographical material on other early horror story writers who made significant contributions to the genre. Needless to say, Bram Stoker and *Dracula* offered some fascinating material. For information on the New York Public Library display on *Visionary Daughters of Albion*, visit http://www.nypl.org/press/1997/mary2.cfm

So, inadvertently, we can thank Frankenstein for this display on *Dracula*.

ASSEMBLING THE DISPLAY

1. The pale gray felt background suggested an overcast and foggy night for this display. The font selected for *Bram Stoker* was Transylvania sized at 300 for the capital letters and 200 for the lower case. To download this free font, visit http://www.type now.net/t.htm

The word *Dracula* was created using the font Frankenstein sized at 250. This free font is available at http://www.grsites.com/fonts/f013.shtml

The letters were printed on cardstock, taped to red foil wrapping paper, glued, then attached with pins and pulled forward. The image of Dracula was inspired by a cover illustration on the book *Tales of Terror* retold by Nicola Baxter. It was drawn freehand on black poster board using white poster board to outline.

The bats, fiberfill and spiders were recycled from the display *Tales of Horror.* A section of a horse whip was cut and attached with pins to Dracula's right hand.

2. On the top left was the quote introducing this display. Under that was a brief biography of the life and times of Bram Stoker. Next was some historical data on vampires. This information is available at: http://www.chebucto.ns.ca/~vampire/vhist.html

Under that was an explanation of *The Undead* which was based on information found at http://www.utexas.edu/features/archive/2003/vampires.html

Vampire teeth, found on a Google image search, were cut out and glued above the title of that passage. All of this was printed on white cardstock and mounted on black, cranberry or silver poster board.

3. On the top right was this quote from *Dracula*:

> I only slept a few hours when I went to bed, and feeling that I could not sleep any more, got up. I had hung my shaving glass by the window, and was just beginning to shave. Suddenly, I felt a hand on my shoulder, and heard the Count's voice saying to me "Good morning." I started, for it amazed me that I had not seen him, since the reflection of the glass covered the whole room behind me ... but there was no sign of a man in it, except myself.
>
> —Jonathan Harker's journal

An image of a vampire, found through a Google search, was mounted on silver poster board and affixed to the top of the quote.

A passage titled *Dracula Considered* was compiled from information found in *The Origins of Dracula: The Background to Bram Stoker's Gothic Masterpiece* by Clive Leatherdale.

Under this was a color image of the actual Dracula: Vlad Tepes, Prince of Wallachia, and information about his life. This was printed on white cardstock, and mounted on cranberry and silver poster board. For this background data on Count Dracula, visit http://www.fortunecity.com/roswell/seance/500/vamps/vlad/intro.html

4. On the base of the display, Styrofoam blocks were stacked to provide different elevations for the books. The blocks were covered with black fabric. A wooden cross and cardstock stake were placed among the books. The stake was found through a Google image search. A holy water bottle and several garlic bulbs surround the book *Dracula*.

Books included in the display were *Bram Stoker and the Man Who Was Dracula* by Barbara Belford, *Dracula* by Bram Stoker, *The Lady of the Shroud* by Bram Stoker, *Best Ghost and Horror Stories* by Bram Stoker and *Beyond Dracula: Bram Stoker's Fiction and Its Cultural Context* by William Hughes.

BIGGER AND BETTER

Obviously, this display would be an exciting one to mount around Halloween. If your space permits, focus on horror stories and incorporate some other tales, in addition to Dracula. Include characters from Rip Van Winkle's *The Legend of Sleepy Hollow,* Robert Louis Stevenson's *Dr. Jekyll and Mr. Hyde,* or Arthur Conan Doyle's *Hound of the Baskervilles,* and don't forget Freddie Kreuger from *A Nightmare on Elm Street!* Check out your party store for inspiration.

Choose *Frankenstein* and research the fascinating life and times of Mary Shelley, wife of a famous poet, and daughter of a pioneering feminist. Choose both women as your focus, and mount a display around Mary Wollstonecraft and Mary Wollstonecraft Shelley. For information on the Anglo-Irish feminist, intellectual and writer Mary Wollstonecraft, visit http://www.historyguide.org/intellect/wollstonecraft.html

For the compelling backstory on Mary Shelley, her turbulent childhood and passionate romance with Percy Bysshe Shelley, visit http://www.kirjasto.sci.fi/mshelley.htm

MICHENER AT 100

I love writing. I love the swirl and swing of words as they tangle with human emotions.

—James A. Michener

There is little certainty surrounding the birth of James Albert Michener. He was born in New York City early in 1907, but was abandoned shortly thereafter. It is known that he was raised by an adoptive mother, Mabel Michener, in Doylestown, Pennsylvania. Some have argued that she was actually his biological mother, but she denied it and it was never proven. The economic circumstances of Michener's childhood were dire. There was minimal food and nothing frivolous. As a child there simply were no sleds, no baseball gloves, no bicycles, no little wagon, not even a new pair of sneakers. He reflected on his childhood in an interview held in St. Petersburg, Florida in 1991: "I didn't have anything. And do you know at about seven or eight, I just decided, 'Well, that's the way it is. And I'm not going to beat my brains out about it.'" This compelling interview can be found if you visit http://www.achievement.org/autodoc/page/mic0int-1

It was rumored that as a schoolboy his sneakers were so worn that his toes protruded through the fabric. His attitude toward money and material possessions was formed at that time. He decided to deal with life as it was dealt to him, and began to focus on the possibilities.

As a young teenager with a few coins in his pocket, Michener began hitchhiking across America, sometimes with a friend, but often on his own. He wrote fondly of those years of wonder and enchantment in his autobiography, *The World Is My Home*. From those adventures grew Michener's enduring curiosity about people, cultures and lands across the globe.

A natural athlete, Michener played both basketball and baseball for Doylestown High School. He was awarded an academic scholarship to Swarthmore College, a small private institution near Philadelphia, where he savored his education and graduated with highest honors. Michener studied at St. Andrew's University in Scotland and returned to his home town to teach at the George School, a prestigious independent boarding facility. He also taught at Colorado State Teachers College and later became an assistant visiting professor of history at Harvard University. In 1940, he took a position as a social studies editor for Macmillan publishing company in New York, a position that would prove quite profitable and alter the course of his life.

Although Michener was a practicing Quaker, he genuinely felt that Hitler and Japan posed serious threats to the world. Consequently, he did not register as a conscientious objector with the Selective Service. Aware that he held a high draft number, he chose to sail rather than march into war. Michener joined the U.S. Navy at age 36, in the final years of World War II. He was commissioned a lieutenant commander

Michener at 100—The vintage typewriter holds a passage from Michener's first endeavor, the Pulitzer Prize winning *Tales of the South Pacific*.

and assigned to the South Pacific as a naval historian to investigate and report problems with troops stationed on various islands.

As he observed the interaction of the two contrasting cultures, and inspired by the breathtaking beauty of the Solomon Islands in the South Pacific, Michener formulated his ideas and tapped into some of his actual wartime experiences. The result of this enterprise was his first novel, titled *Tales of the South Pacific*.

Because Macmillan had a rule against publishing the works of an employee, Michener submitted the manuscript to his employer under a nom de plume. He felt that his leave of absence for military duty provided something of an exemption to the policy. His first literary effort, which was finally published by Macmillan, won a Pulitzer Prize in 1948. It became the basis for the musical *South Pacific*. This production enjoyed an extended run on Broadway, and was later made into a major motion picture.

Michener went on to travel extensively and kept copious notes about places that had an emotional impact on him. He published four dozen books, including the texts of five art books. His works of fiction, such as *Chesapeake* and *The Covenant,* and non-fiction, namely *Sports in America* and *Kent State: What Happened and Why,* have been issued in virtually every language. Hardcover and paperback sales have exceeded 75 million copies.

Michener's passions were formed in childhood. He developed a love of opera, a quest for travel, and a keen interest in politics. He campaigned for John Kennedy in the 1960 elections, but was unsuccessful in his own quest for a congressional seat in the 1962 election.

Michener and his third wife, Mari Yoriko Sabusawa, shared a profound appreciation of art. They favored contemporary American artists, whose works they collected throughout their marriage.

Although he never fathered children, Michener believed strongly in the value of education and underwrote the tuition of many of his friends' children. He was an ardent philanthropist and gave $30 million for the establishment of a creative writing program at the University of Texas at Austin. He also gave generously to his alma mater, Swarthmore College, and a variety of other institutions including libraries and museums.

To ensure the University of Texas could continue adding the paintings of emerging American artists to the sizable art collection that the Micheners donated, James and Mari each gave $5 million toward the construction of a new building for the Blanton Museum of Art. Michener's directive was that the collection continue to be dynamic and that new acquisitions reflect trends in contemporary American painting. For more information about the Blanton Museum of Art visit http:www.utexas.edu/features/ archive/2002/michener2.html

Michener's marriage to Mari, a second generation Japanese-American, lasted 39 years, until her death in 1994. Decorated in 1977 with America's highest civilian award, the Presidential Medal of Freedom, Michener also held honorary doctorates in five fields from thirty leading universities. In his last years, Michener lived in Austin, Texas, where he died at age 90 on October 16, 1997.

CREDITS

Doylestown, Pennsylvania, is a charming and historic town nestled in picturesque Bucks County. There are several museums of note located there. One of my favorites bears the name of James A. Michener. It houses some wonderful memorabilia which previously belonged to the many literary and musical personalities who lived in the town and sought a peaceful haven away from New York City. The museum also has an impressive collection of the works of many Pennsylvania Impressionists.

As you enter the facility, you are immediately drawn to the anteroom, a reproduction of Michener's actual library, which features his desk, typewriter, photographs, and mementoes of his life, as well as his many publications printed in numerous languages. There is also a video montage of the movies that were made based on Michener's books. The year 2007 marked the 100th anniversary of the birth of James Michener, so he seemed an ideal subject for inclusion in this book. The personnel at the museum were very accommodating and provided the drawing, photographs, and the memoir *Michener and Me*, written by his close friend, Herman Silverman. This memoir provided excellent material for the display.

ASSEMBLING THE DISPLAY

1. The background of the display was black felt. The sheet of red poster board provided the proper scale for the poster that was created. The sketch of Michener was framed by an 11" × 14" black mat which was affixed to the background with rubber cement. On the bottom left of the mat was a color reproduction of the Medal of Freedom found through a Google image search. Centered on the bottom of the mat was:

Presented by President Gerald Ford in 1977
to James A. Michener

At the top of the poster was the name Michener printed on cardstock using TW CEN MT font at 280. This is available in MS Word. The signage at the bottom right, Centennial 1907–2007, was the same style but at a lower font size. All caps were used for emphasis. The words *Traveler, Citizen, Writer* used mixed cases, but the same font, sized at 100. The signage was printed on white cardstock and framed in black poster board. Long thin strips of black and white poster board were arranged to suggest a frame. The quote introducing this topic was included in the display, along with the quote regarding his childhood poverty, which was found at http://www.achievement.org/autodoc/printmember/mic0bio-1

Additional quotes by Michener that flanked the poster were found at http://www.brainyquote.com/quotes/authors/j/james_a_michener.html

> I think young people ought to seek that experience that is going to knock them off center.
>
> —James Michener

Information about the Medal of Freedom, found though a Google image search, was printed on card stock and mounted on red and black poster board. The illustration of Michener's alma mater, Swarthmore College, was found through a Google search, printed on cardstock and mounted on an oval of red poster board.

2. On the top left was a brief biography of Michener. This information can be found if you visit either of these sites: http://www.grandtimes.com/michener.html or http://www.achievement.org/autodoc/page/mic0bio-1

Under that were selections from the text *Talking with Michener*, by Lawrence Grobel. This interview can be found if you visit http://www.upress.state.ms.us/books/t/talking_michener.html

Both documents were printed on white cardstock and mounted on red and black poster board.

3. On the top right was a poster for the musical *South Pacific*. This was found through a Google image search. Below that was a poignant farewell letter written by Michener to his friends in the final days of his life. This was found in the memoir *Michener and Me*. These were printed on white cardstock and mounted on black and red poster board.

4. At the base of the display case was a vintage typewriter which held the opening paragraphs of *Tales of the South Pacific*, the author's first novel. The text used was

Mom's Typewriter, font size 12. This font can be found at http://simplythebest.net/fonts/fonts/m_typewriter.html

The typewriter was placed on a Styrofoam form covered with black felt, which elevated it to a height that made it visible and permitted Michener's quotation about the importance of rewriting to be featured:

> I have never thought of myself as a good writer. Anyone who wants reassurance of that should read one of my first drafts. But I'm one of the world's great rewriters.

The quote was printed on white cardstock and mounted on red poster board. A globe turned to the South Pacific was placed to the left along with two operatic CDs, which reflected his lifelong passion for opera. A small American flag was set behind a brass pen holder. To the right, a clock was mounted on Styrofoam covered with black felt. Two photographs, one of both the Micheners, and the other of James Michener at 2 months old, were framed and placed behind a baseball and stand. A brass letter opener and passport were set in front of the photographs.

The Michener books featured in the display were *Alaska, Mexico, Japanese Prints, Texas, The Novel, Tales of the South Pacific,* and *The World Is My Home.*

BIGGER AND BETTER

When mounting a display on Michener, you could choose to feature his works set in the South Pacific such as *Rascals in Paradise, Return to Paradise, Hawaii,* and *Tales of the South Pacific* to create a tropical exhibit. Or, you could select a patriotic theme and focus on *Centennial, America, Texas, Chesapeake, Alaska,* or *Hawaii.*

Since Michener wrote four books on Japanese art, and several books set in wartime, either of those categories could be chosen as central themes.

"NOT FOR MYSELF ALONE": CELEBRATING JEWISH-AMERICAN AUTHORS

The opposite of love, I have found, is not hate, but indifference.
—Elie Wiesel

Many immigrants' initial introduction to America comes in the form of a poem composed by the Jewish-American writer Emma Lazarus. Her words are emblazoned on the base of the Statue of Liberty Enlightening the World. Located on a 12 acre island, this monument was a gift of friendship from the people of France to the people of the

United States and is a universal symbol of freedom and democracy. Dedicated in 1886, it was designated a National Monument in 1924.

Emma Lazarus was fortunate to have had a privileged upbringing as the daughter of a prosperous sugar merchant. After the Civil War, her father arranged for private tutors to give his daughter a classical, secular education. She later wrote that she was "brought up exclusively under American institutions, amid liberal influences, in a society where all differences of race and faith were fused in a refined cosmopolitanism" (Vogel 14).

Lazarus sought the "truth" of Judaism and its relevance to her writing. The words of her famous poem, "Give me your tired, your poor, your huddled masses yearning to be free," are familiar to the American people. Georgia Schuler, a patron of the arts in New York City, discovered Lazarus' verse within a packet of poems written in 1883 for a fund-raising project related to the construction of the Statue of Liberty's pedestal. Mrs. Schuyler was moved by the sentiments expressed in this poem, and arranged to have the last five lines engraved on the pedestal of the statue. These words by Emma Lazarus represent the freedom to come to the United States and create a new life without religious or ethnic persecution.

Much has been written about the process of Jewish immigrants finding their niche in the world. Irving Howe, past president of both Brandeis and Stanford universities, said that without the dynamic of immigration and the assimilation of Jews struggling to tell the story of their transformation into Americans, Jewish literature would quickly lose it energy, even its raison d'être. Howe seemed to believe that the Jewish contribution to literature was universalistic, and reflected a peoples' situation as outsider, an avant-garde in the struggle to create a better world.

Cynthia Ozick was quoted as saying that American Jewish literature would thrive only if it resisted the impulse to be quintessentially American, to be assimilated. For her, American Jewish writers would survive within the Jewish law only if they adhered to the liturgical—the religious, spiritual and moral matters of Jewish life.

The intent of this display was to document the impact of Jewish-American writing on various levels of American life, from the stage to cinema, journalism and academia.

CREDITS

We are fortunate to have excellent resources on the topic of Jewish-American authors at a nearby New Jersey institution. The Princeton University Milberg Collection traces the path of Jewish-American literature from the work of immigrant writers who sought to understand their adopted home within the confines of their heritage, to those contemporary writers who would alter the American literary horizon, giving American writing its Jewish legacy.

The original exhibit Not for Myself Alone: Celebrating Jewish-American Writers was presented by the University's Firestone Library several years ago. The object was to assemble poetry, fiction, drama, essays, artwork, and correspondence from over

Jewish-American Authors—The cropped Star of David is a bold graphic that pulls you into this celebration of notable Jewish-American authors.

70 men and women who have contributed to two centuries of American culture. This exhibition featured selected works from the Leonard L. Milberg (Princeton '53) Collection of Jewish-American Writers.

My husband and I were fortunate to visit the university library when this exhibit was installed. I thought it would be a subject of interest to our college community and picked up some informative material while we were there.

ASSEMBLING THE DISPLAY

1. The font Seven Swordsmen was used for the title *Jewish-American*. It was sized at 500 and can be found at http://www.1001fonts.com/font_details.html?font_id=2826

The word *Authors* was created using Courier New (available in MS Word) sized at 500. The letters were printed on cardstock, traced on to black poster board, and pinned to the background of blue felt, slightly overlapping the top of the flag.

The Star of David was drawn freehand on dark blue poster board. The American flag was sketched onto white poster board and painted with watercolors. Both of these images were pinned to the light blue felt background.

2. On the top left of the display was a poem written by Maxine Kunin titled *Looking for Luck in Bangkok*. This can be found in her collection *Looking for Luck* (New York: Norton, 1992). All of the items included on the display sides were printed on white cardstock and double mounted on red and blue poster board. Below that was a quote from playwright Neil Simon:

> The way I see things, life is both sad and funny. I can't imagine a comical situation that isn't at the same time also painful. I used to ask myself: What is a humorous situation? Now I ask: What is a sad situation and how can I tell it humorously?

This quotation and a list of Simon's work is available at http://www.msu.edu/~pelowsk1/neilsimon/plays/

At the bottom right was a quote from *Reading Myself and Others* by Phillip Roth:

> Between first discovering the Newark Bears and the Brooklyn Dodgers at seven or eight and first looking into Conrad's Lord Jim at age eighteen, I had done some growing up. I am only saying that my discovery of literature, and fiction particularly, and the "love affair"—to some degree hopeless, but still earnest—that has ensued, derives in part from this childhood infatuation with baseball. Or, more accurately perhaps, baseball—with its lore and legends, its cultural power, its seasonal associations, its native authenticity, its simple rules and transparent strategies, its longueurs and thrills, its spaciousness, its suspensefulness, its heroics, its nuances, its lingo, its "characters," its peculiarly hypnotic tedium, its mythic transformation of the immediate—was the literature of my boyhood.

For this quote and biographical information about Phillip Roth, visit http://www.kirjasto.sci.fi/proth.htm

3. On the top right was an excerpt from Bernard Malamud's novel *The Assistant*:

> "If you live, you suffer. Some people suffer more, but not because they want. But I think if a Jew don't suffer for the Law, he will suffer for nothing." "What do you suffer for, Morris?" Frank said. "I suffer for you," Morris said calmly.

For this quote and others from his novel, visit http://www.sparknotes.com/lit/assistant/quotes.html

Below that was a brief description of the Statue of Liberty and the poem by Emma Lazarus which is inscribed on the base. Clip art of the statue was inserted under this information. Visit this site for the entire poem entitled *The New Colossus*: http://www.factmonster.com/ipka/A0874962.html

A passage from Arthur Miller's *Death of a Salesman* was attached under the poem:

> Don't say he's a great man. Willy Loman never made a lot of money. His name was never in the paper. He's not the finest character that ever lived. But he's a human being, and a terrible thing is happening to him. So attention must be paid. He's not to be allowed to fall into his grave like an old dog. Attention, attention must finally be paid to such a person.

4. At the center of the display base is the Hebrew phrase "To Life!" found on a Google image search. This was printed on cardstock and mounted on black poster board. Stars of David, found on a Google image search, were sized four on a page, printed on paper, cut out and placed among the books. Because of the vast number of titles available for this display, the books were arranged both vertically and horizontally.

The small red and blue metallic topped toothpicks were actually patriotic cupcake decorations, available at a local craft shop. These were placed atop the books and at other strategic points to unify the background colors.

Books featured in the display were *The First Wives Club* by Olivia Goldsmith, *Lilly: Reminiscences of Lillian Hellman* by Peter Feibleman, *War and Remembrance* and *The Hope* by Herman Wouk, *Memoirs: All Rivers Run to the Sea* by Elie Wiesel, *Rewrites* by Neil Simon, *Anne Frank: The Diary of a Young Girl* by Anne Frank, *The Hope* by Herman Wouk, *Patrimony* and *Sabbath Theater* by Phillip Roth, *The Waterworks* and *Billy Bathgate* by E. L. Doctorow, *Satan in Goray* by Isaac Bashevis Singer, *Atlas Shrugged* by Ayn Rand, *Harlot's Ghost* by Norman Mailer, *Opus 200* by Isaac Asimov, and *Albert Einstein: Love Letters* by Marie Mileva.

BIGGER AND BETTER

There are so many Jewish writers and artists from whom to choose. You may decide to narrow the topic to just poets, or non-fiction writers, or perhaps art through Jewish eyes.

You could select a topic such as the Holocaust and feature books related to that period of history. Should you choose that topic, be sure to visit http://www.ushmm.org/

You may have some local Jewish artists or craftsmen who would be willing to lend their pieces to you as a focal point of your display. If you feature noted artists of Jewish descent, consider these names: Modigliani, Frida Kahlo, Louise Nevelson, Marc Chagall, Judy Chicago, Roy Lichtenstein, Annie Libovitz and Lee Krasner. You can find this information at the Jewish Art Network if you visit http://www.jewishart-network.com/JewishArt/Index.asp

LEWIS CARROLL AND ALICE

He was the last saint of this irreverent world: those who have surrendered the myths of Santa Claus ... of Jehovah, hang their last remnants of mysticism on Lewis Carroll and will not allow themselves to examine him dispassionately.
—*Florence Becker Lennon*

Charles Lutwidge Dodgson was born in 1832 near the village of Daresbury, England. His father was a minister in the Anglican church, and his family grew to include three brothers and seven sisters. His parents shared the same grandfather, and this close genetic link probably explains the speech problems inherent among the Dodgson children.

Charles boarded at the Rugby School, where he excelled as a student, but wrote of some "nocturnal annoyances." Later he studied at Oxford University, where he would both live and teach.

Although ordained an Anglican deacon, he never fully became a priest. There were several reasons for this. First, his passion for the theatre was not shared by the church, and second, his partial hearing loss and speech impediment made both reading aloud and preaching difficult. A "gentle shrinking celibate," as described by Alexander Woollcott, he was said to be fussy, prim, and eccentric by some, and brilliant by others. He communicated primarily through writing and photography. His prolific body of literature included poems, letters, and essays on a broad range of topics. At the time of his death, in 1889, his records indicated that he had written close to 99,000 letters.

The enchanting tale of Alice, who follows a large white rabbit into a wondrous land, actually began as a fairy tale. It was intended to be recited aloud for the amusement of Alice Pleasance Liddell and her two sisters. In 1862, Dodgson was invited to a boating picnic with the Liddell family on the river Thames on a sunny afternoon in Oxford, England. It was here that the story-telling took place, and *Alice in Wonderland* came to be.

The Reverend Dodgson, a shy mathematician and Oxford don, later wrote down the story which he originally titled *Alice's Adventures Under Ground*. The manuscript, written under the pen name Lewis Carroll, was to be formally published by Macmillan in 1865 as *Alice in Wonderland*. Although

Lewis Carroll and Alice—The playful arrangement of playing cards surrounding the Mad Hatter's hat is reminiscent of Alice tumbling into the rabbit hole.

originally illustrated by the author, the images that we associate with this work were drawn in pen-and-ink by Sir John Tenniel. In order to maintain some level of control, Tenniel's illustrations were closely monitored by Lewis Carroll.

Since that memorable summer afternoon, both *Alice in Wonderland* and the 1871 sequel, *Through the Looking Glass*, have entertained both children and adults for almost 150 years. The latter publication was inspired by yet another Alice, eight-year-old Alice Raikes, a fetching child Lewis Carroll had met in London in 1868.

Set in Victorian England, these amazing literary flights of fancy have sustained the test of time, and are, in many ways, rather modern. With Alice's adventures, which transfer her through a rabbit hole to Wonderland, or through a mirror into a game of chess, Carroll tells stories that are both bizarre, yet amusing—and absurdly profound. Although Carroll would have preferred his legacy be his treatises on mathematics and logic, posterity has a way of making its own choices. *Alice* has grown to become one of literature's darlings and the primary fictional character with whom the author is most associated.

Although Alice was the central character of this famous tale, the language itself formed something of a "character." W. H. Auden supports this idea in the following passage:

> [In the Alice books], one of the most important and powerful characters is not a person but the English language. Alice, who had hitherto supposed that words were passive objects, discovers that they have a life and will of their own. When she tries to remember poems she has learned, new lines come into her head unbidden and, when she thinks she knows what a word means, it turns out to mean something else [Draper 64].

Early reviews of the Alice books emphasized Dodgson's skill as a linguist, his gift for parody and distinguished literary style. After his death, critics analyzed the stories from many perspectives—political, philosophical, metaphysical and psychoanalytical—often suggesting that the stories were the result of his neuroses, and his response to Victorian mores. Because of the disturbing nature of Alice's adventure, and their harsh and sometimes sadistic elements, some critics have suggested that they are not appropriate for children. Consequently, these stories are not always experienced by the very audience for whom Lewis Carroll intended. The literary world has applauded the author's seamless meshing of the logical and illogical in two tales that have captivated generations of readers of all ages.

There is much written on the life of Lewis Carroll, the art of *Alice In Wonderland*, and the political, religious, and philosophical implications of this work. There are also many contrasting views on the lifestyle of this author and the significance of his friendships with and preference for young girls.

There are some excellent sites on the author and his works. Here are some which were referred to in the display: http://catlin.clas.virginia.edu/shadows/carroll/dodgson.html and http://www.todayinliterature.com/biography/charles.dodgson.asp

CREDITS

The idea for this display came as a result of a visit to the Pierpont Morgan Library in New York City several years ago. Both a museum and a center for scholarly research, the Morgan Library is an extraordinary complex of buildings located in the heart of Manhattan. The facility was undergoing a renovation at the time, so they had cleaned house and offered old posters of previous library exhibits free to the visitors.

At first glance, I felt that the *Lewis Carroll and Alice* poster would provide a good focal point for a library display. Researching the background information on the author, for this display, was most interesting and even compelling.

ASSEMBLING THE DISPLAY

1. The black felt background was selected to offset the tan, green, brown and blue tones of the poster. The latter was double mounted on both bright green poster board and then metallic gold. It was placed at the top center of the case as the focal point of the space and straight pins were used to secure it.

An antique pocket watch was attached with pins under the poster, at the bottom left. This was suggestive of the one carried by the Mad Hatter in *Alice in Wonderland.*

The Mad Hatter's hat was made from black poster board in three pieces. The main section was formed like a megaphone and the top piece had notches cut that could be folded inside the top of the hat and taped. The hatband was bright green poster board. The font chosen for the price tag "In this style..." was Rage Italic, sized at 100 bold. This phrase was printed on white card stock and slipped through the hatband. The hat was mounted on the inside with straight pins.

The playing cards were printed on cardstock and can be found at www.gambler.ru/sukhty/decks/0343/0343j.htm

These cards were positioned around the hat so that it would pop out of the display. The placement of the cards is suggestive of Alice tumbling into the rabbit hole. Gold hearts were cut from poster board and attached with pins.

The W. H. Auden quote, previously cited, was printed on off-white cardstock and double mounted on gold and green poster board. This was placed below and to the right of the hat. The quote uttered by the Queen of Hearts in *Alice in Wonderland* was placed in the top center of the poster. It was printed and mounted as above: "Off with her head."

2. On the top left was a quote by Florence Becker Lennon which can be found at the introduction to this display.

Below that was an image from *Alice in Wonderland* found through a Google search.

Next came a passage titled *Lewis Carroll and the Liddell Family* which was taken from *The Making of the Alice Books* by Ronald Reichertz.

Under that was a quote from *Alice in Wonderland:* "Why is a raven like a writing desk?" This passage came next:

> Still she haunts me phantomwise
> Alice moving under skies
> Never seen by waking eyes
> —*Alice Through The Looking Glass*, chap. 12.

The font Chiller, sized at 36, was used for the above quotation to given an eerie effect. These quotations were double mounted on black and gold poster board and placed throughout the display.

Lastly, an explanation of the phrase "Mad as a Hatter," found in *The Annotated Alice* by Martin Gardner, was included. All of this information was printed on off-white cardstock and mounted on black or gold and black poster board.

3. On the top right was a reproduction of a photograph of Alice Liddell found through a Google image search. Next came a summation of the making of *Alice*. This was taken from the *Quotable Alice* by Lewis Carroll. After that was a biography of Charles Dodgson, from taken from *Quotable Alice* by Lewis Carroll. Under that was this quote:

> I could tell you my adventures-beginning from this morning, but it's no use going back to yesterday, because I was a different person then.
> —*Alice in Wonderland*, chapter 10

All of this information was printed on off-white cardstock and mounted on black and/or gold poster board.

4. A velvet covered circle of polyurethane was placed on the bottom of the display case, and served as a stand for the bottle labeled "Drink Me" and some of the gold hearts which were scattered throughout the display.

The books featured in the display case were: *All Things Alice* by Linda Sunshine, *The Making of the Alice Books* by Ronald Reichertz, *The Complete Stories and Poems of Lewis Carrol, Alternative Alices* edited by Carolyn Sigler and *Alice's Adventures* by Will Brooker.

The sheet music that was included was "Alice in Wonderland" by Charlie Tobias, Jack Scholl, and Murray Mencher.

BIGGER AND BETTER

There are many other items that could have been featured in this display. A croquet mallet, a child's tea set and/or miniature teapot, gloves, or a fan—all of these would tie into the book's storyline. A quill pen and inkwell, reproductions of Lewis Carroll's many letters or diary entries, or a framed reproduction of a photograph of the author would enhance the display. There are also Web sites for the purchase of items related to Lewis Carroll and Alice, such as http://images.google.com/images?q=alice+in+wonderland&hl=en

Collectibles are also available on eBay.

Pop Culture

ALL THAT JAZZ

"What is jazz?" "...if you hafta ask, you ain't never gonna know!"
—Attributed to Fats Waller

The music we call jazz originated sometime around 1895 in the city of New Orleans. The jazz sound incorporated elements of ragtime, blues, and music played by marching bands. The unique contribution jazz made to the world of music stemmed from the improvisation it allowed the musicians involved in the performance. Previously, Western music traditions required scores to be played exactly as they were written. In a jazz piece, the song becomes a point of reference around which musicians ad lib. The end result often had little resemblance to the piece as written. The fact that many of the musicians lacked proficiency in reading music and relied on their "ear" made improvisation inevitable.

Buddy Bolden is considered the first real jazz musician. Freddie Keppard, Bunk Johnson and Clarence Williams followed. Despite their contributions, these names are not generally known. However, their ideas provided the foundation for jazz as we know it today. Most of these men worked other jobs, as they were not able to make their livings strictly with their music.

The jazz eras can be defined in many ways. The following breakdown is fairly standard and can be found at this Web site: http://www.hypermusic.ca/jazz/fusion.html

Ragtime (1880s–early 1900): Composed mainly for the piano, it combined a sixteenth-note-based syncopated melody with the form and feel of a march.

The Blues (1900s–1920s): A highly expressive, predominantly vocal tradition, the blues communicated the stories and emotions of African-Americans of the time. Usually blues vocalists accompanied themselves on the guitar or sang with the instrumental accompaniment of guitar, piano, harmonica, or even homemade instruments.

Dixieland (1917–1920s): Also known as traditional or New Orleans jazz, Dixieland

All That Jazz—A tri-color background sets the tone for this tribute to the Jazz Age. Instruments give dimension to the display and the erratic lettering used for the title suggests the creative improvisations of this musical genre.

combined blues and ragtime, along with a rich brass band sound and various other influences.

Big Band Music: The Early Years (1920s): This new style performed by a large ensemble usually consisted of 10 layers or more. These bands relied more on saxophones, instead of clarinets, and featured sectional playing. The music performed by big bands was called "swing," a type of music that people could dance to easily.

Big Band Boom (1930s–1940s): Musicians played together in jam sessions at after-hours bars and clubs. Radio was highly instrumental in spreading interest in big band music. New York City ballrooms provided great venues for listening and dancing to big bands.

Latin Jazz (1930s–present): This is characterized by Latin dance rhythms combined with jazz melodies and chord progressions. Congas, bongos, timbales, claves and cowbells can be seen and heard in this genre of jazz.

Bebop (1940s–1950s): This musical style featured a small group of musicians—four to six players—which allowed more solo performances for the players. Bebop was characterized by more complicated melodies and chord progressions, as well as more emphasis on the role of the rhythm section.

Cool Jazz (1940s–1950s): This music was more subtle, moody, muted, and restrained than bebop and may have drawn on the harmonies of composers Stravinsky and Debussy.

Free Jazz (1960s): Experimental, provocative and challenging for many listeners, free jazz was characterized by a high degree of dissonance. Pitch and tone quality were manipulated by musicians on their instruments to produce shrilling and wailing sounds.

Fusion Jazz Rock (1970s–present): This era combines jazz improvisation and chord progressions with the rhythms of rock. It is more electronic than acoustic, featuring synthesizer, electric bass, electric guitar, electronically-processed woodwind and brass instruments. It is characterized by a great deal of percussion.

The noteworthy performers of jazz read like a Who's Who of the musical world: Scott Joplin, Louis Armstrong, Dizzy Gillespie, Ella Fitzgerald, Artie Shaw, Count Basie, Dave Brubeck, Jelly Roll Morton, Miles Davis, Billie Holiday, Duke Ellington, John Coltrane, Lester Young, and Bessie Smith. The list goes on and on. *Jazz: A History of America's Music* by Geoffrey C. Ward and Ken Burns, and *The Illustrated Encyclopedia of Jazz* by Brian Case and Stan Britt were excellent resources for this display.

CREDITS

Our son, Jeff, began playing the trumpet in the third grade. At first we feared that he was tone deaf. The sounds that emanated from his instrument were painfully discordant. Family members found reasons to run errands or planned outside activities when trumpet practice began. Thankfully, with his growth and the passage of time, harmony happened and, finally, family members could hold their heads high at the annual spring concert.

When I think of jazz, I think of Jeff and the joy he found when his friends (and their instruments!) visited and a jam session erupted. The trumpet, shown here, belongs to Jeff.

ASSEMBLING THE DISPLAY

1. An image search on Google yielded some colorful jazz festival posters. Many used variations of the word jazz—jass and jaz with interesting font styles and contrasting colors. The lettering became the focal point of the display and dictated the color palette. The "j" was black, the "a" orange, the tall "z" purple, and the final "z" a bright green. The orange was repeated in the thin rectangle in the upper left of the display. The lower left rectangle was white. Black felt cover the right portion of the case.

A clarinet was wired with thin dark craft wire around the keys and hardware, then attached to the plastic grill which hangs at the top of the display case. Another wire was placed around the instrument about 5" from the bottom and the wire was secured with a straight pin inserted into the corkboard.

A history of the jazz clarinet can be found at this Web site: http://www.answers.com/topic/list-of-jazz-clarinetists

Information was printed on white cardstock, mounted on black poster board and hung to the right of the instrument.

Next to the clarinet was a replica of a keyboard made from poster board. The keyboard was mounted with straight pins and pulled away from the background to give it more prominence. The saxophone was sketched from an illustration found on a Google image search. It was cut out of gold poster board, attached with pins and pulled forward.

This quotation was printed on white cardstock and mounted on black poster board above the saxophone:

> What we play is life.
>
> —Louis Armstrong

At the upper right of the display case, a sepia toned photo of Frankie Trumbauer holding a sax was cut into the shape of a circle and mounted on a circle of brown poster board. Flanking the photo were two miniature color replicas of posters. One announced a performance by Thelonious Monk and others, which was held at a theatre on Broadway. Another, from the year 1910, invited music lovers to the grand opening of Dixie Park where an open air concert, moving pictures and a big minstrel show would take place. All of these items were found in *Jazz: A History of America's Music* by Geoffrey Ward and Ken Burns.

At the lower left of the display, CDs by Sarah Vaughan, Ella Fitzgerald, and Glenn Miller were grouped and attached to the white and black background.

2. On the top left, these items could be found:

> Jazz came to America three hundred years ago in chains.
>
> —Paul Whiteman

> I say, "Play your own way. Don't play what the public wants. You play what you want and let the public pick up on what you're doing—even if it does take them fifteen, twenty years."
>
> —Thelonious Monk

Under that was a photograph of Billie Holiday easily found through a Google image search. This was mounted on black poster board.

A synopsis of the eras of jazz beginning with ragtime and ending with fusion-jazz-rock was printed on white card stock and mounted on black poster board. The description of these eras can be found if you visit http://www.hypermusic.ca/jazz/fusion.html

Interspersed among these descriptions were black musical notes found through a Google image search. All items on the left were printed on white cardstock and mounted on black and/or gold poster board.

3. On the top right was a short biography of Frankie Trumbauer which can be found if you visit http://www.pbs.org/jazz/biography/artist_id_trumbauer_

This was followed by a biography of Louis Armstrong which can be found if you visit http://www.redhotjazz.com/louie.html

Next was a photo of Louis Armstrong.

Under that was the following quote:

Jazz went from the classics to ragtime to Dixieland to swing to bebop to cool jazz, ... But it's always jazz. You can put a new dress on her, a new hat, but no matter what kind of clothes you put on her, she's the same old broad.

—Lionel Hampton

A photo of the Hellfighter's Band, who played throughout Europe during World War I, was next. Under that was a description of the band which can be found if you visit http://www.redhotjazz.com/hellfighters.html

All items on the right were printed on white cardstock and mounted on black and/or orange and gold poster board.

4. On the base of the display, a trumpet was placed on a black velvet covered Styrofoam disk to give it additional height. Books featured in the display were: *Jazz: A History of America's Music* by Geoffrey C. Ward and Ken Burns, *The Oxford Companion to Jazz* by Bill Kirchner, *Black Bottom Stomp* by David A. Jasen and Gene Jones, *The History of Jazz* by Ted Gioia and the CD *Faith* by Kenny G. A white feather boa was woven through the items on the display base. Musical notes were placed within the folds of the boa.

BIGGER AND BETTER

If your space is larger, you could add additional jazz instruments, some hats of the various eras, cocktail glasses, early 78 records or 45s, a phonograph or period radio, sheet music, music journals or musical scores. You could choose a particular era in jazz, and highlight the national events or political newsmakers of the time, as well as the specific music and musicians of those years.

Since the language of jazz is so colorful, you may want to visit this site for additional quotations: http://www.stmoroky.com/reviews/music/jazz/htm

BASEBALL AS AMERICA

I think there are only three things that America will be known for 2,000 years from now when they study this civilization: the Constitution, jazz music and baseball. They're the three most beautifully designed things this culture has ever produced.

—Gerald Early, scholar

The national celebration of America's love for the sport of baseball was found in a traveling exhibition organized by the National Baseball Hall of Fame and Museum. The unprecedented tour criss-crossed the country visiting ten major cities over a four-year period which ended in 2006. The exhibition is currently back in its permanent home in Cooperstown, New York.

The dawn of the modern game of baseball can be traced to a divided America engaged in a bloody civil war. Despite many political differences and contrasting social principles, the North and South shared a surprising common interest: baseball. Michael Aubrecht, Civil War author and baseball essayist, summarizes the feelings of soldiers on both sides of the Mason Dixon line regarding baseball and the battlefield during the course of the War Between the States. To view the soldiers' sentiments, visit: http://www.baseball-almanac.com/articles/aubrecht2004b.shtml

> The parade ground has been a busy place for a week or so past, ball-playing having become a mania in camp. Officer and men forget, for a time, the differences in rank and indulge in the invigorating sport with a schoolboy's ardor.
>
> —Private Alpheris B. Parker,
> 10th Massachusetts Regiment

An unnamed Confederate counterpart recalled:

> It is astonishing how indifferent a person can become to danger. The report of musketry is heard but a very little distance from us.... Yet over there on the other side of the road most of our company, playing bat ball and perhaps in less than half an hour they may be called to play a ball game of a more serious nature.

Sometimes, games would be interrupted by the call of battle. A Union soldier, George Putnam, wrote of a game that was "called-early." The reason for that was a surprise attack on their camp by Confederate infantry:

Baseball as America—The growth of the sport of baseball parallels the evolution of social change within the American culture. This display chronicles the significance of the sport during wartime, disasters and troubling financial times.

Suddenly there was a scattering of fire, which three outfielders caught the brunt; the centerfield was hit and captured, left and right field managed to get back to our lines. The attack ... was repelled without serious difficulty, but we had lost not only our centerfield, but ... the only baseball in Alexandria, Texas.

There has always been much controversy about who was the "father of the modern game." The city of Coopersburg, New York, dedicated Doubleday Field in 1920 as the "official" birthplace of organized baseball. However, baseball historians reject the notion that Union General Abner Doubleday originated the game, since nothing in his writings supports this theory. It has been documented that Doubleday did organize several exhibitions among the Union regiments. These games garnered front-page news that rivaled reports on the progress of the Civil War.

Baseball has always enjoyed a broad appeal across America. From the youngest children who became acquainted with the game in backyards and neighboring playgrounds, to the ardent lifelong fan—this sport has a loyal following which includes people of every age and ethnicity. The growth of the sport of baseball parallels the evolution of American culture. The impact of immigration, the Industrial Age and modern technology can be seen in the development of our society as well as in the game itself. Cherished national values, such as patriotism and ingenuity, have a unique place within this sport.

Baseball's impact on the country is undeniable. More than just a sporting competition, the game has been responsible for bringing people together in times of crisis. During wartime, amidst natural disasters, through periods of tumultuous social change, and in troubling financial periods, baseball has provided an escape for scores of people able to make their way to the comfort and familiarity found at the baseball park.

The culmination of a season of baseball is the race for the championship between the American and National leagues. Better known as the World Series, this "fall classic" began in 1903 and continues to excite and involve a nation of fans to this day.

CREDITS

I am married to a collector of sports memorabilia. An area of our home is dedicated to his passion. Signed bats and baseballs, prized Cal Ripken souvenirs, Wheaties boxes featuring sports figures, baseball cards, ticket stubs, mugs, mitts and buttons have all found a place in an alcove adjacent to our home library. Being surrounded by these mementoes has given my husband great pleasure during the time he spends in his study. Since this collection was readily available for a display, I was eager to feature it in a display at Cressman Library.

I found the 2002 National Geographic publication *Baseball as America* at our local bookstore. Not merely an overview of the history of the game, this publication provided an interesting slant on the evolution of the sport. There is a well-designed and user-friendly Web site for this exhibition which compliments the material in the text. Both the book and the Web site provided excellent background material for all aspects of the history of the sport. They examine how the American landscape, language, literature, movies, and summer lifestyle all reflect baseball's mark on American hopes and values. The book included excellent photographs and graphics. To gain access to this Web site, please visit http://www.baseballasamerica.org/

ASSEMBLING THE DISPLAY

1. The 18" baseball was drawn on white poster board with pen, ink and watercolor. The moisture found in the materials used to color the ball allowed it to curve. When it was mounted with pins to the black felt background, some fiberfill was placed behind it to round out the shape.

The rectangular sign was cut from blue poster board. The word *Baseball* was created using Franklin Gothic Heavy, upper case, sized at 300. The word *as* used the same font, in lower case letters. It was sized at 100. *America* was created by using a 4½" stencil and tracing the letters on scrapbooking paper with a flag design. The stencil was placed in positions that would assure that the stars would appear at a different point in each letter.

The baseball cards were attached with straight pins. Double sided tape was used to attach the circular buttons to the background. The Civil War quotations cited earlier were printed on white cardstock and some were mounted on blue poster board, while others were framed with the flag motif paper. The following quote by 19th century Hall of Fame pitcher, Albert Spalding, was also featured:

> Modern baseball had been born in the brain of an American Soldier, it received its baptism in the bloody days of our Nation's direst danger, it had its early evolution when soldiers, North and South, were striving to forget their foes by cultivating, through this grand game, fraternal friendship with comrades in arms.

2. On the top left there was a photograph of congressional pages choosing up sides in the shadow of the Washington Monument. It was dated circa 1922, and was found in the *Baseball as America* publication. This photo was mounted on blue and black poster board attached with double sided tape to the left side of the display case.

Baseball as America also included a copy of the letter from President Franklin Roosevelt to the baseball commissioner, Hon. Kenesaw M. Landis of Chicago, Illinois, urging him to continue playing baseball despite the recent attack on Pearl Harbor. The letter, dated January 15, 1942, cited the need to keep people employed, and for the country to have a healthy recreational outlet during trying times. This was printed on white cardstock and mounted on blue poster board.

3. On the top right was text that included the origins of the game. This can be found if you visit http://www.baseball-almanac.com/articles/aubrecht2004b.shtml

Under that was a summation of the concept of "Baseball as America" which can be found on their Web site. For that information, visit http://www.baseballasamerica.org

All of this was printed on white cardstock and mounted on either blue poster board or flag motif paper.

4. Styrofoam forms were placed on the base of the display case and covered with black fabric. These blocks provided varied elevations for the items featured. The bat, ball, gloves, batting helmet, and mug were placed among the books. Additional baseball cards were randomly placed throughout the base of the display, along with cut-up stars from a roll of plastic flag tape found in a local dollar store.

The following books were included in this display: *Wait Until Next Year* by Doris Kearns Goodwin, *Baseball's Great Experiment* by Jackie Robinson, *Summer of '49* by David Halberstam, and *Players of Cooperstown: Baseball's Hall of Fame* by David Nemec.

BIGGER AND BETTER

There are many other items that you could feature in your display space, such as a catcher's mask, a Wheaties box featuring a prominent baseball player, a plaque, a jersey, some baseball caps, posters, prints, cleats, programs, ticket stubs, poems such as "Casey at the Bat" by Ernest Lawrence Thayer, the sheet music for "Take Me Out to the Ballgame," a flag or banner, newspaper sports headlines, pennants, baseball magazines, DVD cases for baseball themed films and short biographies of Hall of Fame standouts.

Include a list of baseball firsts, which is available if you visit http://baseball-almanac.com/frstmenu.shtml

The original rules of baseball would be interesting to include and are available at this site: http://www.baseballasamerica.org

FROM PAGE TO SCREEN

> The spell was broken. My uncle learned to laugh, and I learned to cry. The secret garden is always open now. Open, and awake, and alive. If you look the right way, you can see that the whole world is a garden.
> —Mary, *The Secret Garden*, 1993

Since novels and films were prominent entertainment art forms for many decades, it makes sense that the two are linked. Writers were critical of movie studios, which were always in search of new material. Often, the motion picture rights were more lucrative than book sales for the authors. Consequently, writers willingly sold the rights to studios that were intent on maintaining control of their projects.

The conversion of multiple pages of plot within a novel to a few lines of film dialogue presents a challenge to the screenwriter. In a successful adaptation, elaborate detail must fuse into several captivating images, and lengthy character development meld into just a few scenes. The screenwriter's challenge is to provide an outline and dialogue that the collaborators will interpret while being mindful of the talents of the studio's players. The director, cast, editor and production crew unite to interpret the story that the screenwriter develops.

From Page to Screen—Projection reels of varying sizes add a touch of reality to this homage to novels that have found their way to the big screen. Smell the popcorn!

Since film is a visual medium, the screenwriter must avoid telling the story, but rather must show it. He is charged with the task of writing what the audience will see, as well as what they will hear. He needs to make allowances for the actor to improvise, to interpret, to give that "certain look" which ultimately will speak volumes.

Neil Sinyard summarizes his thoughts about noteworthy book to movie adaptations in the comprehensive text *The Classic Novel: From Page to Screen.*

> The most successful screen adaptations of literature have, I would argue, one or all of three main characteristics. They aim for the spirit of the original rather than the literal letter; they use the camera to interpret and not simply illustrate the tale; and they exploit a particular affinity between the artistic temperaments and preoccupations of the novelist and filmmaker [Giddings 147].

Sinyard also adds that an effective film adaptation may diverge from the story, if doing so paves the way for an alternative and possibly superior narrative strategy. Obviously, a film should make certain changes from the primary source. A simple duplication of the original structure would deem the film redundant.

Great classics like Tolkien's *Lord of the Rings*, Mark Twain's *Adven-*

tures of Huckleberry Finn, and Victor Hugo's *Les Miserables* are some examples of the type of literary work worthy of transformation to the silver screen. Recent books made into film include the Harry Potter series, *Bridget Jones' Diary*, *Memoirs of a Geisha*, *Pride and Prejudice*, *High Fidelity*, and *Chicken Little.*

Thousands of books have been translated into film with varying results. The Internet Movie Database is a rich source of titles of films "based-on-novel." To view these titles visit http://www.imdb.com/

Credits

I really enjoy a good film. I particularly enjoy the verbal exchange that follows the movie, as each of us sorts through our personal interpretation of the experience we shared.

My husband recently installed a home theatre in our basement. Obviously this new space required many decisions with regard to design and décor. As the project drew to completion, a local university eliminated their film collection, and we were given the opportunity to acquire a variety of old projection reels at no cost.

We proceeded to spray the reels silver and black, left some with their original gray patina, and hung them at various heights on the stairway wall which descends into the theatre. These reels added some dimension and created an interesting entry to the space. Ultimately, they provided the main focus for the *From Page to Screen* display.

As an avid reader and movie buff, it became apparent to me that many of the films selected for viewing in our home theatre were based on books. And so, the idea for *From Page to Screen* was born.

Assembling the Display

1. The background was lined with red felt, which provided a contrast to the silver, gray and black projection reels. The reels were of three different diameters and arranged so that they filled the entire background surrounding the title signage. Film was woven through all of the reels to connect and unify them.

The title sign font was created using Goudy Old Style, available in MS Word. The words *From* and *To* were in both upper and lower case letters and sized at 100. The word *Page* used just upper case letters and was sized at a 240 font. *Screen* was sized at 230 font using only upper case. These were printed on white card stock and glued to a background of red poster board, and then framed in a 2½" border of black poster board. Finally, this was affixed to a 24" × 15" piece of white poster board which was framed in black. One inch squares of white cardstock were placed on the black frame both above and below the title to represent film.

2. On the top left of the display was the quote introducing this display and the paragraph by Neil Sinyard cited above.

The following quotations were also included:

> You never really understand a person until you consider things from his point of view—until you climb into his skin and walk around in it.
> —Atticus to Scout, in *To Kill a Mockingbird* by Harper Lee

> You live on—in the hearts of everyone you have touched and nurtured while you were here.
> —Morrie to Mitch, in *Tuesdays with Morrie* by Mitch Albom

A photograph of the famous Hollywood sign was found through a Google image search. A description of the sign and its origins was attached. This information can be found if you visit http://www.npr.org/programs/morning/features/patc/hollywoodsign

All of the above were printed on white cardstock and mounted on red and/or black poster board. Clip Art images of projectors and film or film reels were inserted on some of the documents featured in the display.

3. On the top right of the display was the following passage:

> To write dialogue well, it is important to understand what it really is, what it isn't, and why. *The primary function of dialogue is to convey information to the audience.* The information may relate to plot, to character revelation, to locale— anything from the simple fact of what day it is, to the profundity of what a character believes his or her life is all about. In actuality, dialogue is not spoken from one character to another, but from the author to the audience, via the character [Bronfeld 74].

The following quotation was included:

> Many book-to-movie transfers do a disservice to both mediums. The psychological depth that makes good novels tick is surprisingly tough to capture visually. *Midnight in the Garden of Good and Evil*, anyone? Or, consider the gorgeous wreckage that was *The English Patient*, which swapped author Michael Ondaatje's multilayered complexity with jumpy incoherence on the big screen.
> —Kimberly Potts

For this and more thoughts regarding books made into movies, visit http://www.eonline.com/Features/Topten/Bookmovies/

A selected list of Print to Film titles was included. This list can be found if you visit http://www.bookspot.com/features/moviefeature.htm

All of the documents on the right were printed on white cardstock and glued to black and/or red poster board. A border of film was created and affixed at the top and bottom of the Print to Film list. The final film quote was on screenwriting. This and other good quotes on that subject can be found at http://chatna.com/theme/screenwriting.htm

> The challenge of screenwriting is to say much in little and then take half of that little out and still preserve an effect of leisure and natural movement.
> —Raymond Chandler

4. DVDs selected for the display were attached with rolled packing tape to the lower left and right of the display case. They were *About a Boy*, *Frankenstein*, *How the Grinch Stole Christmas*, *The Joy Luck Club*, and *The Postman Always Rings Twice*.

5. Popcorn was strewn among the display books. Movie tickets, found on a Google image search, were printed on cardstock and placed on the center front of the display. A full box of popcorn was elevated on Styrofoam which was covered with black felt.

Books included were *The Accidental Tourist* by Anne Tyler, *Cold Mountain* by Charles Frazier, *The War of the Worlds* by H. G. Wells, *Waiting to Exhale* by Terry McMillan and *The Rainmaker* by John Grisham.

BIGGER AND BETTER

There are many other aspects of film on which you could concentrate. Femme Fatales of Film, Films of the Decade, Behind the Scenes (focusing on directors), Giants of the Silver Screen (highlighting actors), Blockbusters, Silent Films, Golden Age of Film, Song and Dance, Make Me Laugh, Epics and Films and Fantasies are just some ideas that might work in your space.

If you have one available, a director's clapboard would make a great focal point for a film display. Should your space allow, a director's chair would enhance your display.

THE AWESOME 80S

Trust, but verify.

—Ronald Reagan,
President, USA, 1981–1989

The 1980s were marked by a dramatic shift toward more conservative lifestyles after the considerable cultural revolution that prevailed throughout the 1960s and 1970s. American citizens, during this period, elected the oldest man ever to serve as president. This was the decade that officially recognized the AIDS virus (Acquired Immune Deficiency Syndrome), a deadly threat that gripped a nation and the world.

Estimates of homelessness reached record highs by mid-decade, and Americans looked to the sky in shock and disbelief, as the space shuttle *Challenger* exploded 73 seconds after liftoff. We witnessed the Chernobyl nuclear power plant disaster, severe droughts and the largest one-day plunge in stock market history (October 19, 1987), which sent waves of panic across Wall Street. We bade farewell to legends: John Lennon, Princess Grace of Monaco, John Belushi, Cary Grant, Lucille Ball.

The decade opened and closed with major environmental events. 1980 saw the eruption of the Mount Saint Helens volcano, and 1989 endured the Exxon Valdez oil spill, the worst in U.S. history. Medical science attempted to transplant the heart of a baboon into a fragile newborn baby. An artificial heart extended one man's life another 112 days. The Human Genome Project began, and the first plutonium pacemaker was introduced.

Timeline of the '80s

1980: The popular TV show *Dallas* asked, Who shot JR? The U.S. boycotted the summer Olympics in Moscow, Post-It Notes were introduced by 3M, CNN debuted as the first twenty-four hour cable news service, John Lennon was assassinated, smallpox was eradicated by the World Health Organization, Saddam Hussein launched a war against Iran over oil rights, Japan passed the U.S. as the largest automaker, the U.S. suspended grain sales to the Soviet Union in response to their support of the war in Afghanistan, President Carter oversaw a failed helicopter rescue attempt of hostages in Iran, and the US hockey team beat Russia for the gold medal at the winter Olympics.

1981: The shuttle *Columbia* was first launched, President Reagan fired striking air-traffic controllers, Pope John Paul II shot, Sandra Day O'Connor became the first female Supreme Court justice, Mitterrand was elected president of France, Prince Charles married Diana Spencer, ketchup was declared a vegetable by the USDA, the first IBM-PCs were manufactured, MTV was born, Pac-Man was introduced, fifty-two American hostages were released in Iran, there was an assassination attempt on President Ronald Reagan, and AIDS was linked to homosexual behavior in men.

1982: Helmut Kohl became chancellor of Germany, Leonid Brezhnev died, Reverend Sun Myung Moon married 4,150 followers at Madison Square Garden, Prince

The Awesome 80s—Famous images of this Decade of Plenty can be found within the large numerals. Cabbage Patch dolls and Trivial Pursuit are nostalgic reminders of this era.

William was born to Prince Charles and Lady Diana, Mexico's economy collapsed, Liposuction was introduced, the telephone monopoly was dissolved, the Equal Rights Amendment died, and the Vietnam Memorial was erected in Washington, DC.

1983: The Cabbage Patch doll debuted, the "Just Say No" campaign against drug abuse was introduced, the U.S. invaded Grenada after a coup, Karen Carpenter died of anorexia nervosa, the final episode of *M*A*S*H* aired to record number of TV viewers, Sally Ride became the first American woman in space, camcorders and compact discs were introduced, Australia won the America's Cup for the first time in 132 years, and HIV was discovered by French scientist Dr. Luc Montagnier.

1984: Indira Gandhi was assassinated, Ronald Reagan was re-elected in a landslide, Congress cut off aid to Nicaragua, Bell Labs produced the first megabit chip, infomercials appeared on TV due to FCC de-regulation, the Soviet Union boycotted the summer Olympics in Los Angeles, rap music was introduced, Apple Computer released the Macintosh PC, and the term *cyberspace* was coined by author William Gibson.

1985: Live Aid in London and Philadelphia was beamed around the world, crack cocaine appeared, an earthquake in Mexico and a volcano in Columbia killed thousands, Gorbachev became the last president of the Soviet Union, the *Titanic*'s wreckage was found and filmed by a robotic camera, the hole in the ozone layer became an indisputable fact, the Nintendo system was introduced, leaded gas was banned, and Rock Hudson died of AIDS, the first major public figure known to do so.

1986: The Iran-Contra scandal was reported, Halley's Comet returned, the Statue of Liberty turned 100, Oprah Winfrey began her televised syndicated show nationally, Martin Luther King, Jr., Day was established, supermodel Gia became first woman known to die of AIDS in the U.S., and President Corazon Aquino ended the corrupt Marcos regime in the Philippines.

1987: "Baby Jessica" was rescued from a well in Midland, Texas, after a three day ordeal, the battle for "Baby M" brought reproductive technology to the forefront, Margaret Thatcher was re-elected prime minister of the United Kingdom, condom commercials began to appear on TV, Robert Bork was denied a Supreme Court appointment, scandals which involved Jim Bakker and Gary Hart dominated the headlines, Klaus Barbie was convicted of Nazi war crimes, and world population reached a record 5 billion.

1988: Pan Am flight 103 exploded over Lockerbie in Scotland, Prozac was introduced as an anti-depressant, work began on the Chunnel, Benazir Bhutto became the first woman to head an Islamic nation, the Iran-Iraq war ended, Australia turned 200, and Yellowstone Park endured severe fires.

1989: The Berlin Wall fell, Iran began its hunt for Salman Rushdie, students protested on Tiananmen Square, where thousands were killed, the trade of ivory was banned worldwide, the Stealth bomber was completed, Pete Rose was banned from baseball, Vietnam ceased its occupation of Cambodia, and the Soviet Union withdrew fully from Afghanistan.

CREDITS

I have fond memories of the '80s. My children experienced their pre-teen and teen years during this decade. The '80s were indeed the decade of plenty in pop culture. *Wham, Star Wars, The Cosby Show, The A-Team, Punky Brewster*, the *Thriller* album, *Rainbow Bright, New Kids on the Block, M*A*S*H, The Facts of Life, Born in the USA, MTV* and the Sony Walkman come to mind when reflecting on this period. Included in this display were images from scanned photos housed in the archives of the Cressman Library, Cedar Crest College. These were photographs of our alums involved in various college related activities during the 1980s.

The display received very positive comments from our college students. It was a decade they remember and to which they could relate. The Cabbage Patch dolls and Rubik's Cube seemed to be highlights of the display.

ASSEMBLING THE DISPLAY

1. The black felt background provided a contrast for the large numerals, "80," which were cut out of yellow poster board. Photographs of events of the 1980s were found through a Google image search and glued to the poster board. For guidance in your search for '80s nostalgia, please visit http://www.80snostalgia.com/index.php

Nineteen-eighties photographs from the college library archives and yearbooks were scanned, then cut to fit into the collage, along with images of political figures, national events, members of royalty, pop culture slogans, popular games and toys, and entertainment personalities.

Title signage was drawn freehand on red poster board and outlined with black magic marker.

2. On the left and right of the display case was a timeline for each year of the decade. This was created in Microsoft Publisher. The numbers for each year were inserted using Word Art and selecting the shadow style. Text boxes with the date and description of each event were positioned under the heading. Twelve black squares signifying the months of the year were inserted along the bottom using clip art. Arrows were drawn from the appropriate square to the event in the text box. In Microsoft Publisher choose *insert, picture, autoshapes, lines* and then select the arrow graphic to attach arrows.

3. At the center of the display were two Cabbage Patch dolls with miniature boxes of doll cookies and cereal. To the right was a Smurf lunchbox. In the front of the dolls were the following media: the CDs of *The Big Chill* and Steve Winwood's *Back in the High Life*, the videos *Heartburn* and *Accidental Tourist*, and the DVD of *Raging Bull*. A Rubik's Cube sits atop a Plexiglas stand behind a second edition of Trivial Pursuit, complete with game pieces.

Books displayed were *20th Century Pop Culture: The 80s* by Dan Epstein, *Decades of the 20th Century: The 1980s from Ronald Reagan to MTV* by Stephen Feinstein, *The 1980s* by John Peacock, *A Cultural History of the United States Through* the Decades: The 1980s* by Stuart A. Kallen, and *Totally Awesome 80s* by Matthew Rettenmund.

BIGGER AND BETTER

Your display of the '80s might feature Movies of the Decade, Headlines of the '80s, Best Sellers or Notable Books, Women's Fashions of the 1980s, Musical Tribute to the Decade, Classic TV Shows, or 1980s Politics. There is a great deal of information relevant to all of these topics in books on the decade, particularly *20th Century Pop Culture: The 80s* by Dan Epstein, and *Pride and Prosperity: The 80s*, a Time-Life book publication.

For online information, visit http://www.mables.com

For events, prices, people and pop culture for any given day in the 1980s, visit http://dmarie.com/timecap/

NO PUN INTENDED

Analyzing humor is like dissecting a frog. Few people are interested and the frog dies of it.

—E. B. White

In the last decade or so, there has been an explosion of interest in the concept of humor. Many of the current best selling paperbacks are books of cartoons. Comedians have become authors of numerous witty memoirs. Television networks continue to develop dozens of situation comedies for viewers each fall. Nothing *but* humor is featured on some cable channels. Comedy clubs abound in cities throughout the nation.

In addition to the pleasure derived from the simple exercise of laughter, there is a medical interest in the other benefits that can be attained. Researchers have been studying the effect of humor on the immune system in recent years. Tens of thousands of nurses subscribe to the *Journal of Nursing Jocularity*. Hundreds of corporations hold seminars on the importance of humor with respect to stress reduction in the workplace and in promoting cooperation among co-workers.

Our Puritan forefathers believed in a no-nonsense, hard-work ethic, and, more accurately, a dedication to the achievement of goals. The only justifications for laughter and play were if they managed to refresh us for more work, or were channeled into goal-oriented activities. One way that society found to achieve the latter mission was to organize team sports such as hockey and football, which were truly "goal" oriented. Many parents, when commenting on their child's performance at the end of a Little League game, are heard referencing the work ethic by saying "good work," or "good job!"

However, the philosophy of a strict work ethic is no longer effective in today's workplace. Employers now want and need employees who engender enthusiasm,

No Pun Intended—A rubber chicken is a great sight gag that sets the tone for this display on the importance of humor within the workplace and in society.

are risk takers, will engage in higher level thinking, and can be objective and creative problem solvers. Other important traits in the workplace are versatility, and the ability to create rapport and motivate others. Wise managers encourage a spirit of fun in the workplace. As David Ogilvy, head of a major advertising agency, said: "When people aren't having any fun, they seldom produce good advertising. Kill grimness with laughter. Maintain an atmosphere of informality. Encourage exuberance" (Peters and Waterman 291).

A high profile example of the link between fun, creativity and output is Thomas Edison. During his lifetime, he applied for and received almost 1100 patents registered in his name. This renowned inventor would frequently comment that he never did a day's work in his entire life—it was all fun! Edison honestly believed that his best creative efforts, the most effective and valuable work, were indeed fun.

Some people disregard the importance of a sense of humor. They consider it trivial. However, these are the same individuals who find it difficult to adapt to environmental changes and tend to be oblivious to the humor in situations. Their tendency is to react harshly when events do not go as planned. On the contrary, there are those individuals whose sense of humor permits them to rise above the negative and maintain a spirit of optimism when plans do not progress as expected.

No matter where you find it, laughter is great medicine. Its benefits seem the most therapeutic when we laugh because we need to. Laughter's positive effects are greatly enhanced when we chuckle because someone who loves us reminds us how. It might happen at a life altering point, or a door-slamming moment, or even after withstanding a monumental loss. Humor may just be the long term key to healthy survival.

Looking at life with humor is like viewing Earth from afar. In that situation we would not be overly attached to material possessions or specific events. When mishaps occurred we would stay levelheaded and on task, instead of reacting to feelings. Humor is a thoughtful response rather than an emotional one. As the eighteenth century novelist and political commentator Horace Walpole said: "The world is a comedy to those who think, a tragedy to those who feel."

There were some informative and entertaining sources which were relevant to this display. *Humor Works*, by John Morreall, gave insight into humor and the workplace. *The 776 Stupidest Things Ever Said* by Ross and Kathryn Petras offered a collection of brainless, ridiculous and witty misstatements and doublespeak attributed to people in the public eye.

Other valuable sources were *Humor at Work* by Esther Blumenfeld and Lynne Alpern, and *Humor Me: The Geranium Lady's Funny Little Book About Big Laughs* by Barbara Johnson.

CREDITS

I have always had a personal philosophy that it is beneficial to create a work environment where humor is accepted and encouraged. I actually have no choice. I supervise college students who would rather be sleeping, have only been shown the task three times, have a test in an hour, never went to bed last night, just flunked a quiz, caught what their roommate has, accidentally turned off the snooze button, or just broke up with their boyfriend. Whatever the excuse, I am reminded daily that their prime focus is not their minimum wage job in the library. Life is what matters.

So, the decision to mount a display on humor was a no-brainer.

ASSEMBLING THE DISPLAY

1. Two-inch black adhesive-backed commercial letters were used to create the title "No Pun Intended." These were attached to white poster board. Surrounding this phrase were cutout caricatures with smiling faces which were located through online image searches. On the top right, a rubber chicken was hung from the ceiling grate and integrated into the poster design. At the very top was a caricature of Groucho Marx, which was found at www.proclassics.de/lasalle.htm and printed on off-white card stock. The quote captioned above him read:

> I could dance with you until the cows come home. On second thought, I'd rather dance with the cows until you come home.
>
> —Groucho Marx

Below the title poster were three reproductions of comedy video covers found through Google image searches. These were printed on off-white card stock, attached with pins and pulled forward.

Under these were quotations surrounded by laughing mouths found on image searches and printed on off-white card stock. These were also pulled forward on pins. The quotes were embedded in "speech bubbles" as seen in comic strips:

> Have you ever noticed? Anybody going slower than you is an idiot, and anyone going faster than you is a moron?
>
> —George Carlin

> Tom Seaver: "What time is it?"
> Yogi Berra: "You mean now?"

> Nobody goes there anymore, it's too crowded.
>
> —Yogi Berra

These were printed on white cardstock and pulled forward.

2. On the top left of the display was a Far Side cartoon found through a Google image search. Under that was a synopsis, "Humor in Life," mainly taken from *Taking Laughter Seriously*, by John Morreall, PhD. Two cartoons found on a Google image search were positioned above and below this quote printed in a speech bubble:

> If crime fighters fight crime, and fire fighters fight fires, then what do freedom fighters fight?
>
> —George Carlin

All items on the left were printed on white cardstock and mounted on black and/or red poster board.

3. On the top right was a passage titled "Skunk Works" from *Humor Works* (Morreall 19) which describes an unorthodox work setting used by a branch of the Xerox Corp. which promoted openness,creative thinking, and humor along with team spirit. An illustration of a skunk, found on a Google image search, was printed on off-white card stock and attached to the bottom right of the text. Under that was a comic strip which can be found if you visit http://www.otherarena.com/htm/cgi-bin/comicstrip.cgi?007

Next was the quote introducing this display and another Yogi Berra quote:

> "If you ask me anything I don't know, I'm not going to answer."

A passage on humor in the field of advertising which could be found in *In Search of Excellence* (Peters 291) was next. All of the items on the right were printed on white cardstock and mounted on black and/or red poster board.

4. The bottom of the display was lined with black velvet material which covered Styrofoam forms. At the top was a face which was found through a Google image search and printed on off-white card stock, then mounted on poster board. A triangle of black poster board served as a stand. Groucho Marx glasses, nose and eyebrows were hung over the face. A reproduction of a yellow whoopee cushion (found on a

Google image search) was printed on cardstock and mounted on black poster board. This was positioned among the books featured, which were *The North Beach Diet*, by Kim Bailey, *Jokes* by Ted Conen, *Humor Me* by Barbara Johnson, *Laughter* by Robert R. Provine, *The Mammoth Book of Humor* by Geoff Tibbals, and *Fierce Pajamas: An Anthology of Humor Writing* from the *New Yorker*, by David Remnick. Interspersed among these items were various colored "happy faces" found on a Google search and printed on off-white card stock.

BIGGER AND BETTER

Should your space permit, you could use additional sight gags such as an arrow piercing a head, a nail through a finger nail, a real whoopee cushion, the classic text of "Who's on First?," and actual video or DVD cases of comedy programs and films. You could also include clown faces or the comic face in literature. You could choose a specific subject around which to create your display, such as the Three Stooges or Abbott and Costello, or perhaps a favorite contemporary comedian.

Genres

Wild, Wild West

At sunset hour the forest was still, lonely, sweet with tang of fir and spruce,
blazing in gold and red and green; and the man who glided on under the great
trees seemed to blend with the colors and, disappearing, to have become a part
of the wild woodland.

—*The Man of the Forest* by Zane Grey

There is a unique and magical aura that surrounds the American West. Its geography is massive in scope. The snow-capped peaks of the Teton Range, the red rock monoliths of Monument Valley, the treeless expanses of the prairie, towering cowboys, tall tales and turbulent history all add to the allure that this region has had for those who have sought to explore and conquer it.

The story of the West includes the historical idea of the victory of civilized man over the barbarian, of pioneers conquering not only the perceived enemy, but a menacing terrain that over time has exacted a hefty human price. For these brave men and women, the promise of acquiring land and newfound riches overshadowed the perils of the daily journey. American historians are fortunate to have autobiographical accounts, which were chronicled in both diaries and letters, that weathered not only the expedition, but also the passage of time.

An America without the West is unfathomable. Still, there were no assurances that the newcomers would, or could, make a claim to it. Others had prior ownership of this land. They certainly had the will to preserve their possession and mount a strong resistance.

The United States could easily have remained a nation east of the Mississippi. However, our forefathers were visionaries who sought to explore and annex the existing territory. Their resolve, coupled with the courage of those early pioneers, made the exploration of this region inevitable.

It was only a matter of time before the historical accounts of the passage west made their way to the country's literature. Western genre books, by definition, are set in the American West, almost exclusively in the 19th century, and take place generally between the Antebellum period and the turn of the century. Their settings may extend back to the American colonial period or forward to the mid 20th century. Geographically, they may span North America and range from Canada to Mexico.

Many Westerns are set on the brink of emerging technology—such as the printing press, the telegraph and the railroad. The stories usually suggest an impending end to the nostalgia associated with the frontier days and the emergence of a more modern era.

It is interesting to note that Western fiction got its start in publications that were called "penny dreadfuls," which were later upgraded to "dime novels." These inexpensive books were published to profit from the true stories that were being recounted by the mountain men, settlers, villains and heroes who pioneered the movement west. Pulp magazines also capitalized on the folk tales of these adventurous easterners.

The Western in American literature emerged with the novels of James Fenimore Cooper. However, Westerns weren't considered a separate genre until the publication in 1902 of *The Virginian*, written by Owen Wister. This was followed a decade later by *Riders of the Purple Sage* by a newcomer named Zane Grey.

Of all of the notable authors of Western genre, Louis L'Amour was by far the

Wild, Wild West—The steer's skull offers a compelling focal point for this celebration of the old West. The portrait of John Wayne provides a balance to the imposing artifact.

most prolific. At the time of his death, it was estimated that he had published 101 novels, short story collections, and poetry and non-fiction. The reason L'Amour had such success with this genre is that he traveled the West, knew the people, and fully understood the culture and the mind-set. For the interesting account of the life and times of Louis L'Amour, visit http://www.kirjasto.sci.fi/lamour.htm

Tony Hillerman, Annie Proulx, Barbara Kingsolver, Elmore Leonard and Larry McMurtry are successful contemporary writers who frequently place their stories in the West. Several of these authors have had their works successfully adapted for TV and film.

The popularity of Western movies during the majority of the twentieth century helped spur the Western genre. Some decades later, these tales ultimately made their way to the small screen with popular TV shows such as *The Lone Ranger*; *Maverick*; *Gunsmoke*; *Have Gun, Will Travel*; *Little House on the Prairie* and *Bonanza*.

With its heroes and villains, misdeeds and triumphs, truths and legends, the story of the American West, as told in fiction and non-fiction, in print and on film, has left an indelible mark on the world and continues to intrigue us.

CREDITS

Although I am not a fan of Western genre movies, it was hard to avoid all the hype given to the 2005 film *Brokeback Mountain*, written by Annie Proulx. Beautifully filmed in the U.S. and Canada, and adapted for the screen by Larry McMurtry, the movie enjoyed a successful run in 2005, taking in over $170 million at the box office here and abroad. This modern-age Western told a revolutionary love story. After experiencing this film, I decided to focus on the Western as a genre for a library display.

The portrait of John Wayne, painted in 1972 by Lehigh Valley artist Russ Famulary, found its way to my home several years ago. When considering what props to include on a display featuring the West, it became clear that this painting would make a great backdrop.

PBS serves as a rich source of material useful for library personnel responsible for displays. New Perspectives on the West is an excellent Web site that contains many resources which will help to bring your display to life. The companion volume, *The West: An Illustrated History* by Geoffrey C. Ward and Dayton Duncan, will provide letters, diaries, memoirs and 400 photos that chronicle the wave of newcomers into the western landscape. For this PBS site visit http://www.pbs.org/weta/thewest/

ASSEMBLING THE DISPLAY

1. The black felt background combines with a camel felt irregularly cut on the diagonal to suggest the look of the mountainous terrain symbolic of the American West. The portrait of John Wayne hangs to the left of the title of the display. The font Fisticuffs, sized at 250, was used for the lettering of the word *Wild* and sized at 500 for the word *West*. The letters were printed on white cardstock and traced onto red

poster board, then attached with straight pins and pulled forward for a 3 dimensional effect. To obtain this font visit http://www.1001fonts.com

A cactus, drawn on green poster board, hangs under the title and to the right of the display. Both a black permanent marker and a yellow highlighter were used to add detail to the cactus.

Posters titled *Lawmen of the American West* and another called *Wanted: Outlaws of the West* were created. They each included characters appropriate to these categories, and gave a brief description of the subject's relevance. Included under *Lawmen* were Wyatt Earp, Bat Masterson, James Butler Hickok, and the members of the Pinkerton National Detective Agency. *Outlaws* featured the likes of Billy the Kid, the Dalton Gang, Jesse James and the James Gang, as well as Butch Cassidy and the Wild Bunch.

Factual information on *Lawmen* and *Outlaws* can be found at http://www.line camp.com/museums/americanwest/hubs/gun_fighters_lawmen_outlaws/gun_fighters_ lawmen_outlaws.html

These posters were printed on off-white card stock, and the edges were scorched with a lighter to give an irregular singed border. A bullet hole was fashioned on the *Outlaws* poster. This was glued to red poster board and positioned on the diagonal to the right of the painting. A feather from a bird of prey connected the two.

2. On the top left of the display is a poem titled *Finale of the Puncher* by E. A. Brininstool. This was printed on off-white card stock and attached to red poster board. This poem and many others on the American cowboy and the Western experience can be found by visiting http://www.cowboypoetry.com

Below the poem was a replica of *Harper's Weekly: A Journal of Civilization* from September 27, 1877. This was mounted on black poster board. This front page illustration depicted Chief Joseph and his followers being pursued by U.S. troops through the mountains of Idaho in 1877 (Josephy).

3. On the right side of the display case are two documents: one titled "The Western Genre" and the other "Western Literature." Information for both essays can be obtained if you visit http://en.wikipedia.org/wiki/Western

This information was printed on off-white cardstock which had Western clip art from MS Word inserted at the bottom center. This was then attached to red poster board. Between these two documents hangs the following quote:

> I am probably the last writer who will ever have known the people who lived the frontier life. In drifting about across the West, I have known five men and two women who knew Billy the Kid, two who rode in the Tonto Basin war in Arizona, and a variety of others who were outlaws, or frontier marshals like Jeff Milton, Bill Tilghman, and Chris Madse, or just pioneers.
> —Louis L'Amour, *Education of a Wandering Man, 1989.*

This was printed on off-white cardstock and mounted on olive green poster board.

4. Just off center of the display base is a large steer's skull.

This was placed on a wine and ecru striped woven southwestern rug. Styrofoam blocks were placed under the rug to elevate the skull. Cacti and a rock surround the skull, along with a Western belt buckle. One cactus was elevated 4" on a piece of Styrofoam. Sand and stones were interspersed over the rug. Coarse rope was strewn over the books and skull to unify the tableau.

5. Books featured in the Wild, Wild West were *The Frontier in American History* by Frederick Turner, *Finding the West: Explorations with Lewis and Clark* by James Ronda, *The Real Wild West: The 101 Ranch and the Creation of the American West* by Michael Wallis, *Beyond the Great Snow Mountains* by Louis L'Amour, *The West: An Illustrated History* by Geoffrey Ward and Dayton Duncan, *Cowboy Folk Humor: Life and Laughter in the American West* by John West, *Dead Man's Walk* by Larry McMurtry, *Bad Dirt: Wyoming Stories* by Annie Proulx, and *The West: The Making of the American West* by Jon Lewis.

Lying in front of the Turner book is the following quote by Frederic Remington, famous painter, sculptor and illustrator of the American West:

> Art is a she-devil of a mistress, and if at times in earlier days she would not even stoop to my way of thinking, I have persevered and will so continue.

This was printed on off-white cardstock and attached to olive poster board.

BIGGER AND BETTER

There were many alternative props that could have been incorporated into a display on the subject of the American West, namely cowboy boots and apparel, a small saddle, large rocks, dried leaves and weeds, weapons, lassos, textiles, sheriffs' badges, period maps, Native American headdresses, beads, gold pieces, horseshoes, vintage money, a wagon wheel, snakes, and mounted animal heads or skins.

The subject could be narrowed to the Lewis and Clark expedition, featured the California Gold Rush or just one geographical area of the movement westward. Or, your display could highlight one of the authors of this genre. The focus could be on the Native American resistance, or one of the many and famous battles, such as the Alamo, which were central to the story of the acquisition of this region. Centering on the subject of the lawmen or the outlaws would make an interesting display. Notable military personnel or famous chiefs would also work as a theme.

Posters or Western art could be used in place of the portrait central to this display. Period maps or flags would make an effective background.

TALES OF HORROR

> People want to know why I do this, why I write such gross stuff. I like to tell them I have the heart of a small boy ... and I keep it in a jar on my desk.
> —Stephen King

It has been said that the genre of horror fiction is the branch of literature which is most concerned with pushing the limits. It is the form of fantasy that provides the least escape for its readers. The criterion for this genre is that it be frightening and repulsive with elements of horror, fantasy and the supernatural. Horror fiction presents us with sights that we would otherwise find grotesque, or a perceptivity we would prefer to ignore. It invites strangers into our world and introduces a freakish dimension into our lives. It acknowledges our fears, and continues to traumatize. Horror works its way into the science fiction, fantasy, and crime fiction genres, and sometime even finds its way into more mainstream literature.

Generally speaking, horror fiction is that literature which intends to scare, unnerve, or terrify the reader. The genesis of the horror experience has frequently been the infiltration of an otherwise unremarkable event by a demonic, or, perhaps a misconstrued paranormal element. This writing frequently explores the evil side of humanity. Often, the main characters are people with whom we can identify, even though there is a hint of estrangement present. Frequently the mood of the work is foreboding, which demands an emotional reaction from the reader. The main ingredient in horror fiction is the unexpected followed by dread.

Violence and explicit sexuality are frequently present. Traditionally, horror is associated with demons, ghosts, vampires and witches, although it has branched out to include other paranormal events. Elizabeth Peake gives some excellent pointers on writing horror. She warns that if you want to write horror, think about the things that really frighten you. Ponder those subjects that cause your mouth to go dry, and your insides to get queasy. Peake theorizes that if you go to that certain place where you would

Tales of Horror—The graveyard setting is sure to create an eerie tone for books designed to shock. Flying bats, crawling creatures and one lone wolf complete this tableau of terror.

not usually venture and face your fear, you will then have the mindset to work in this genre. For more information about what makes a horror writer, visit http://www. writing-world.com/sf/peake.shtml

Fear is the secret weapon held by those who write the macabre and craft the sinister story. Horror writers such as Stephen King look to dredge up the whole fright syndrome that is outside our day to day experiences. Do you dare chance being scared? Perhaps it will serve a purpose. Reacting to that which shocks us can provide an outlet for the real fears that permeate our daily lives.

Horror: 100 Best Books, edited by Stephen Jones and Kim Newman, was a very helpful source for developing this display. As you peruse the contents of this monograph, several authors stand out as particularly noteworthy. Historically, there were Jane Austen *(Northanger Abbey)*, Edgar Allan Poe, Bram Stoker *(Dracula)*, Nathaniel Hawthorne *(Twice-Told Tales)*, Mary Wollstonecraft Shelley *(Frankenstein)*, Robert Louis Stevenson *(Dr. Jekyll and Mr. Hyde)*, and H. G. Wells *(Island of Dr. Moreau)*. Current writers of this genre are Stephen King, Clive Barker, Anne Rice, Dean Koontz, Thomas Harris, Peter Straub, and Jay Anson.

CREDITS

The idea for this display came from a recent Halloween purchase. The wolf's mask, coupled with grandmother's nightgown (with Red Riding Hood in tow) provided an easy costume for a neighborhood theme party. The wolf mask has always generated a powerful reaction from neighbor children trick or treating, and so it seemed a natural item to include in a display called Tales of Horror.

An online image search provided some guidance for the final design of the gravestone, bat and spider.

ASSEMBLING THE DISPLAY

1. The background was divided into two sections. The top black felt suggested night, and the olive green poster board was meant to serve as the graveyard grass. The 13" white circular moon was cut from poster board, with a crescent yellow poster board highlight glued to the left side. Bats of two sizes (9" and 4" wide) were attached to the moon with pins and pulled forward for effect. The black poster board had an orange reverse side which created a soft glow with the display case light on. The bats were initially printed on cardstock and traced on black poster board.

The gravestone measuring 20" wide and 28" high was made out of silver poster board. A section of red poster board was attached to give the illusion of depth. A black permanent marker was used to embellish the poster with a rectangle to frame the words *Tales of* and also to add cracks that gave a weathered effect. The font used was Creeper sized at 300 for the "H" and 250 for the remainder of the word Horror. This was printed on card stock and traced onto red poster board. The font selected for the words "TALES OF" was Frankie sized at 250. This was printed on card stock and traced onto black poster board. Grass was fashioned from 3 different shades of green poster board and construction paper. Fiberfill was placed throughout the display to represent fog.

2. On the top left of the display were thoughts by Stephen King about the place of horror writing in finding an outlet for your personal fears. *Contemporary Authors New Revision Series*, Vol. 1, has an excellent entry on this subject by King. A synopsis of his thoughts was printed on white cardstock and glued on red poster board.

Below that was a quote by Mary Shelley from *Frankenstein*:

> It was already one in the morning; the rain pattered dismally against the panes, and my candle was nearly burnt out, when by the glimmer of the half-extinguished light, I saw the dull eye of the creature open.

The quotation was printed on white cardstock and double mounted on red and black poster board. Bats of varying size cut from black poster board were strategically placed on both of the above items.

These items on the left were printed on white cardstock and mounted on red and/or black poster board.

On the lower left was a reproduction of the poster from the 1955 horror film *Tarantula!* The poster and a passage that described the movie were found in *Science-Fiction and Horror Movie Posters in Full Color*, edited by Alan Adler. The descriptive passage was printed on cardstock and both were mounted on black or red poster board.

3. On the top right of the display is a quote by Bram Stoker from *Dracula:*

> Then a dog began to howl somewhere in a farmhouse far down the road, a long, agonized wailing, as if from fear. The sound was taken up by another dog, and then another, till, borne on the wind which now sighed softly through the Pass, a wild howling began, which seemed to come from all over the country, as far as the imagination could grasp it through the gloom of the night.

An essay on horror writing located through a Google search was printed on white card stock and mounted on red poster board. For this information visit http://www.writing-world.com/sf/peake.shtml

All of the above items on the right were printed on white cardstock and mounted on red and/or black poster board.

At the bottom right of the display is a reproduction of the poster, also from the Adler book, for the 1956 film *Not of This Earth*. A synopsis of the plot, taken from that source, was printed on white cardstock. Both of these items were mounted on black or red poster board.

Below that, printed on white card stock and double mounted on red and black poster board, was a quote by Clive Barker:

> To you who have never died, may I say: Welcome to the world!

4. On the base of the display the rubber wolf mask was elevated with Styrofoam draped in black felt and stuffed with a balloon. Additional fiberfill and some spiders, found on an online image search, were placed in and around the books. The books

featured in this display were *Nightmares and Dreamscapes* by Stephen King, *The Monster Show* by David J. Skal, *Horror: 100 Best Works* edited by Stephen Jones and Kim Newman, *Memnoch the Devil: The Vampire Chronicles* by Anne Rice, *Horror Stories* by Susan Price, *Horror: A Thematic History in Fiction and Film* by Darryl Jones, and Clive Barker's *Days of Magic, Nights of War*.

BIGGER AND BETTER

This display would obviously work well for Halloween. Walk through the party store or the dollar store for ideas relevant to a display on the macabre.

You could piggyback on a current popular film of the genre for your horror display. Or, you could choose a particular author's works and build the display solely on his or her body of work. If you chose Edgar Allan Poe, for example, you could use a raven as your primary graphic. For useful educational information about Poe at a nominal charge, visit http://www.poemuseum.org/educational_resources/index.html

Your display could include skulls, a skeleton, eyeballs, an arm rising from the ground, ghosts, a mummy, rats, a witch's hat, goblins, a bloody knife, and a vampire cape, coffin and teeth.

If your horror display centers on science fiction, you could include a flying saucer or spaceship, and a head shaped like an alien. Check some old covers of publications such as *Analog* or *Fantasy and Science Fiction* for ideas relevant to this type of display.

Be sure to consult this colorful source for your display: *Horror Poster Art* edited by Tony Nourmand and Graham Marsh. It is sure to help.

HOT NIGHTS, COOL READS

> Best sellerism is the star system of the book world. A "best seller" is a celebrity among books. It is a book primarily (sometimes exclusively) known for its well knownness.
> —Daniel Boorstin, Librarian of Congress Emeritus

Reading for pleasure is the ultimate great escape. Entertainment does not come in a more portable or accessible form than books. And, remember, no batteries required! Any time that you can snatch a few minutes, while you travel, or while you wait, you can become immersed into your current selection. Dive into books—experience other lives, other centuries, other worlds. Leave your cares behind for a while and go, absorbed or entranced, into the world of the written word.

Those who were fortunate enough to have learned the joys of reading at an early age, usually under the guidance of a parent or that special teacher, know that there will never be a substitute for a really good book. All of the wisdom of the ages, all the tales that delight, are available at negligible cost, to be selected and savored, or put aside as your whim dictates.

Reading for pleasure can lead to laughter or tears. This experience provides us with exciting alternative perspectives. It serves to move us away from the center of the specialized circles inherent in our required work related reading material. This activity broadens our objectivity and challenges us to consider new ideas, or strengthen personal views. Books are the fantasies we would love to have. Like dreams, they have the ability to change our consciousness. Let's face it, at the end of the day, readers are just looking for good stories!

The hot books of summer are as varied as the shades of the sea, but will frequently include the newest Harry Potter book; those tried and true mystery stories from veteran writers such as Elmore Leonard and Michael Connelly, the hottest tell-all biography, and a particularly potent saga of forbidden love. Serious reads need not apply to the summer book list.

Summer suggests a slower pace, perhaps more leisure time, and certainly some outdoor alternatives to the more sedentary lifestyle the colder months allow. This is the time to track down the runaway hit atop the best-seller list, the original work upon which that summer blockbuster movie was based, or, perhaps, that classic that has always intrigued. The pleasure reader concludes, at the book's end, that he may indeed

Hot Nights, Cool Reads—What is a day at the beach without palm trees, sand and shells? This setting is a perfect scenario for that lazy summer day where a cool drink and an easy read are high priorities.

be wiser, yet is still amazed that he had been drawn through these soundless pages into some amazing dreams, all the while absorbed by the story.

Elizabeth Hardwick, New York novelist and journalist, summarized her feelings about the written word: "The greatest gift is the passion for reading. It is cheap, it consoles, it distracts, it excites, it gives you knowledge of the world and experience of a wide kind."

For additional quotes on reading, go to http://www.brainyquote.com/quotes/key words/reading.html.

CREDITS

Those of us who have raised families know the difficulty in finding a few moments to ourselves. "Soccer Moms," as they have become known to be, have learned to keep a book and/or magazine handy to maximize the time they inevitably spend waiting for practice to end, books to be retrieved from lockers, or social interactions to be completed.

Most of us savor the idea of having the time to sit on the beach with the a book we have set aside for just that purpose. We anticipate doing absolutely nothing but savoring the sun rays while our eyes follow the unfolding saga. Choose a paperback; they pack well, and can be stashed in a tiny section of your overstuffed suitcase. Remember, summer means fun—save the weighty bestsellers and more serious literary works for fireside reading next winter!

This display, which celebrates books at the beach, is dedicated to my oldest and dearest friend, Joan Allen. An avid reader, she not only graciously shared her beach house all these years, but often provided the books!

ASSEMBLING THE DISPLAY

1. The large palm trees dominate the space and set the mood for this tongue-in-cheek display. The trees were secured to the background with straight pins and staples. Directions for making these trees can be found in the Resources section. The title of the display, *Hot Nights*, was done with the Arial font, size 150, bold. The font for *Cool Reads* was Agency FB, size 150, bold italic. Both were printed on white card stock and glued to cloud patterned poster board. The clouds were attached with pins and pulled away from the background for emphasis. The background for this display was light blue felt, which represented the bright summer sky.

2. Quotes were printed on white cardstock and glued to the cloud patterned poster board which was then cut in the shapes of clouds. Two clouds were hung on the left side panel, with three clouds on the right of the display cases. Colorful animated butterflies were found using an online image search and selecting the term "butterfly cartoon." They were printed on cardstock, cut, and attached with double sided tape to the cloud tableau. In addition to the quote introducing the text of this display, the quotation by of Elizabeth Hardwick, previously cited, was included among the quotations. The other featured quotations were

The great blessing of my youth was that I grew up in a world of cheap and abundant books.

—C. S. Lewis

A great book should leave you with many experiences, and slightly exhausted at the end. You live several lives while reading it.

—William Styron

I divide all readers into two classes: those who read to remember and those who read to forget.

—William Lyon Phelps

3. A one inch layer of sand was spread across the base of the display case. On the right a child's beach chair was positioned at an angle and covered with a colorful beach towel. Books were arranged against the back of the chair and propped on the seat. Sea shells, starfish, colored glass stars, flip-flops, and two containers of suntan oil were placed around the chair. A small cooler filled with bottles, cans and cereal bars sits to the left of the chair. A canvas bag holding four books is angled on the extreme left. Sunglasses were attached to the strap, and a starfish was leaning against it. A portable radio was placed in front of the canvas bag at an angle. Ladybugs were strewn throughout the sand and shells. These were found through a Google image search and printed on cardstock.

Books featured in the display were *Haunted* by Chuck Palahniuk, *The Hitchhiker's Guide to the Galaxy* by Douglas Adams, *The Sisterhood of the Traveling Pants* by Ann Brashares, *Three Junes* by Julia Glass, *Up Island* by Anne Rivers Siddons, *The Notebook* by Nicholas Sparks, *Harry Potter and the Chamber of Secrets* and *Harry Potter and the Sorcerer's Stone* by J. K. Rowling.

BIGGER AND BETTER

If your display space permits, you could add a hat or visor, swim fins, a beach ball, a body board or raft, goggles, artificial sand crabs or lobsters, a picnic basket, a bottle of wine, a flyswatter, an oar, a beach mat, a beach ball, a bucket and shovel, a small boat (or other sand toys), surfing music CDs, an iPod, and a beach umbrella. A hammock could be positioned between the palm trees in lieu of the beach chair. Larger props (bigger cooler and boom box, larger chair) could be used to fill a larger space, or an actual sand castle might be created. A first aid kit could also be included along with some netting and volleyball or badminton items.

You could title your display Beach Books and Beyond. Add a steering wheel to the display, and take it on the road. Name it Armchair Travel. Create a display using books the particular authors favor. Call it Authors Advise. For information on this topic, visit http://www.authorsontheweb.com/Reading_Lists/

Set your books in a treasure chest and name it Books: A Treasure! This was the title of a recent New York State summer reading program. For access to this information, visit http://www.summerreadingnys.org/

There are many online sources for titles that would work in your display. For a wealth of great summer reading suggestions that include books of all genres, be sure to visit either of these sites: http://bookreporter.com/summer/index.asp or http://www. coudal.com/ftb/

NINE LIVES OR MORE: CATS IN LITERATURE

Of all God's creatures, there is only one that cannot be made the slave of the lash. That one is the cat. If man could be crossed with a cat it would improve man, but it would deteriorate the cat.

—Mark Twain

There are a myriad of literary cats. They are featured characters in Aesop's Fables, fairy tales, nursery rhymes, and modern children's stories. Felines are featured in popular mainstream mysteries as well as general adult fiction. Cat tales have earned a prominent place in the literature of most cultures beginning in ancient times, through the medieval period, and even to modern times.

The first form of literature to feature a feline was the animal fable. Every culture has its amusing stories about animals, but the most famous of these are attributed to Aesop. His stories, in which animals take on human characteristics in order to highlight morals to the human world, originated in Greece. It wasn't until the fifth century that they became associated with Aesop. New fables were added to the canon just as familiar ones became part of the folklore and literature of the world. Spanish poet and dramatist Lope de Vega (1562–1635) penned the epic *Battle of the Cats* in which a cat bride is abducted on the day of her wedding. This narrative served to elevate the cat to literary renown in Renaissance Europe.

Writers have celebrated the cat in all of its guises. These animals factor into fiction and real life, whether contributing in small measure, or being central to the plot. Some fortunate felines are assigned a lead role and become a vital element of the narrative. Cats not only appear in stories, they have been known to publish them, albeit through a human ghost writer. The cat memoir has earned its place in literature, especially *The Cat Chronicles*, written by Tom Howard, in which nine different cats all tell their tales.

Many writers have paid tribute to their own pets in essays and memoirs. Poets, however, have memorialized the cat above all animals. They have noted the amazing transformation from hunter-carnivore to docile kitten, often in the blink of an eye.

Joyce Carol Oates writes in her book *The Sophisticated Cat*:

Male, female, "romantic," coolly skeptical—we are mesmerized by the beautiful wild creatures who long ago chose to domesticate us, and who condescend to live with us, so wonderfully to their advantage; and, of course, to ours [Oates and Halpern xii].

Whether fanciful, as in the Mother Goose nursery rhyme of a pussycat's royal visit, or uncompromising, as in T. S. Eliot's whimsical "The Rum Tum Tugger," felines in literature do as they want, when they want. Just as cats are forever interested in their surroundings, the literary world was, is, and will remain, deeply curious about cats.

CREDITS

Our family adopted a highly independent cat when the children were small. Samantha, we soon learned, lacked the commitment and loyalty we expected in a pet. On several occasions, she left our home and sought refuge with other families in the neighborhood, often staying for months at a time. In most cases, her temporary digs were quite impressive. These houses were larger and better appointed. One was positioned high above the cove complete with a river view. It was apparent that our cat was upwardly mobile!

Several years ago, on a trip to Manhattan, we found ourselves in the gift shop at New York's Pierpont Morgan Museum. Included in the clearance merchandise was a poster illustrated by Rudyard Kipling for his story *The Cat Who Walked by Himself*. The title of the museum's 1980 exhibit was *Nine Lives or More*, and it featured the cat in early children's literature. Since those monographs weren't readily available to the average library, the theme of this display was broadened to include simply cats in literature.

Nine Lives or More—A striped tabby cat assumes a familiar pose while observing the antics of the scurrying mice. Felines have been a central theme in literature for hundreds of years.

And so, this display is dedicated to the memory of our notorious Samantha, a cat unafraid to "walk by herself."

ASSEMBLING THE DISPLAY

1. Black felt was attached to the rear of the display case. *The Cat Who Walked by Himself* poster was mounted on black poster board and attached to the top right section of the display case. A description of the illustration by Rudyard Kipling was printed on white card stock and mounted on black poster board. This information was easily found through an online search.

White poster board was cut 5" wide and affixed to the felt. Although the mice were an original design, similar mouse graphics and cats' paws can be found through online image searches. The mice were cut out of black poster board, and the cats' paws were printed on white card stock and cut in circles. The mice and paws were randomly glued on the white sections. The poem was mounted on black and gold poster board. On the bottom left of the display was a color photocopy of *Tinkle, a Cat* by an unknown American artist. To the right was a poem, *The Mysterious Cat* by Vachel Lindsay. Both were mounted on gold and/or black poster board. Above those items was the word *Meow*, created using the font Papyrus, sized at 150 and printed on cardstock. Three cat paws separate the two items.

2. On the top left of the display was another *Meow* created using a smaller font size. These "meows" were scattered throughout the display. Next was a copy of a black and white cat looking head-on, found on a Google image search. Under that was the poem "Rum Tum Tugger" by T. S. Eliot. The poem was printed on white card stock and glued to yellow poster board. Under that was a copy of a color lithograph postcard titled *Woman, Child, Cat* by an unknown artist (Austria, ca. 1910). This image can be found in *Curious Cats: In Art and Poetry* by William Lach. This was mounted on black poster board. Similar images are available online.

Quotes featured in this display, in addition to the one by Joyce Carol Oates previously mentioned and the quote introducing the text on this display, were

> Cats are connoisseurs of comfort.
>
> —James Herriott

> The more people I meet the more I like my cat.
>
> —Anonymous

3. On the top right side of the display case was a passage from *Feral Cat* by Jalma Barrett which traces the history of feline domestication by the Egyptians. A black cat's eyes are pictured above the text. Next are two poems: *The Stray Cat* by Eve Merriam, and *True* by Lillian Moore. These were printed on white card stock, and mounted on black poster board. A side view of a cat, found through an image search was cut out and glued to the bottom right section of the page.

A fable titled *Belling the Cat* was printed on cardstock and mounted on black and gold poster board. This fable can be obtained if you visit http://www.xmission.com/~emailbox/fables.htm

4. A 16 inch cat silhouette was located through an image search and drawn on orange poster board. Stripes were added using black magic marker. The cat was placed at the bottom right front of the display case so that he appears to be looking at the scattered mice. A twelve inch ruler was taped to the front of the cat figure, which permitted him to stand upright. Balls of cranberry and orange yarn were placed to the left of the cat, and then strewn throughout the books. A ball of twine was also included.

Books featured in the display were *99 Lives: Cats in History, Legend, and Literature* by Howard Loxton, *Cats Are Cats* by Nancy Larrick, *The Mythology of Cats: Feline Legends and Lore Through the Ages* by Gerald and Loretta Hausman, *The Sophisticated Cat: A Gathering of Stories, Poems, and Miscellaneous Writings about Cats* by Joyce Carol Oates and Daniel Helper, and *Minoa* by Mindy Bingham.

BIGGER AND BETTER

Should your display space allow, you could have a fishbowl next to a cutout of a cat. A window, flower pot, and stuffed cat combination would also be effective. Instead of mouse cutouts, rubber or stuffed mice could be placed throughout the display, and a border of larger cat paws could be mounted around the perimeter, and serve as a frame. Have your display focus on fables and call it Feline Fables. Feature cat mystery stories and call it Hidden Paws. Feature cats in poetry and title it Purrfect Poetry.

WHODUNIT?

It is an old maxim of mine that when you have excluded the impossible, whatever remains, however improbable, must be the truth.
—Arthur Conan Doyle, *Adventures of Sherlock Holmes*,
"The Beryl Coronet"

Everyone loves a good mystery. Readers are compelled by the conflict, the plight of the fallen, the turmoil and the killer—the disorder that ensues.

Michael Connelly writes: "The reason we love mystery novels is that they reassure us. They tell us that indeed the puzzle can be carefully constructed and put back together, that order can always be restored, that chaos does not win the day."

Visit this Web site for more on Michael Connelly: http://www.twbooks.co.uk/crimescene/connelly.htm

The killer is caught. Justice prevails. The pace is relentless and suspense abounds! The mystery reader's ultimate challenge is to arrive at the final solution using logical deduction with regard to the evidence put forth.

Whodunit?—The silhouette of a pipe-smoking Sherlock Holmes is a highly recognizable image for this display on mystery books. A magnifying glass, daggers, a letter opener and a bottle of poison are paraphernalia associated with stories that intrigue.

Since the detective has become as fascinating as the story in which is he involved, the writer must create a protagonist that has the physical and intellectual capacity necessary to capture the villain and compel the reader. The expectation is that the investigator will be fearless, resourceful, shrewd, complex, and definitely more interesting than the villain.

It was the 1892 publication of a series of short stories by Arthur Conan Doyle titled *The Adventures of Sherlock Holmes* that first captured the public's interest in the famous detective, "with his keen sense of observation, his lean face and hooked nose, his long legs, his deerstalker hat, his magnifying glass, and his ever-present pipe. This personality is what caught the reader's imagination." When Holmes was killed off in "The Final Problem" (1893) the public response was so great, Conan Doyle was forced to bring him back to life!

Agatha Christie introduced Hercule Poirot in 1920. This Belgian detective had a long and illustrious career in thirty-three novels and sixty-five short stories. When he made his final appearance in the 1975 novel *Curtain*, his obituary appeared on the front page of the *New York Times*, the only fictional character to be so honored!

P. D. James' Chief Inspector Adam Dalgliesh is a quiet, intense and detached individual who could be characterized as formidable. His popularity stems from the level of complexity of his cases and the unorthodox speed with which the crimes are solved. A published poet with a tragic past, this chief inspector handles only the most sensitive of murder cases.

Mystery lovers are of a certain breed. For readers who favor this genre, there can never really be enough to satiate their appetite for the next new and compelling murder mystery. Happily, mystery writers abound!

CREDITS

I have been a supervisor and mentor of college students for twenty-plus years. In that capacity, I have frequently been in a position to serve as a reader's advisor to my young assistants. Often I come across a member of my student staff who has lost her desire to read, or, perhaps, never really developed a strong affinity for the written word. I always have a couple of favorite books to lend that are designed to excite and engage the apathetic reader.

Loves Music, Loves to Dance by Mary Higgins Clark invariably makes an impact on my students. The book has a great pace and immediately draws the reader into the mystery. The victim is a woman in her early twenties with whom they readily identify.

Really more of an international thriller than strictly a mystery, *The Day After Tomorrow*, by Allen Folsom, provides as much excitement and mystique as any book that I have read. In this debut thriller, the author delivers in full and involves the reader in an unforgettable journey with an ending sure to surprise.

I also keep a stash of books by Janet Evanovich, Sue Grafton, David Balducci, and Elmore Leonard in my small lending library.

ASSEMBLING THE DISPLAY

1. The title Whodunit? summed up this display, which featured renowned British and American mystery writers. The font Monotype Corsiva was selected and the word was enlarged to a font size of 400, bolded, and shadowed. This was mounted on black poster board. The colors used in this display were red, black, and white with some gold. The background was black felt. The quotation under the title was "... when you have eliminated the impossible, whatever remains, however improbable, must be the truth." (Sir Arthur Conan Doyle, *Sherlock Holmes*)

To retrieve the image of Sherlock Holmes' head in profile, go to http://www.sherlock-holmes.co.uk

A magnifying glass was attached with tacks, connecting the detective's image to the title.

The quotes featured under *Whodunit* were the one introducing the display, and

> At least half the mystery novels published violate the law that the solution, once revealed, must seem to be inevitable.
>
> —Raymond Chandler

Other content material for the center of the display was an essay titled *The Mystery of Mystery Writing*, by Michael Connelly. In it he describes the art of writing mysteries and gives a great analysis of his approach to the process, and the evolution of the genre. This information can be found at http://www.michaelconnelly.com/index.html

A biography of Agathia Christie was included and can be found if you visit www.agathachristie.com/essentials/crime.shtml

Below that was a witty statement by Rogers Turrentine, writer for *Northern Exposure*, a popular TV show in the 1990s. This can be found if you visit http://www.quotationspage.com/quotes/Rogers_Turrentine

The design for the daggers was found through a Google image search. These images served as an inspiration for the hand drawn version in the display. These were created using colored markers on white poster board and were then attached with pins.

Circles the size of a quarter were cut out of red poster board and pinned to connect Sherlock Holmes and the text. Directions for creating these images can be found in the Resources section of this book under Techniques.

2. On the top left was a passage by P. D. James. The author states her feelings about the detective novel in a comprehensive paragraph which can be found at http://www.contemporarywriters.com/authors/?p=auth193#authorstatement

Below that were these quotes:

> Writing is like getting married. One should never commit oneself until one is amazed at one's luck.
>
> —Iris Murdoch

> It was one of those perfect English autumnal days which occur more frequently in memory than in life.
>
> —P. D. James

3. On the top right was a quote by Stephen King:

> Fiction is the truth inside the lie...
>
> —Stephen King

Under that was a biography of Arthur Conan Doyle which can be found at www.sherlockholmesonline.org/biography/index

Other quotations may be selected from sites such as www.memorablequotations.com and www.great-quotes.com/cgi-bin/author.cgi

There is an interesting paragraph that was selected for the display which describes Richard North Patterson's sentiments on courtroom thrillers. This was part of a larger interview that can be found at www.bookpage.com/9809bp/richard_north_patterson.html

All of the text material was printed on white cardstock and mounted on red and/or black poster board.

4. At the base of the display was a bottle containing poison, and a letter opener. To recreate the bottle, see the Resources section under Techniques. Also included was an annotated booklist published by the Free Library of Philadelphia titled "Women of Mystery."

Monographs selected for this display were *Libre* by Elmore Leonard, *The Children of Men* by P. D. James, *You Belong to Me* by Mary Higgins Clark, *The Complete Sherlock Holmes* by Arthur Conan Doyle, *Master of the Moore* by Ruth Rendell, and Sara Paretsky's *A Woman on the Case*.

BIGGER AND BETTER

Should you have additional room in your display, you could add some handcuffs, a pipe, a detective's badge, a toy gun or dagger, and a Sherlock Holmes cap or fedora.

You may want to focus on either women or men in mysteries. Or, set it at the shore and title it Mysteries for the Beach. Choose mysteries that are set during the holidays and call it Secrets of the Season. Set your display in an international venue and call it Secrets and Spies. Feature detective novels and choose a title such as Daunting Detectives.

Traditions

CELEBRATE THE NEW YEAR!

For last year's words belong to last year's language
And next year's words await another voice.
And to make an end is to make a beginning.
—T.S. Eliot, "Little Gidding"

As each calendar year comes to a close on a sentimental note and with much personal reflection, a new year appears on the horizon which fills us with hope and possibilities. The transition from one year to another is sometimes bittersweet, as we tally the highlights and passages that will be forever historically linked to that segment of time.

In America, neighbors, friends and families gather together in the late evening hours on New Year's Eve to acknowledge this transition. Events such as dance parties are customarily thrown on December 31st to welcome in the New Year. Times Square in New York City is famous for the large crystal ball that drops at the stroke of midnight before a large and enthusiastic crowd of onlookers. People don hats, hug, kiss, blow paper horns, set off firecrackers, bang pans and noisemakers, honk car horns, toss confetti and watch televised fireworks displays set in major cities throughout the world. It is indeed a time for celebration!

On January 1st, the transition to the new year usually begins with the tradition of making resolutions, a custom that dates back to the time of the early Babylonians. Each New Year's Day determined citizens vow to lose weight, stop smoking, reassess priorities, work on relationships, and set goals that will improve their overall state in life. Although many of these commitments are likely to be forgotten in short order, the idea of assessing one's life and attempting to make some positive changes is admirable.

Football games, parades and festivals mark the New Year's holiday in the United States. The Tournament of Roses Parade has a long history that dates back to 1886, when members of the Hunt Valley Club decorated their carriages with flowers to celebrate the ripening of the orange crop in California.

Although the Rose Bowl game was first played in conjunction with the Tournament of Roses in 1902, it wasn't until 1916 that the game returned to the spotlight and became the sports highlight of these festivities. The Rose Bowl competition, held in the city of Pasadena, California, is a highly anticipated event which showcases the top football teams in the nation.

The city of Philadelphia, Pennsylvania, hosts the unique and colorful Mummers Parade on New Year's Day. Members of string bands dress in flamboyant feathered costumes, in keeping with the current year's theme, and march down Broad Street before animated throngs of loyal admirers. Other parade participants are divided into the following categories: Comic, Fancy, and Fancy Brigade. Mummery has traditionally been a family affair where members receive moral support and achieve a certain level of status and recognition within the community for their involvement. The tradition of using a baby to represent the new year began in Greece around 600 B.C. It was their custom to celebrate Dionysus, the god of wine, by showcasing a baby in a basket. This young child symbolized the rebirth of Dionysus as the badge of fertility. Other cultures, such as the early Egyptians, also used a baby as a spirit of rebirth.

Many superstitions accompany the onset of the new year. There are reasons why we toast to the new year, make loud noises, kiss at midnight, and perhaps even clean the house and wind the clocks on New Year's Eve. To learn more about New Year's superstitions visit http://www.oldsuperstitions.com/new_years.html

Celebrate the New Year!—Fireworks, confetti and New Year's noisemakers combine to create an explosive display for this international holiday.

CREDITS

Those of us born in the City of Brotherly Love, aka Philadelphia, have fond memories of attending the annual Mummers Parade held in the heart of the city on New Year's Day. Inevitably, the crowd was spirited and the temperatures bitingly cold. Still, this unique spectacle was not to be missed. Parents and children, with blankets and hot chocolate in tow, would find their way to bleachers set up for the occasion. The parade proceeded throughout the day and ended with the setting sun.

This childhood fascination with the Mummers was the impetus for the display Celebrate the New Year! It was interesting to research other customs surrounding this holiday. A visit to the party and dollar stores provided the color scheme used as well as some of the items included.

ASSEMBLING THE DISPLAY

1. The black felt background was selected to provide a contrast to the brightly colored fireworks. Heavy duty foil wrapping paper in metallic gold, bright red and vibrant blue were used for the arcs of the fireworks. Circles of foil in several sizes were placed in the center and throughout the explosion. The word *Celebrate* was printed on cardstock and traced onto red poster board. The font selected was Elephant and was sized at 700 using bold italic lower case letters. Holiday bows made of gold curly ribbon were taken apart and individual strands were attached to the protective grill at the top of the display case. A gold party horn was attached to the top left on an angle complementing that of the title.

2. At the top left of the display was information about the history of the Philadelphia Mummers Parade. This, along with a photo of a member of the Quaker City String Band, was found online. All of this was printed on white cardstock and mounted on red and gold poster board. For additional information about this unique Philadelphia extravaganza visit any of these sites: http://www.phila.gov/recreation/mummers/mummers_history.html or http://www.fieldtrip.com/pa/53363050.htm or http://philadelphia.about.com/library/weekly/aa010300.htm

Two New Year's quotes were posted below the Mummers information. They were:

> As we look into 2006 we look at a block of time. We see 12 months, 52 weeks, 365 days, 8,760 hours, 525,600 minutes, 31,536,000 seconds. And all is a gift from God. We have done nothing to deserve it, earn it, or purchase it. Like the air we breathe, time comes to us as a part of life.
>
> —Stephen Cloud, *A Year of Time*

Visit this site for more words of inspiration from Stephen Cloud: http://www.appleseeds.org/newyear3.htm#TOP

> I do think New Year's resolutions can't technically be expected to begin on New Year's Day, don't you? Since, because it's an extension of New Year's Eve, smokers are already on a smoking roll and cannot be expected to stop abruptly on the stroke of midnight with so much nicotine in the system. Also dieting on

New Year's Day isn't a good idea as you can't eat rationally but really need to be free to consume whatever is necessary, moment by moment, in order to ease your hangover. I think it would be much more sensible if resolutions began generally on January the second.

—Helen Fielding, *Bridget Jones's Diary*

For additional quotes on New Years visit http://www.basicquotations.com/index.php?cid=209

3. On the top right of the case was a list of New Year's traditions. These were found at http://www.fathertimes.net/unitedstatesnewyear.htm and http://new-years.123holiday.net/new_years_traditions

Below that was information about luck in the new year. This can be found if you visit http://wilstar.com/holidays/newyear.htm

All of the information was printed on white cardstock and had clip art, found in MS Word, inserted.

4. Two stainless steel martini glasses, filled with red confetti, were elevated on a Styrofoam disk covered in black velvet. This was raised with Styrofoam blocks to attain the proper height. A text box was used to create the black background and gold lettering used in the wording *the New Year*. The font chosen was Elephant sized at 72. This was printed on cardstock and placed in front of the martini glasses. Below that were the words to "Auld Lang Syne" by Rabbie Burns. Clip art of toasting glasses was inserted below the lyrics to this New Year's Eve song. The cardstock was glued to red poster board and positioned at an angle with two red cardboard horns flanking it. Visit this site for the lyrics to this favorite New Year's Eve song: http://wilstar.com/xmas/auldlangsyne.htm

On the base of the display case red and gold confetti was strewn among the red and yellow balloons. The books featured in Celebrate the New Year! were *We Celebrate New Year* by Bobbie Kalman, *New Year's Eve* by Lisa Grunwald, *The New Year's Eve Compendium* by Todd Lyon, *Chinese New Year* by Judith Jango-Cohen and *Folklore of American Holidays* by Hennig Cohen.

BIGGER AND BETTER

Should your display space permit, you could emphasize worldwide New Year's customs. Cities such as Sydney, Paris, Madrid and Buenos Aires, and many countries located in the Far East, have unique and colorful customs and celebrations ranging from eating twelve grapes at midnight to intricate paper cutting rituals. Featuring the Chinese New Year, complete with appropriate animal for "The Year of..." would make a dynamic and eye-catching showcase.

Your display might feature multiple New Year's hats arranged in a pyramid. You could include a bottle of champagne and flute glasses filled with colored water, noisemakers, maracas, clackers and paper blow-outs. Balloons filled with helium could fill the top space of your display. Attach colorful streamers and add Mardi Gras beads. Ready made signage is available for the New Year's holiday at both the party and dollar stores and is a great time saver.

Obtain a copy of *The Art of the Party: Design Ideas for Successful Entertaining* by Renny Reynolds for some dramatic party ideas that could be incorporated in a display on celebrations. Should you decide to feature a California tradition, consult *America's New Year Celebration: The Rose Parade and Rose Bowl Game* edited by Darcy Ellington. For more information of this topic visit http://www.topics-mag.com/internatl/holidays/new-years-page1.htm

SANTA BLUE: THE LEGEND BEGINS

I will honor Christmas in my heart and try to keep it all the year.
—Charles Dickens, *A Christmas Carol*

Probably the most celebrated holiday in the world, our modern Christmas is a product of hundreds of years of both secular and religious traditions from around the globe. The Christmas traditions we observe in the United States today stem from those that were prevalent in the 1860s, Victorian times.

The traditional Santa, dressed in a red ensemble and trimmed in white fur, is the stereotype with whom American children identify. However, the international versions have dozens of names and varying costumes. From Saint Nicholas, to Papa Noël, to Father Christmas, to Grandpapa Indian, to Che Lao Ren, Santa has a host of interpretations.

We can attribute these backgrounds to two of the Santas dressed in blue.

1. Saint Nicholas became the patron saint of Russia shortly after he was canonized in the 9th century, some 500 years after his death. It was 987 ad when the life and times of Saint Nicholas became known to the Russian people. Duke Vladimir wanted to wed Princess Anna of Byzantium, but he had to publicly accept Christianity in order to win Anna's hand. Vladimir returned to Russia from Byzantium with a portrait of Saint Nicholas. He also brought with him legends surrounding his life, including tales of the many miracles reputed to him. These legends, passed down to each succeeding generation, were instrumental in gaining Saint Nicholas the honor of being recognized as the patron saint of such diverse people as sailors, maidens, packers, and even pawnbrokers! The Russian depiction of Saint Nicholas is generally that of a bearded man, an image which is probably based on the portrait Duke Vladimir brought from Byzantium. For more information visit http://www.christmas-treasures.com/duncan_royale/Collection/Santal/RussianSaintNicholas.htm

2. The Mongols were wandering herdsmen of Central Asia. They traveled with their herds of sheep, goats, horses, camels and cattle, moving them from season to season while seeking fresh pastures. In the early 1200s, under the direction of Genghis

Khan, the Mongol herdsmen were forged into a warlike horde. They became fearful of losing their grazing land to the ever expanding Chinese. Genghis Khan so inspired his followers that they subsequently became victors over many lands.

The Great Wall of China, built as a barrier to warring tribes, was no deterrent to the onslaught of the vast strength of the Mongols. Under the rule of Genghis Khan, Mongolia extended from the Pacific Ocean to the Caspian Sea.

Even though they were warriors and nomads, the Mongols ended their year with a celebration of Herdsmen's Day. This was a day of feasting and merriment. The men exhibited their skill in horsemanship and the women dressed in their best finery, adding silver and trinkets to their headdresses. Gifts of trinkets and products of the time were exchanged within the family much like our current holiday traditions.

Orientals, those touched by the Mongols, may have been influenced by these year-end festivities. One Chinese God, Tsai Sen Yeh, appears at the end of the year and gives money gifts to the children. He carries the traditional sack on his back and is a favorite of the children to whom he makes his rounds. It is believed that Marco Polo, a close friend of Genghis Khan, may have introduced Christian ideals and customs while he was living in China. For more information visit http://www.christmas-treasures.com/duncan_royale/Collection/Santil/Mongolian.htm

There are references to the German Saint Nicholas also being clothed in blue garb. These carved wooden figures

Santa Blue—Create an effective display featuring an array of holiday figures. Cluster them and add greens and stars and a snowflake or two.

were hollow so that candy could be stored in the removable boots. For more information on the German Santa, visit http://www.stnicholascenter.org/Brix?pageID=87

CREDITS

I have always been fascinated by blue Santas. This collection of Old World figurines, which began in the early 1990s, has largely grown as a result of the generosity of family and friends who have shared and encouraged this interest over the years.

People have wondered where to find blue Santas. The answer is that they are everywhere! In the area of southeastern Pennsylvania where I live, there are a number of country, craft, and folk art stores, as well as specialty gift shops who cater to collectors. Online shoppers will find many sites for these figures. Although pricier than the figures found locally, they are quite unique. Some of the most interesting Santas can be found at http://www.christmas-treasures.com/duncanroyal.htm or http://www.victoria-dove.com/flsanta.htm or http://www.christmasinternational.com/santa/russian.html

Some beautiful hand carved Santas are available at this site: http://www.hometown.aol.com/carveshop/world

These blue Santas are prominently displayed throughout my home during the holiday period. It is with pleasure that I share this collection, via the display titled Santa Blue: The Legend Begins.

ASSEMBLING THE DISPLAY

1. The felt background material chosen for the display case was ecru. This color created a warm tone that worked well with the blues, silvers and "greens" that would be added. The title *Santa Blue* was created using Matura MY Script which was printed on the PC and enlarged on the photocopier. This was glued to navy and ecru pillow ticking wallpaper and mounted on black poster board. The blue sequined star was mounted to the lower left portion of the title, and provided a contrast to the hanging silver stars.

2. The swag of greens with small pinecones was hung on the top left of the case, and secured with straight pins. About 2 ft. of blue and beige gingham ribbon was threaded throughout the swag. The 15" artificial tree was situated on the right in order to balance the visual weight of the swag. Clear plastic stands were placed in the rear of the display to permit the figures to stand at varying heights. Lastly, the silver stars were hung from open paper clips which slipped over the plastic grate that served as a cover for the top interior light.

3. The larger artificial tree, which measured 40", was placed at the base of the display case. The large wooden Santa was already mounted on a stand, so it stood upright. Artificial greens with large pinecones and red berries surround this tableau. The shelf was positioned so that the collection was eye level (for the majority of our patrons). Small vertical slits were cut into the felt to allow for the shelf supports to be inserted.

4. The silver stars were hung from thread and secured with transparent tape to the underside of the acrylic shelf. Greens and large pinecones were laid at the bottom of the case. A 1989 antique reproduction of *The Night Before Christmas, or A Visit of St. Nicholas* by Clement Clarke Moore was placed under the large tree along with an antique box imprinted with blue Santas and wrapped in ribbon. Information about the Russian Santa was printed on white cardstock and mounted like the title signage just above the large wooden Santa of the display.

5. Flanking the top section of the display were the names of international Santas. They were printed in black and blue, using various fonts with an "Old World" feel. They were cut in 2"–3" strips and hung on to the left and the right of the blue figures. The foreign names for St. Nicholas can be found at http://Instar.com/mall/main-areas/santafaq.htm

6. On the lower left of the display was a synopsis of Santas around the world. Information on this subject can be found if you visit http://www.christmas.com/pe/1378

7. On the lower right "Saint Nicholas the Legend Begins" was featured. This can be found at http://www.christmas.com/pe/1376

The pieces in #6 and #7 were printed and mounted as was the title (see #1, above).

BIGGER AND BETTER

Figures of Santas around the world, dressed in gold, white, green, blue and red would make a colorful seasonal display. There is much information regarding the dress and traditions associated with these international symbols. Flags of the countries represented could be featured.

Should your display area be larger, any number of seasonal books could be added. Holiday decorations such as bells or Christmas balls could be substituted for the silver stars. If your collection is of traditional red Santas, the ribbon and paper should be similarly coordinated. Those who live in coastal areas can incorporate sand dollars, shells, fishing lures and starfish. Large and small wrapped presents would also work well with your Santa display.

Other holiday collections could be featured: trains, vintage Christmas cards, nutcrackers, antique ornaments, cookie tins, or snowmen. The classic editorial *Yes, Virginia, There Is a Santa Claus* by Francis P. Church, which was first published in *The New York Sun* in 1897, could be the heart of your display. This can be found online.

ONE THOUSAND CRANES

Peace comes from within. Do not seek it without.

—Buddha

On August 6, 1945, the United States dropped an atomic bomb on Hiroshima, Japan. Three days later a second bomb was released over the city of Nagasaki. It is impossible to know for certain, but estimates of causalities run as high as 250,000 dead and 100,000 wounded. Many of those who survived the burns from the attack initially, ultimately died from atomic radiation disease over a period of years following the end of World War II.

Word of the terrible suffering that resulted from the bomb, which had destroyed a whole city in a single flash of fire, spread around the globe. Many were touched in particular by the story of Sadako Sasaki, who was just under two years old when the bomb fell on Hiroshima. She and many of her family survived the initial blast. Sadako grew to become a strong, courageous and athletic girl. However, after a period of ten years she was stricken while practicing for a track event at school. Sadako was eventually diagnosed with leukemia, also known as the Atomic Bomb Disease.

As Japanese legend has it, anyone who uses the ancient art of origami and folds a thousand paper cranes will be granted a wish. The crane is a symbol of long life and good fortune in Japan. According to folk lore, one crane represents a thousand years of happiness, and a thousand cranes translates into one million years. While hospitalized, young Sadako endeavored to fold 1,000 cranes. She believed that completing this task would ensure a quick and healthy recovery. Sadako was only able to fold 644 cranes before her tragic death on October 25, 1955. Her friends gathered together with the purpose of completing the remaining cranes so that 1,000 could be buried with her, thus ensuring her eternal peace.

As a permanent memorial to the life of this courageous young girl, her classmates joined forces and raised money for a monument that was erected

One Thousand Cranes—Involve your volunteers or staff members in a enjoyable origami project which symbolizes peace in the world. Almost 300 cranes were crafted to create this circle of hope.

in her honor, and in memory of all the children who shared a similar fate. Enough money was raised to erect a statue of Sadako holding a large golden crane high above her head. The statue was unveiled in 1958, and stands today close to the site of the Atomic Bomb Museum in Peace Park, Hiroshima, Japan. The sentiments of the children are inscribed at the base of the statue. The plaque reads "This is our cry: this is our prayer, Peace in the world."

Today, children from Japan and all over the world continue to send thousands of paper cranes to Hiroshima to be placed at the foot of Sadako's monument to honor the life she led and the dreams they shared. The cranes form huge mountains around the monument as a colorful but silent prayer for the end of war.

Originally made in China in the first century, the art of paper making was brought to Japan in 610 A.D. by Buddhist monks who produced it for the purpose of writing sutras, scriptural texts regarded as discourses of the Buddha.

Washi is the Japanese word for the traditional papers used in the authentic art of origami. This paper is made from fibres of the inner barks of three plants, all native to Japan. The translation of this word is apparent: *wa* means Japanese and *shi* is paper. Washi is no longer made strictly by hand. Machines are capable of pro ducing a product that is similar-looking, but that has certain qualities which differ from the authentic *washi*. In order to maintain the original tradition, there are roughly 325 families in Japan today who are still engaged in the production of paper by hand.

To learn more about the features, history and methods of paper production, visit http://www.japanesepaperplace.com/about_jap_paper/about_washi.htm

Instructions for creating cranes can be found in almost any book on origami. *A Thousand Cranes* by Florence Temko has excellent graphics and clear directives. For more information on the subject visit http://www.csi.ad.jp/suzuhari-es/1000cranes/paperc/

CREDITS

Several years ago, Cedar Crest College offered information about the life story of Sadako Sasaki. They also provided colorful origami paper with instructions for folding paper cranes. Students became familiar with the events of Sadako's life and untimely death. They were encouraged to make as many cranes as they wished. The completed cranes were threaded together and strewn throughout the lobby area and stairwells of the student center. The results were a colorful visual celebration of the life of this young girl.

I found the story of Sadako to be very compelling. Since I had a staff of talented college students at my disposal in the library, I decided to involve them in the creation of the cranes, which were the heart of this display. It was a great bonding experience for the students. They enjoyed the process and were pleased that their creative endeavors would be a part of this publication.

ASSEMBLING THE DISPLAY

1. The black felt background provided a contrast for the blue and green globe featuring the continent of Asia, which is centered among the two rings of pastel paper cranes. The globe was made of poster board, attached with straight pins, as were the cranes. The arms cradling the globe were hand drawn on blue poster board, attached with pins. All of this was pulled forward in relief. A flag of Japan, found by a Google image search and printed on white cardstock, was centered between the arms and pulled forward.

The title *One Thousand Cranes* was printed in black on off-white cardstock using the font Papyrus Bold, which was sized at 150 font. This was mounted on blue poster board, attached with pins, and pulled forward. The signage was positioned in the bottom half of the display, creating a frame for the collage. Included in this tableau was an illustration by Ronald Himler of Sadako, found in *Sadako and the Thousand Paper Cranes* by Eleanor Coerr. This was printed on cardstock and mounted on blue poster board. The Japanese symbol for the word *peace* was drawn on off-white card stock using an image found on Google as a guide. This was mounted on green poster board along with a photograph of the Hiroshima Memorial found in *A Thousand Cranes* by Florence Temko. An illustration of an actual crane was found through a Google image search and printed on card stock.

The pagoda can be found at this site: http://en.wikipedia.org/wiki/pagoda

It was printed in black on card stock and mounted on green poster board. All of the images in the collage were pulled forward on straight pins. Four cranes were attached around the tableau.

2. On the top left side of the case was an explanation of the concept behind the tradition of one thousand cranes. This can be found if you visit http://www.sadako. org/sadakostory.htm

Next was the quotation introducing this display.

Under that was an illustrated guide for folding paper cranes found in *One Thousand Paper Cranes* by Takayuki Ishii.

Below that was the following quotation:

> If we are to teach real peace in this world, and if we are to carry on a real war against war, we shall have to begin with the children.
>
> —Mahatma Gandhi

Next was information relevant to the sun goddess and Japanese culture, which is available at http://ancienthistory.about.com/od/ameratsumyth/

Finally came the Chinese proverb:

> The more you sweat in peacetime, the less you bleed during war.

All this information was printed on off-white cardstock and mounted on blue and/or green poster board.

3. The top right side of the case featured a history of the pagoda (see above mentioned Web site), printed on off-white card stock and mounted on blue poster board. Under that was the English word *Peace* printed on card stock and using black French Script at 200 font.

A color photocopy of a trio of Buddhist statues was mounted on gold poster board. Above that was information regarding various figures sacred to Buddhism. All information was found in the *Pictorial Encyclopedia of Japanese Culture.*

Lastly, these quotations were included:

> Everything is changeable, everything appears and disappears; There is no blissful peace until one passes beyond the agony of life and death.
>
> —Buddha

> When the character of a man is not clear to you, look at his friends.
>
> —Japanese proverb

Quotations such as those cited can be found if you visit http://www.quotations page.com/quotes/Japanese_Proverb/ or http://en.thinkexist.com/quotations/peace/

Items on the right were printed on off-white card stock and mounted on blue and/or green or gold poster board.

4. Origami cranes were placed randomly throughout the lower portion of the display. At the base, elevated atop a block of Styrofoam covered in velvet, was a sundial mounted on a plate stand. This represents the significance of the symbol of the sun in the Far Eastern culture. Additional origami cranes were placed in front of the sundial, just as they can be found at the base of the Sadako memorial.

Books featured in the display were *The Dawns of Tradition* by Nissan Jid-osha Kabushiki Kaisha, *Sadako and the Thousand Paper Cranes* by Eleanor Coerr, *Pictorial Encyclopedia of Japanese Culture* published by Gakken, *Easy Origami* by John Montrall and *Children of the Paper Crane: The Story of Sadako Sasaki and Her Struggle with the A-bomb Disease* by Masamoto Nasu.

BIGGER AND BETTER

You may decide to have the cranes appear to be in flight, in which case you will probably need more than the 280 cranes used in this display. Crisscross them across the display case.

You could go into more background on the creation of the atomic bomb, or the impact that this decision had on the ending of World War II. Include newspaper headlines which chronicled this event, as well as photographs of Hiroshima and Nagasaki.

Your display could include information on the current state of diplomatic relations between Japan and the United States following the ending of the World War II.

DAY OF THE DEAD:
DIA DE LOS MUERTOS

The Mexican is familiar with death, jokes about it, caresses it, sleeps with it,
and celebrates it. It is one of his favorite playthings and his most steadfast love.
—Octavio Paz, writer

A commonality present among people in all cultures is a struggle between life and death. Life is vibrant, holding bright possibilities, while death is bleak and silent. Life holds promise; death engenders fear. Funeral rites encompass both the denial and the acceptance of these extremes. Mourning precedes the feast.

In Mexico, once a year, death becomes a celebration! In mid-autumn, the living invite the deceased members of their families to return and join them in a festival which pays homage to the lives they once shared. When the spirits of children come to visit, they are feted in their earthly homes. Adult spirits, however, are hosted in cemeteries, at their individual graves.

The *Day of the Dead* is a holiday with a complex history, and therefore its observance varies quite a bit both by region, and, also, by degree of urbanization. It is not a morbid occasion, but rather a time of celebration. Traditionally, people welcome back the souls of the departed to family hearths with lavish meals, new clothes, and delightfully elaborate altars called *ofrendas*. During this celebration the lives of the deceased are commemorated. Families share food and drink with their relatives and neighbors.

These feasts include everything from figurines and skulls made of sugar and chocolate to special breads, stews, and tamales. Fresh fruits, beer, soda pop, and even junk food are served. The food and beverage selection is based on the particular tastes of the living as well as the dead.

During the *Day of the Dead* celebration, the altar is lavishly adorned with pictures and portraits of the deceased, important saints, and/or Mary and Jesus. Flowers, especially marigolds, fruit, and lacy paper cutouts depicting skulls and skeletons are placed on the *ofrenda*. A novel feature of the holiday décor are papier-mâché dolls of skeletons doing everything from dancing and singing, to cycling, or riding in cars and buses, and even cooking!

Rural displays tend to follow tradition, celebrating the holiday with a more serious intent. But in the cities, there are no limits to the imagination, and displays there often diverge far from the personal commemorative purposes. In recent years, due to the timing of this celebration, the festival has begun to merge with the celebration of Halloween.

Starting on the evening of November 1, families arrive at the cemetery, prepared to sit and wait for the arrival of the spirits. Candles are lit commemorating the lives

Day of the Dead—This display on the Mexican holiday of the Day of the Dead addresses the dichotomy of the struggle between life and death. The base of the case is transformed into an altar, or *ofrenda*, which pays homage to the deceased ancestors. The 3-dimensional skeleton is an imposing figure.

of their loved ones who have passed. The genders then separate, with men engaging in political discussions and local problem solving, and women sitting in silence amidst the graves. Children frolic until they tire and fall asleep. Teenagers sometimes bring a radio or a small television to entertain themselves and pass the time.

In larger towns and cities, food stands are set up outside the cemetery. An energy permeates those present. They eat and drink heartily throughout the night. A nearby church is open and available as a shelter for the people, whether or not mass is being celebrated. By sunrise, the men are generally a little hung-over, the women tired and hungry. On the third of November, when the celebrating has come to an end, the remaining *ofrendas* are taken to the homes of friends or relatives. Now is the time for the living to enjoy the fruits of the tradition.

There are many good books which chronicle these special days for the Latin culture. *Dia de Muertos en Mexico,* by Mary Andrade, includes recipes and poems relevant to this celebration, along with vibrant, colorful photographs. *The Skeleton at the Feast: The Day of the Dead in Mexico,* by Elizabeth Carmichael and Chloe Sayer, is an excellent and comprehensive resource for this contemporary annual celebration.

CREDITS

Although I had heard of the *Day of the Dead,* I had no real idea of the particular customs involved in the celebration. An exhibit mounted at my husband's university introduced the tradition.

This colorful display is the result of the generosity of Marilyn Fox, director of the Freyberger Gallery at Penn State–Berks. Marilyn's original exhibit was mounted in October 2004 at the Penn State–Lehigh Valley campus. Her display included a tribute to the Mexican artist Frida Kahlo, in addition to commemorating *The Day of the Dead*. Marilyn had involved the Penn State students in the decorating of sugar skulls which were featured in her display. As a result, the exhibit engendered interest among the students and the tradition took on new meaning.

Marilyn graciously lent the papier-mâché skeletons, a book, flowers and skulls, all of which formed the core of this display. Her enthusiasm for this tradition assured me that it would have broad appeal and was worthy of mounting in our library.

ASSEMBLING THE DISPLAY

1. The first consideration in designing this display was to make it colorful. Black felt was attached to the rear of the display case. Then hot pink poster board, slightly larger than the dimensions of the skeleton, was stapled to the felt. This background color provided a stark contrast to the black and white 3-dimensional figure. After creating a black perimeter from poster board, two shades of bright green paint were applied at regular intervals with a sponge. Small sections of foam board were positioned behind the black frame and secured with extra-long straight pins to allow the border to appear in relief. The 4' papier-mâché skeleton was then positioned within the rectangular "coffin."

The skeleton was attached to the poster board with thin white string wrapped around the neck and ankles, then secured with straight pins. String was attached to the wrists to create the position which would work within the available space. Two small pieces of foam board were attached with long straight pins. These served as tiny shelves for the two miniature papier-mâché skulls that flanked the large skeleton.

2. Original limited edition linoleum reduction ink prints of brilliantly colored abstract skeletons on mulberry paper were hung at the top left and right of the display case. Under that, on the left, was a description of *Todos Santos*. Information on that subject can be found if you visit http://deguate.xoopiter.com/traditions.htm

The quotation introducing the display and a several pictures of *ofrendas* came next. These pictures were easily located via a Google image search. Lastly, information about the celebration in Mexico was included. This Web site was helpful: http://www.public.iastate.edu/~rjsalvad/scmfaq/muertos.html

All of these items were printed on white cardstock, mounted on black poster board, and attached with double sided tape.

3. Under the linoleum print on the right was a passage titled "Tradition." It included information found at this Web site: http://www.intelnet.com.mx/queretaro/muertos/

This material was printed on cardstock with black borders inserted. This is available under "format" in MS Word.

Next was a quote by the writer Octavio Paz:

> The Mexican is familiar with death, jokes about it, caresses it, sleeps with it, and celebrates it. It is one of his favorite playthings and his most steadfast love.

Under that was a touching photograph of a young couple from Cuernavaca, with arms intertwined, standing amidst the tombstones in the cemetery while paying tribute to their deceased family members.

Finally, there were color photographs of bakers' trays filled with special loaves of bread, *pan de muertos*, which have bones decorating the top crust; marzipan "coffins" housing white chocolate skeletons; sugary ghouls with confectioner's hair; and chocolate and sugar skulls, which often jokingly bear the name of one of the living.

Images of Cuernavaca and *pan de muertos* were easily found through a Google search.

All items were printed on white cardstock and mounted on black poster board.

4. Styrofoam blocks were positioned on the base of the display case at varying heights, and then covered with a black shawl. This formed the altar upon which were positioned a candelabra, two sugar skulls, a standing skeleton, fruits and flowers.

The books featured had colorful covers. They were *The Days of the Dead* by Rosalind Rosoff Beimler (photographs by John Greenleigh) and *Dia de Muertos* by Jermain Argueta.

BIGGER AND BETTER

If your space permits, you may want to include some colorful paper banners, which are prevalent at these festivals. Patterns for these are available within the pages of *The Skeleton at the Feast*. There are many online sites which have good information and an array of items relevant to this festival, available for sale. Some excellent sites are http://www.directfrommexico.com/mexican-folk-art-dod.html and http://www.mexicansugarskull.com/mexicansugarskull and http://www.lafuente.com/new/dead.php and http://www.ebay.com

There are also sites with step-by-step directions for creating relevant 3-dimensional papier-mâché items. For those procedures, go to http://www.papiermache.co.uk/exec/cms-documents/s-tutorials/p-view/id-23/page-1/

Patriotism

SAGE OF MONTICELLO

I cannot live without books.

—Thomas Jefferson

Thomas Jefferson was born in 1743 at Shadwell plantation, in Albemarle County, Virginia, to Peter Jefferson, a planter and surveyor, and Jane Randolph, daughter of a prominent Virginia family. Peter Jefferson invested wisely in land in the Charlottesville area. His initial 1,000 acres grew to double that amount over the years and became the core of the estate later named Monticello, Italian for "little mountain."

Among other accomplishments, Peter Jefferson and his friend Joshua Fry were responsible for preparing a map of the state of Virginia in 1751. That map became the accepted standard for many decades, a fact which made his son quite proud. In fact, Thomas Jefferson reprinted this map in *Notes on the State of Virginia* in 1787.

Jefferson's early education occurred locally. His father's prosperity permitted him to enroll in a boarding school twelve miles away at the school headed by the Reverend James Maury in Fredericksville Parish. It was during these years that Jefferson was exposed to foreign languages, in which he grew to excel.

From 1760 to 1762, Jefferson attended the College of William and Mary in Williamsburg, the capital of Virginia. He was greatly impressed with the quaint town of Williamsburg. Although small in comparison to the major European cities of that era, Williamsburg seemed a great metropolis to young Jefferson. During his years at college he was introduced to a network of wealthy and well-traveled mentors who were instrumental in altering the course of his life.

Upon graduation from William and Mary, Jefferson studied law under a former college professor, George Wythe. The new law school graduate was considered one of the nation's best legal minds of the time. He gained admission to the bar of the General Court of Virginia in 1769.

In 1768, construction of Jefferson's home, Monticello, began. The original design was based on the classical style of Palladian architecture. The house was his own design and is situated on the summit of an 867-foot-high peak in the Southeast Mountains, near the family home in Shadwell.

In 1772 Jefferson married the widow Martha Wayles Skelton, age 23, and brought her to his home. At the time of their marriage, Monticello left much to be desired, as it was still in the construction stage. Martha's considerable dowry almost doubled Jefferson's land holdings and slaves. Historians record that the Jeffersons' marriage was a happy one. Martha bore him six children, only two of whom survived until adulthood.

As a member of the Continental Congress in 1776, Jefferson drafted the Declaration of Independence along with John Adams, Benjamin Franklin, Robert Livingstone and Roger Sherman. Writing this document, vital to our ultimate freedom, was one of the major achievements of his life.

Tall, shy and somewhat awkward, the sandy-haired Jefferson was never comfortable in the role of public speaker. Jefferson's contribution throughout his life was not as a great orator. Rather, his writings would be his legacy.

At age 25, Jefferson served in the Virginia House of Burgesses, and later as governor of the state of Virginia from 1779 to 1781. In 1782, Martha died during childbirth. Two years later, Jefferson departed for Europe where he served as minister to France until 1789. Upon his return, he accepted George Washington's appointment as

Sage of Monticello—The display case *becomes* Thomas Jefferson's portico at Monticello. Columns flank a portrait of our third president who is surrounded by that which he loved most in this world: books.

the first secretary of state. This was a position he held until 1793. He was elected vice president in 1797 and served two terms as president (1801–1809).

Visit this Web site for a brief, comprehensive account of the life of Thomas Jefferson: http://www.americanpresident.org/history/thomasjefferson/

Jefferson never remarried. He retired to care for his plantations. In addition to Monticello, Jefferson built a similar but smaller home on a large parcel of land overlooking the Peaks of Otter. The home and property, located in Bedford County, Virginia, was named Poplar Forest. For information on this historic home, currently under restoration, visit http://www.poplarforest.org/

From 1817 until his death in 1826, he was heavily involved in designing and establishing the University of Virginia in Charlottesville. For photographs of this architectural feat visit http://www.bc.edu/bc_org/avp/cas/fnart/fa267/Jeffersn.html

Jefferson's genius was apparent is every phase of his life. He read the ancient philosophers in the original Latin and Greek texts, yet he also knew and appreciated the modern thinkers. He assembled the finest library in America, which became the core collection of the Library of Congress. Jefferson built an exceptional private residence, designed the first republican statehouse and the finest new state university. To observers, all of these accomplishments seemed effortless.

Jefferson served as governor and author of a new Virginia constitution, minister to Paris, first secretary of state, leader of the first political party and third president. His public service was unmatched.

It is interesting to note that on his grave in the family cemetery at Monticello, an obelisk of gray stone omits Jefferson's service as U.S. president, but includes other accomplishments:

Here Was Buried
Thomas Jefferson
April 2, 1743 O.S.–July 4, 1826
Author of the Declaration
of Independence
and of the Virginia Statute for
Religious Freedom,
and Father of the University
of Virginia.

As a politician and statesman, Jefferson was the center of much controversy. Historians have conjectured that this may explain the omission of his tenure as president on his tombstone.

The burial site at Monticello is a peaceful place. Tourists who visit the cemetery treat it with reverence. The silence is what Jefferson craved during his lifetime. It was said that he yearned for a life of tranquil contemplation, spent in his library, among his architectural drawings and his science research, better known in his era as natural philosophy.

It is widely known that Thomas Jefferson and John Adams engaged in frequent correspondence during the later years of their lives. It is interesting to note that they both died within hours of each other on July 4, 1826, exactly fifty years after the Declaration of Independence was signed.

CREDITS

Several years ago my husband took a group of Penn State University freshman scholars on a weeklong trip that included visits to the Library of Congress, Monticello, and the archives of the University of Virginia. The purpose of this experience was to have a task that involved reading, writing and rhetoric. The students were introduced to a Thomas Jefferson they may not have previously known. They were expected to absorb and communicate the philosophy and accomplishments of this complex individual. The students were genuinely positive about the merits of the experience and submitted papers based on their overall experiences.

Several years ago, my husband and I visited both Monticello and Thomas Jefferson's summer home in Bedford County, Virginia. It was interesting to note that Poplar Forest was similar in design to Monticello, but smaller, and the ornamentation less formal. These decorative choices were made because heads of state would not be entertained at Poplar Forest. It was interesting to learn that Jefferson did some of the brickwork himself at his summer home. He wanted to be assured that the workmen he contracted understood and could duplicate the quality of brickwork that he expected.

The engraving by Thomas Johnson, based on a painting by Gilbert Stuart, was purchased in Charlottesville, Virginia, and now hangs in our home library along with several other Jefferson portraits and the small bust included in the display. After taking stock of our historical memorabilia and reflecting on both trips to Virginia, it seemed apparent that a display on Jefferson and Monticello would be an interesting choice.

ASSEMBLING THE DISPLAY

1. The portico of Monticello was recreated using white poster board. Watercolor was applied to change the hue and to give the illusion of architectural detailing on the columns. This was pinned to a black felt background. In the center of the case the Jefferson engraving was hung. Above the portrait was a banner with the title *Sage of Monticello*. The font used was Georgia sized at 170. This was printed on white cardstock and the letters were cut out and glued to the banner. For a small template of the banner, visit http://www.scrapbook-templates.com/banners-001.jpg

The stars were found through a Google image search and cut out of red, white and blue poster board. They were pinned strategically throughout the display, and placed on the cloth banner as well.

2. On the top left of the display was this quotation:

All authority belongs to the people

—Thomas Jefferson

This was printed on white cardstock and mounted on blue poster board. Stars and striped plastic ribbon, available at a dollar store, was cut to flank the quote.

Below that was a photograph of the University of Virginia and a information about the founding of this institution. This was printed on white cardstock and mounted on blue poster board. For this information visit http://www.virginia.edu/uvatours/short history/

3. On the top right of the display was a history of Monticello which was largely drawn from this site: http://www.aboutfamouspeople.com/article1015.html

An image of Monticello, found in MS Word's clip art, was inserted at the bottom center of the document. This was printed on white cardstock and mounted on red and blue poster board.

Below that was the well-known quote which introduced this display, which was mounted in the same manner as the previously mentioned quote.

A timeline on the life of Jefferson was found at this site: http://www.monticello.org/jefferson/timeline.html

Photos of a flag and Jefferson were inserted onto the paper using Microsoft Word. Click on the photo you have inserted, choose "Show Picture Toolbar" and then choose the icon for "text wrapping." Then select the option of "behind text." This will permit you to type the timeline on top of the images.

The timeline was printed on white cardstock and double mounted on red and blue poster board.

4. At the base of the display was a large red, white and blue banner. Styrofoam was placed under the banner to elevate the bust of Jefferson and to give better placement to some of the books. A copy of Jefferson's signature, which was found through a Google image search, was printed on soft gloss presentation laser paper. This was mounted on black poster board and placed in front of the bust.

A quote about the meaning of Monticello was printed on a transparency and mounted on scrapbooking paper with a historical document motif. This was then mounted on black poster board and set on an angle to the left of the signature. The quote was this:

> I am happy no where else, and in no other society, and all my wishes end where I hope my days will end, at Monticello.
>
> —Thomas Jefferson

Information about the origin of the engraving, which was based on a portrait by Gilbert Stuart, was processed in the same manner as the above quote, and placed to the right of the signature.

Books featured in the display were *Thomas Jefferson Architect: The Built Legacy of Our Third President* by Hugh Howard, *American Sphinx: The Character of Thomas Jefferson* by Joseph J. Ellis, *The Paris Years of Thomas Jefferson* by William Howard Adams, *Thomas Jefferson's Library: A Catalog with the Entries in His Own Order* edited by James Gilreath and Douglas L. Wilson, *The Lost World of Thomas Jefferson with a New Perspective* by Daniel J. Boorstin, and *Understanding Thomas Jefferson* by E. M. Halliday.

BIGGER AND BETTER

Your display could be called Thomas Jefferson, Architect and center on those creative endeavors. Or, since he left behind a host of inventions, such as the dumb-waiter, Jefferson: Inventor could be the main theme. Jefferson in Paris might be yet another display. You could center your display on the book collection donated by Jefferson that formed the foundation of the collection of the Library of Congress.

There has been much written of late on Jefferson's relationship with Sally Hemmings, a former slave, who may have given birth to at least one Jefferson offspring. This revelation in combination with his philosophy on slavery would make a provocative display.

TEN DAYS THAT UNEXPECTEDLY CHANGED AMERICA

These ten events "tell the story of rural farmers, gold-seeking forty-niners, immigrant workers, and disenfranchised African Americans all seeking their pieces of the American dream. But it also tells the story of noble statesmen, powerful presidents, decisive generals, and brilliant scientists who almost single-handedly changed the course of history" (Gillon 2).

It is interesting to note that the obvious historical highlights of American history aren't included in this display. No July 4, 1776, no surprise firing on Fort Sumter that ignited the Civil War, no attack on unsuspecting Pearl Harbor, not even a lunar landing! Instead, events included within this display were pivotal days that ultimately transformed the nation.

The History Channel asked leading historians, including Professor Steven M. Gillon of the University of Oklahoma, to suggest lesser-known events that were the catalyst for change in America. Gillon and his panel ultimately chose ten days that tell a story about the democratic principles upon which our country was built. The only parameter for inclusion was that all the events selected had to have occurred prior to 1965. This insured that proper historical perspectives could be applied.

The committee of historians and History Channel producers discussed, and sometimes heatedly debated, the days which should be included on the final list. They made a point of overlooking more apparent choices in favor of events whose importance had been undervalued. The range of topics spanned American history from the days of its early settlement to events in the recent past. Through these events a story unfolds which includes formidable statesmen, commanding presidents, powerful military men and celebrated scientists who made their mark on history.

The events selected by the History Channel for inclusion in their series entitled *10 Days That Unexpectedly Changed America* were as follows:

Massacre at Mystic (May 26, 1637)

On that day, English settlers and their Indian allies attacked Mystic Fort, home of the Pequot Indians, located in Mystic, Connecticut. This event changed the relationship between the colonists and Indians forever. Several hundred Pequot Indians were massacred in this battle, and those who tried to flee were either killed or sold into slavery. Centuries later, the few remaining Pequot Indians challenged the American government in order to acquire land and federal recognition. This tribe made a resurgence through the controversial construction of a bingo hall, and, eventually, a lucrative casino in the northeast.

10 Days That Unexpectedly Changed America—Events included are not those which immediately come to mind when reflecting on our nation's history. Still, they were crucial days in American history that ultimately transformed our country.

Shays's Rebellion (1786–1787)

Following the American Revolution, the farmers in Massachusetts were incensed by their growing debt and increased taxes. The failure to repay debt often resulted in incarceration in a debtor's prison. Farmer Daniel Shays organized a group of approximately 9,000 rebels to confront the government. They managed to close down courthouses and, in turn, freed the rebels of their financial burdens. The aftermath of this successful rebellion was a reevaluation of the Articles of Confederation at the Constitutional Convention.

California Gold Rush (1848)

Early that year, a carpenter named James Marshall happened upon nuggets of gold in a California river. The ensuing gold rush propelled the creation of the new state of California, and fueled massive industrial growth in the newfound West. As a result of the Gold Rush, America became a major economic power in a very small space of time.

Antietam (September 17, 1862)

Fought near Sharpsburg, Maryland, the Battle of Antietam was the first major battle of the American Civil War to take place in the North. The battle left more than 23,000 soldiers dead. The victory of the North gave President Abraham Lincoln the confidence to announce the Emancipation Proclamation, which brought an end to slavery in America.

The Homestead Strike (July 6, 1892)

On that day the union working at Carnegie Steel Company went on strike due to pay cuts and poor working conditions. Just prior to the strike, Andrew Carnegie had left for Scotland. He had appointed his manager, anti-unionist Henry Clay Frick, overseer of the company in his absence. Frick elected to bring in replacement workers, and hired Pinkerton agents to safeguard their arrival. The melee that followed resulted in the death of ten people. Two brigades of Pennsylvania state militia were called out to restore peace. An unsuccessful attempt on the life of Henry Frick resulted in turning public opinion away from the striking workers. Carnegie Steel resumed operations, without the union, using mostly unskilled immigrant workers.

Assassination of President McKinley (September 6, 1901)

On that day, President William McKinley was assassinated by Leon Czolgosz while attending the Pan-American Exposition in Buffalo, New York. Although doctors were able to remove the bullet, his health declined soon thereafter because physicians were unaware of the concept of introducing intravenous fluids. The murder at the fair propelled Theodore Roosevelt into the presidency, and led to a major political shift in the White House.

Scopes: The Battle Over America's Soul (July 21,1925)

On that day, the Scopes Monkey Trial began in Dayton, Tennessee. A substitute biology teacher by the name of John Scopes was represented by renowned attorney Clarence Darrow. Pitted against Darrow was the prosecutor William Jennings Bryan, well known fundamentalist, orator and local hero. The legal matter in question was known as the Butler Act. This piece of legislation had been passed several months earlier by the Tennessee General Assembly. The law stated "that it shall be unlawful for any teacher in any of the Universities, Normals and all other public schools of the State, which are supported in whole or in part by the public school funds of the State, to teach any theory that denies the story of the Divine Creation of man, as taught in the Bible, and to teach instead that man has descended from a lower order of animals." The debate over evolution and divine creation continues to the present day.

Einstein's Letter to FDR (July 16, 1939)

On that day, Albert Einstein drafted a letter to President Franklin D. Roosevelt, informing him of Germany's scientific research of the atomic bomb. Einstein's correspondence convinced the president of the danger which existed in having this technology in the hands of Adolf Hitler. When it was discovered that the newly formed Advisory Committee on Uranium was underfunded, Einstein sent a second letter to Roosevelt. The president then ordered the government to supply the additional funds, which resulted in the creation of the infamous Manhattan Project. Although a pacifist, Einstein never wanted the Nazis to have ownership of this powerful weapon.

When America Was Rocked (September 9, 1956)

Elvis Presley's appearance on *The Ed Sullivan Show* in the mid-fifties signified a whole new culture that involved teenage independence, sexuality, race relations, and a new form of music. The introduction of rock and roll meant that twentieth century America was forever changed.

Freedom Summer (1964)

The murders of three civil rights workers, part of the Freedom Summer Project, on June 21, 1964, by members of the Ku Klux Klan, spurred Congress to pass the Voting Rights Act. This law removed voter registration barriers for both minorities and the poor.

CREDITS

A couple of years ago, our library director shared a packet of information that had been sent to her from the History Channel. The title was *JFK: A Presidency*

Revealed, and the material was sent in advance of the cable TV production. Among the items included in the packet were a replica of a *Life* magazine article on Kennedy, bookmarks, a cardboard cutout of a bust of Kennedy as well as information about his life, presidency and shocking assassination. Grateful for this information, I mounted a library display which featured a retrospective of Kennedy's life and times, and promoted the upcoming television program.

Since that time, I have made it a point to go to the History Channel Web site to track other interesting events they will be featuring. I am grateful for their thorough research and helpful graphics which they gladly share with educators and librarians.

Sign up for free display material by accessing this worthwhile site: http://www.history.com

The idea for the display *Ten Days That Unexpectedly Changed America* was the direct result of the History Channel's April 2006 miniseries on this topic. Each segment gave great insights into the specific historical event featured, and provided a new perspective for viewers to consider.

ASSEMBLING THE DISPLAY

1. The lettering for *10 Days* was created by using Gill Sans Ultra Bold font sized at 300. The phrase *That Unexpectedly Changed* was created using Ariel Black sized at 100. Dumbledore 1 Shadow sized at 130, was used to create the word *America*. The latter can be obtained and downloaded from this site: http://www.grsites.com/fonts/d018.shtml

The entire title was printed on white cardstock and attached to white poster board which was then mounted on black poster board. This was attached with pins and pulled forward on camel colored felt background.

The images for the ten events were found through a Google image search. They were printed on cardstock and attached to black or black and gold poster board.

The quote introducing this display was printed on white cardstock, mounted on black poster board, attached with pins under the historical images, and pulled forward.

A replica of a star was found through a Google image search, printed on cardstock and traced onto black poster board. The stars were attached with pins above the title and below the images, then pulled forward.

2. The left side of the display had a description of the first five events taken from the above text. This information was printed on white cardstock and mounted on black poster board. Appropriate images from clip art were inserted at the top of these descriptions.

3. The right side of the display was created exactly as the left, but featured the latter five events.

4. A replica of the letter sent from Albert Einstein to President Franklin D. Roosevelt, regarding the danger of uranium in the hands of the Germans, was printed on

cardstock, mounted on black poster board and placed on the bottom center of the display case. This letter can be retrieved by visiting http://www.dannen.com/ae-fdr.html

Books featured in the display were *The Age of Gold* by H. W. Brands, *Shays's Rebellion: The American Revolution's Final Battle* by Leonard L. Richards, *All Shook Up: How Rock 'N' Roll Changed America* by Glenn Altschuler, *Freedom Summer* by Doug McAdam, *The Homestead Steel Strike of 1892* by Nancy Whitelaw, *10 Days That Unexpectedly Changed America* by Steven M. Gillon, *Crossroads of Freedom: Antietam* by James M. McPherson, *Einstein's German World* by Fritz Stern, *Freedom Summer* by Doug McAdam, *Last Train to Memphis: The Rise of Elvis Presley* by Peter Guralnick, and *The Pequot War* by Alfred A. Cave.

The star image was traced onto gold poster board. A dozen of these were interspersed among the display books.

BIGGER AND BETTER

Should your space permit, you could add some Native American artifacts reminiscent of the early Pequot nation, or casino chips, cards, etc. to reflect their current enterprise. An historic map of the West, a pan, and chunks of gold could be added to signify the Gold Rush. Civil War artifacts could support the inclusion of Antietam in the display.

Add Elvis memorabilia, or some 45 RPM records, to suggest rock and roll. A labor symbol (retrieved online), lantern, or vintage hardhat, could be included as a visual reminder of the Homestead Strike of 1892. A We Shall Overcome button (available through a Google image search) could be included to suggest Freedom Summer. A colonial hat or old farm implements could be included for Shays's Rebellion.

D-DAY REMEMBERED: PROJECT OVERLORD

Soldiers, sailors and airmen of the Allied Expeditionary Force: The eyes of the world are upon you. The free men of the world are marching together to victory. Good luck.

—General Dwight D. Eisenhower,
in the address to his field commander,
General Bernard Montgomery and his men, June 6, 1944

Operation Overlord was the greatest amphibious attack in history. Nearly 175,000 American, Canadian and British troops landed in Normandy on June 6, 1944, supported by 6,000 aircraft and another 6,000 naval vessels ranging in size from battleships to 32-foot landing crafts. Although the actual numbers of men and machines deployed vary greatly depending on the account, the enormity of the event is obvious. The task was complex. The objective was to win a beachhead in France which would open a second front against Hitler's armies and to use the beachhead as a springboard for the liberation of France and Belgium, and the eventual conquest of Nazi Germany.

As America bowed its head for its men, President Roosevelt wrote an invasion prayer meant to inspire the troops:

> Lead them straight and true;
> give strength to their arms,
> stoutness to their hearts,
> steadfastness to their faith.
> They will need Thy blessings.
> Their road will be long and
> hard. The enemy is strong. He
> may hurl back our forces.
> Success may not come with
> rushing speed, but we shall
> return again and again; and
> we know that by Thy grace
> and by the righteousness of
> our cause, our sons will tri-
> umph" [D-Day 5].

In retrospect, it is hard to visualize the epic scope of this decisive battle which would foreshadow the end of Hitler's dream of Nazi domination. That story was about to unfold.

After years of fastidious planning and non-stop training for the Allied Forces, it all came down to this: When the boat ramp goes down, jump, swim, run, and crawl to the cliffs. Many of the initial troops who entered the surf were carrying eighty pounds of equipment through withering fire and savage resistance. The men faced over 200 yards of beach before reaching the first natural feature that would offer any protection.

D-Day Remembered—Allied Armies land in France and the great invasion of June 6, 1944, began. This display pays tribute to our uniformed forces who fought and won the greatest amphibious battle in history.

D-Day was originally set for June 5, but a storm that day prevented amphibious operations. At the height of the storm, Eisenhower's weather expert predicted that it would soon abate, and that conditions would allow for the invasion. The supreme Allied commander decided to proceed with the mission.

The attack consisted of division strength assaults on five beaches: two British, two American, and one Canadian preceded by a night assault of three airborne divisions to protect the flanks (one British on the left and two American on the right).

The night operation involved the destruction of bridges along with gun emplacements, captured crossroads and routes inland from Utah Beach. At dawn, there was heavy air and sea bombardment. Although they had expected heavy tank support, the tanks were launched too far out in rough seas, and thirty-two out of the thirty-four tanks sank.

When it was over, the Allied forces had suffered nearly 10,000 injured and over 4,000 dead. Yet somehow, due to planning and preparation, and because of the valor, fidelity and sacrifice of the Allied Forces, Fortress Europe had been breached.

On June 6, 1944, thousands of young men sacrificed themselves that future generations might live in freedom. Americans who fought in World War II have been called "the greatest generation." If this is so, D-Day—with its epic bravery, ultimate sacrifice, and brilliant success—might have been the finest minute, our greatest moment.

CREDITS

The History Channel sent an all-inclusive packet to many libraries across America in the spring of 2004 with information concerning an upcoming cable program commemorating the 60th anniversary of D-Day. This comprehensive material became the inspiration for the display.

A visit to see our son Brian, in Bedford, Virginia, included a trip to the recently built National D-Day Memorial. We were fortunate to have a guided tour by a recently retired naval officer. Our guide's seafaring background, combined with his thorough research, brought to life both the utmost horrors and inspired accomplishments that this day represented.

The small southwestern Virginia town of Bedford was selected as the site of this memorial because it lost 19 of its young men in the Normandy landing. This was the greatest single sacrifice of any of our nation's communities. Bedford is symbolic of the proud towns across our country that sent its citizen-soldiers to war.

More information about the memorial can be found at www.dday.org.

Additional data on Operation Overlord can be found at http://www.oxfordrefer ence.com/

ASSEMBLING THE DISPLAY

1. The word *D-Day* was printed using Tahoma bold, sized at 195. *Remembered* was printed using Monotype Corsiva bold, sized at 148. These words were printed

on off-white cardstock mounted on black poster board and attached to the tan felt background. Between the signage hung a 1943 sepia toned photo of an Air Force communications class on graduation day in Camp Edison, New Jersey. Also mounted on black poster board and surrounding this large photo were photographs of other servicemen who served in World War II, and a D-Day headline from the *New York Times* from June 6, 1944. A B-17 bomber, known as a "Knockout Dropper" and flown by the Hell's Angels, was printed on cardstock and mounted on black poster board (complete with bomb!). The plane was affixed to the top right of the collage. Below that was a replica of a Medal of Honor found through a Google image search. This was printed on cardstock and mounted on black poster board. An image of a marine master sergeant insignia was printed on cardstock and worked into the lower left of the collage. Under the featured image was a photo reprint of a sculpture located at the National D-Day Memorial in Bedford, Virginia. This work, as well as and many others at that memorial, was created by artist Jim Brothers and can be found at http://www.dday.org. The word "heroes" was created using Times New Roman, lower case, 100 point bold italic font, and printed on off-white cardstock, then placed in the right of the collage. Two army dog tags were pinned on the left of the center photograph along with an infantry insignia. All of the items in the tableau, except the large photograph, were affixed with pins and pulled away from the background. Above the collage the twelve Allied countries' flags, found on an online image search, were printed on cardstock. These were hung like a banner and were affixed with pins.

Under the heading "Operation Overlord," a C-47 Skytrain was printed on cardstock and mounted on black poster board. The font chosen for the text was Sylfaen bold, sized at 65. Below this plane were the images of the paratroopers which were framed in black poster board. These images were found in the reproduction *Life* magazine commemorative D-Day issue provided by the History Channel, which covered the progress of the war from June through August of 1944.

This quote, from the History Channel packet, was mounted on black poster board and placed just above the paratroopers:

> To save the world you have to jump into hell.
>
> —Anonymous

The rifle was cut from brown poster board and drawn freehand, then mounted on black poster board, attached to the background with straight pins and pulled forward. The green helmet, also drawn freehand, was placed atop the rifle and both were pulled forward on straight pins. These two items are significant as they would have been placed on the battlefield to mark a casualty of war.

2. On the top left was a description of the SHAEF patch. Next was a replica of the Supreme Headquarters Allied Expeditionary Force patch which was worn by SAARF (Special Allied Airborne Reconnaissance Force) personnel on the left shoulder while they were serving in this special unit. The fiery sword represented the

determination of those fighting for freedom. This was created freehand using a graphic found through an online image search.

Below that was the following quote:

> Later, about ten of us were crossing along the edge of a field when we heard sniper bullets whiz by. We all fell to the ground. As we lay there hugging the earth, that we might escape shrapnel from shell fire and bullets from snipers' guns, the birds were singing beautifully in the trees close by. As I lay there listening I thought of the awfulness of it all; the birds were singing and we human beings were trying to kill each other. We are the greatest of God's creation, made in the image of God, and here human blood was being spilt everywhere.
>
> —Chaplain John G. Burkhalter,
> 1st North Shore Regiment,
> June Beach

Under that was a map of the D-Day operation on Normandy found through a Google image search, and also available in virtually all of the books on the topic.

3. On the top right was a lengthy overview of the landing in Normandy taken from the History Channel's *D-Day: The 60th Anniversary* publication. It was printed on cardstock and mounted on black poster board.

Under that was a poster of Operation Overlord purchased at the D-Day Memorial for 39 cents!

Below that was the quote introducing this display. Other D-Day quotes are available if you visit http://americanhistory.about.com/od/worldwarii/a/ddayquotes.htm

4. A marine fatigue uniform and cap was placed at the base of the display. Color cardstock reproductions of 1940s era candy, a hand grenade and period cigarette packs were found though a Google image search and mounted on black poster board.

Books featured in the display were *D-Day: The 60th Anniversary* by the History Channel, *A Private's Diary* by Donald A. Edwards, and *The D-Day Experience: From the Invasion to the Liberation of Paris* by Richard Holmes.

BIGGER AND BETTER

If your display space permits, you could include actual insignias or medals of war, real Allied flags, military boots and a helmet, war-related posters, miniature vehicles such as jeeps, tanks or model planes, diary entries from soldier's memoirs, large maps of the Normandy area, and additional headlines from other newspapers. Family letters or telegraphs from veterans, military bowls and flatware, and MREs (meals ready to eat) could also be included. A toy rifle and helmet could be substituted for the hand drawn ones.

Highly recommended is the book *The D-Day Experience: From the Invasion to the Liberation of Paris* by Richard Holmes. It includes reprints of top secret documents and diaries, pull-out maps, incredible photos, reproductions of signs, francs, newspapers, letters, and even a passport. It is a great resource.

CITIZEN BEN

A little neglect may breed great mischief ... for want of a nail the shoe was lost; for want of a shoe the horse was lost; and for want of a horse the rider was lost.

—Benjamin Franklin

Benjamin Franklin was born in Boston on January 17, 1706, the youngest of 17 children. His father, Josiah, was a soap and candle maker. His mother Abiah Folger was Josiah's second wife. Boston was deeply rooted in Puritan traditions and teachings, which had a significant impact on young Franklin.

Ben Franklin distinguished himself as a child by exhibiting leadership qualities among his peers and developing a deep passion for reading. Although his formal schooling ended at ten years of age, Franklin's literary interests were the result of an apprenticeship which began at the age of twelve. At that time, he was placed under the supervision of his brother James in the local print shop.

At age 17, Franklin fled his native Boston and relocated to Philadelphia. He moved to London for a brief period of time, where he worked as a compositor in a printer's shop.

When he returned to Philadelphia, he began publishing *The Pennsylvania Gazette*. Franklin contributed many original essays to this publication and subsequently became a catalyst for local reforms. He steadily expanded his personal and professional acquaintances, which in turn advanced his publishing business.

Franklin fathered an illegitimate child in 1728, named William. No information remains about the child's mother. In 1730, he and his childhood sweetheart, Deborah Read, agreed to enter into a common law marriage. She could not be legally wed, as she had been previously married to John Rogers. Her husband had absconded with a slave and fled the city of Philadelphia. The union of Franklin and Deborah produced two children, Sarah (Sally) and Francis (Franky) Folger. Their daughter would live a long and full life. Young Franky, however, succumbed to smallpox at the age of four.

By the time Franklin was 42, he had amassed great wealth through his publishing enterprises. With his financial future assured, he devoted the remaining decades of his life to the search for "useful knowledge." To this end, in 1743 he and some friends formed the American Philosophical Society. Throughout his adult years, Franklin would continue the pursuit of self-improvement and, ultimately, the improvement of the community.

In 1732, Franklin began to publish *Poor Richard's Almanac*, which contains adages that are still commonly quoted worldwide. Other milestones included establishing the first volunteer fire department, founding an academy which would become the University of Pennsylvania, obtaining a charter to establish the first hospital in the United States, identifying positive and negative electrical charges through experiments with lightning, signing the Declaration of Independence, and helping to negotiate the Treaty of Paris, in 1775.

Citizen Ben—Franklin's tercentenary was boldly celebrated in the city of Philadelphia in 2006. The kite, key and lightening bolts symbolize the famous experiment which led to his discovery of static electricity.

Franklin can be credited with numerous inventions that continue to improve the quality of our lives. He was responsible for the heat efficient Franklin stove, bifocals, the glass armonica, the medical catheter, lightning rods, swim fins and the odometer.

Politics became of more interest to Franklin in the 1750s. In 1757, he went to England to represent Pennsylvania in its battle with the descendants of the Penn family over representation of the colony. He later represented New Jersey, Massachusetts and Georgia as well. Initially, while abroad, Franklin considered himself an Englishman. He admired England for its philosophers, theatre and more cultured society. Franklin considered staying in England permanently, but his wife was fearful of sea travel and was unwilling to join him.

Franklin first visited France in the fall of 1767 where his celebrity status had previously been established. Each subsequent journey to this country reinforced the people's adulation. The result was a mutual admiration for both Franklin and the French.

In 1772, he was honored to be elected as a member of the French Academy of Sciences. The next year saw the publication of his *Oeuvres,* the first collection of his writings. Franklin arrived in Paris in December of 1776 to serve as a commissioner of

Congress to the French Court. As usual, he was revered by a learned society as well as the royals. Living the high life agreed with Franklin, who was enthusiastic in his appreciation of fine things. Life as he knew it in Philadelphia suddenly seemed insufferably dull.

After forty-four years together, Deborah Franklin died in 1774. Three years later, Franklin presided over the Constitutional Convention in Philadelphia and served on the committee to draft the Declaration of Independence.

During his final years, Franklin signed both the Treaty of Paris, which effectively ended the Revolutionary War, and the United States Constitution. He wrote a treatise on anti-slavery and became president of the Society for the Abolition of Slavery.

Benjamin Franklin died in Philadelphia on April 17, 1790, at the age of 84. A record twenty thousand mourners attended his funeral at the Christ Church Burial Ground.

For comprehensive biographical information on Benjamin Franklin, visit these sites:http://www.ushistory.org/franklin/info/index.htm or http://www.colonialhall. com/franklin/franklin.php

CREDITS

Philadelphia proudly celebrated the tercentenary of its favorite son in 2006. Much was made of this special anniversary. The national celebration honoring the life and legacy of this formidable founding father culminated in an international traveling exhibition entitled *Ben Franklin: In Search of a Better World.* The show had its rightful beginning in the City of Brotherly Love, at the National Constitution Center, in 2005. Over the course of the next few years, it would visit St. Louis, Houston, Denver, and Atlanta and conclude in Paris, France, in March of 2008.

Philadelphia's Franklin Institute is a permanent venue for this forefather's accomplishments. Founded in 1824, it is a true monument to its namesake. The statue of Benjamin Franklin, located in the museum lobby, suggests the focus of this institute, which is to serve as a clearing house for inventors. Those of us who are familiar with the Franklin Institute value its contribution to science and the community, through its innovative and interactive programs, and the broad spectrum of its ever changing exhibits.

I am fortunate to live but an hour away from this facility. If a trip to Philadelphia and the Franklin Institute is not a possibility for you, be sure to experience Ben Franklin and his impact on your world by visiting http://www.benfranklin300.org/exhibition/ _html/0_0/index.htm

ASSEMBLING THE DISPLAY

1. The black felt background suggests the night sky. The title *Citizen Ben* was created by using the font Stone Serif SCIN Sm sized at 390. This was printed on cardstock, cut, and traced on gold poster board, attached with pins, and pulled forward.

A scrapbook page with an American flag design, purchased at a local craft shop, was glued on poster board and cut into the shape of a kite. Thirteen stars were cut out and glued to a square of blue poster board and affixed to the flag to suggest the colonial period. A strip of cranberry and tan striped homespun fabric served as the tail and ties for the flag/kite. A brass key hung from the kite's tail as per the accounts of Franklin's famous experiment.

Bolts of lightning, found through a Google image search, were printed on cardstock, cut, pinned and pulled forward to suggest an electrical storm.

2. On the top left was a reproduction of the first political cartoon which Franklin created using a woodcut. Information on this cartoon titled *Join, or Die*, can be found at this site http://www.thetalentshow.org/history.html

Under the cartoon was a description of the significance of *Join, or Die*.

These quotes by Benjamin Franklin, from *Poor Richard's Almanac,* were printed on off-white cardstock with patriotic clip art inserted:

There are three faithful friends—an old wife, an old dog, and ready money.

If you would not be forgotten
As soon as you are dead and rotten,
Either write things worthy reading,
Or do things worth the writing.

All the items attached on the left were glued to the flag motif paper and affixed to the wall with double sided tape.

3. On the top right was biographical information about Ben Franklin found at the above mentioned Web sites. A clip art image of an American eagle was centered above the text.

These Franklin quotes were attached to the right side of the display case with patriotic clip art inserted:

Necessity never made a good bargain.

Fear not death; for the sooner we die, the longer shall we be immortal.

Items on the right were printed on off-white cardstock and mounted on flag motif paper and attached with double sided tape.

4. On the base of the display case, an artificial cake was placed on a glass pedestal stand. The cake was made from a circular Styrofoam form iced with shortening. The red foil number 300, purchased at a party store, was placed in the cake's center. Red and blue foil cupcake toppers (previously seen in Jewish American Authors) adorn the cake to give a festive feel to the tableau. Blue and red stars were recycled from The Sage of Monticello and applied to the icing and strewn above the vintage red, white and blue banner which surrounded the cake stand, and lined the base of the display case.

A reproduction of the Declaration of Independence, found through a Google Image search, was printed on off-white cardstock and positioned in the forefront of the cake.

Books featured in the display were *Ben Franklin: America's Original Entrepreneur* adapted by Blaine McCormick, *1776* by David McCullough, *Benjamin Franklin: An American Life* by Walter Isaacson, *The First American* by H. W. Brands, *Bolt of Fate: Benjamin Franklin and His Fabulous Kite,* and *Ben Franklin's 12 Rules of Management* by Blaine McCormick.

BIGGER AND BETTER

Your display could focus on one particular aspect of Franklin's life, such as Franklin the Inventor. If controversy interests you, there is plenty written regarding the plausibility of Franklin's kite experiment. There is a wealth of information should you decide that Franklin the Statesman would be an interesting display to mount.

Poor Richard's Almanac could be a display unto itself. Much is written about Franklin and the French. Ben Franklin would be a perfect subject for a 4th of July display. Include the Liberty Bell and fireworks (see the Celebrate the New Year! display under Traditions) if you decide to use this as a theme. For ideas regarding July 4th, visit http://www.american.edu/heintze/postcards.htm

Remember to check the Franklin Institute and National Constitution Center Web sites under Resources for Educators. These are updated regularly and should offer additional ideas for your consideration.

Art and Architecture

TRIBAL TREASURES

Collectors of art, especially tribal art, may well regard themselves as temporary custodians of the objects in their care, which were made in other times and places to change other people's lives and have since become part of our lives. In time, they will become part of someone else's.
—Editor, *Tribal Arts,* Spring 1998

Over the last century, Western culture has made an earnest attempt to understand the population and appreciate the art of the Oceanic Islands and the continent of Africa. The tribal notion of beauty has been long studied by scholars, and was found to differ from the Western concept, which is based solely on aesthetics.

The idea of a beautiful object is that it should adhere to tribal artistic rules and concepts. In addition, it should have the capacity to cure, to curse, to teach or even protect individuals and communities. Much of so called primitive art was created as a direct response to the natives' emotional state.

Tribal art stands on its own merits and must be judged by its own criteria. Since all art is an expression of culture, it is obvious that societies so different from our own will create different art forms. Much of the art generated within tribes is infused with intensity and power which is then revealed through amazing forms using a wide variety of materials and techniques.

Oceania

The prevailing religious beliefs of the natives of New Guinea in the Oceanic Islands include supernatural spirits, often of formidable character, as well as mythological creatures. The power of the ancestors and magical practices are also important components of tribal attitudes about religion. All of these beliefs serve to inform and inspire the natives' creative and artistic endeavors.

Masks from this region can be used to represent specific ancestors and bring the spirits of the deceased to members of the clan. Some are used as protection against black magic. Surprisingly, few masks are actually designed and intended to be worn over the face. Masks are sometimes paired with elaborate costumes in celebratory dances. These rituals were thought to ensure successful hunting and war parties, or bountiful harvests.

Ceremonial shields are frequently fashioned from large pieces of bark and tied to cane frames, which are then prominently displayed within the dwelling. These brightly colored shields are never taken to battle, but serve to ward off thieving spirits from rival villages. Despite the similarity of design themes, no two carvings are alike.

Primitive Art of New Guinea: Sepik River Basin by Sava Maksic and Paul Meskil and *Art of the South Pacific Islands* by Paul S. Wingert were excellent resources which explore the art created in this exotic area of the world.

Africa

Africa's many diverse people and regions have produced a multitude of artifacts including sculpture, decorative arts, masks, shields, textiles, and everyday usable objects.

> African tribal art is not just about an aesthetic, it is also about meaning and function. African objects were almost never created as "art for art's sake," rather

Tribal Treasures—Masks, wooden instruments, carved figures and utilitarian objects form the core of this display on the arts of Africa and Oceania. The font used for the title complements these artifacts.

these objects always related to magical or social rites—to the supernatural world—and were rarely produced by a single individual. Before the making of many artifacts, there was a long, controlled process including close collaboration between the "commissioner," the village diviner and the sculptor [Bacquart 8]."

The predominant art forms in many regions of Africa are masks and figures. These are primarily used in religious ceremonies. Since wood was readily available it was one of the most frequently used materials. Often the wood was enhanced with metal, beads, shells, ivory and feathers.

The human figure is a common subject in tribal art. These representations tend to be naturalistic and clearly recognizable as such.

African artists have made utilitarian objects of great beauty. Conceived to fulfill a specific function, these objects have beautiful visual and tactile designs. Combs, fly-whisks, neck rests, seats, beds, stools, spoons, pipes, bowls, horns, drums, trays, baskets, staffs, scepters, boxes, snuff containers and doors would all fall into the utilitarian category. Each of these objects exemplifies the seamless integration of aesthetics into daily life in Africa. Jewelry making is another area of artistic expression and is widely crafted and valued throughout the continent.

Interest in tribal art is no longer limited to a few artists, critics and historians, but has grown to include those who view art as a conduit to personal growth. Museums worldwide exhibit primitive art to a growing number of appreciative patrons. *Expressions of Belief: Masterpieces of African, Oceanic and Indonesian Art*, edited by Suzanne Greub, was an excellent source for information about the art in these regions.

For more information on the subject of tribal arts, visit http://www.lewiswara.com/resources/nguinea.html

Credits

Cressman Library at Cedar Crest College was the recipient of tribal artifacts from the collection of Marjorie Wright Miller, class of 1930. Her travels to Oceania and Africa are reflected in the items featured in Tribal Treasures.

Living among these treasures is a joy. However, the room in which they are displayed is somewhat removed from the daily activity in the library. I was pleased to be able to feature these artifacts in a special display that, for a period of time, gave them more prominence. I am happy to share them with you in this manner.

Assembling the Display

1. The background was divided into two felt sections: black to showcase the masks and shield, and camel to provide a contrast to the carved wooden artifacts. A 1" strip of poster board was cut and affixed as a horizontal divider to create a straight line between the contrasting fabric colors. The font VTC Tribal Regular was downloaded from the free Web site. To locate this font, visit http://www.highfonts.com/fontsearch.asp?ord=TRIBAL&f=0

The title was enlarged to 130 and printed on white paper which was glued to camel colored poster board. Above the title were carved artifacts from New Guinea which included a wind instrument and a comb. Both masks and the shield are also from New Guinea.

2. On the top left of the display was a description of New Guinea and its native arts which can be found if you visit http://www.lewiswara.com/resources/nguinea.html

Below that is information about tribal art which can be found if you visit http://www.tribalarts.com/

Items on the left were printed on off-white cardstock and mounted on black poster board.

3. On the top right was the following passage:

> The art of the Sepik River region has more variety and is richer than any other section of Oceania. Each of the cultures along the Sepik River hold many religious customs and values the same, although their artistic objects and artifacts may vary. Some of the common elements include: the men's society, the men's club house, and the performance of spectacular ceremonies. The rites include a vast number of carved and decorated objects. These objects are of two kinds: sacred hidden ones, which may be seen only by a particular group, and others that are used and seen by everyone. Some of the ritual objects produced include: stools, neck rests, slit gongs, shields, canoes, lime containers, flute stops, and wooden suspension hooks.

This information was found at http://www.lewiswara.com/resources/nguinea.html

Next came a description of the various types of African masks. This information is available at http://www.rebirth.co.za/African_mask_history_and_meaning.htm

Last was this quote on ethnocentricity:

> Ethnocentricity cuts both ways. We can see another culture only in terms of our own and, from lack of imagination, not see very much at all. Or we can place that other culture inside our purview and deny ourselves the right to take a look [Ginzberg 3].

All of this information was printed just as the documents on the left.

4. On the base of the display and to the left were two ebony carvings of human forms from Tanzania. In the center were 5 carved African elephants placed on Styrofoam blocks covered with camel felt. These forms created different elevations to showcase the figures. To the right is a figure resembling a totem pole and a carved human form from Africa. To the left of the large elephant is a pouch crocheted in the shape of an elephant with shells and ivory husks attached. To the right of this figure is a passage titled "Treasures of a Continent" (Fisher 602). Two beaded necklaces and 3 miniature carved figures were interspersed. Strings of raffia were placed throughout the display to add texture.

Books featured in this display were *Arts of the Pacific Islands* by Anne D'Alleva, *Kamoro Art: Tradition and Innovation in a New Guinea Culture* by Dirk Smidt, *Oceanic Art* by Nicholas Thomas, and *The Tribal Arts of Africa* by Jean-Baptiste Bacquart.

BIGGER AND BETTER

The items available to you will necessarily differ from those included in Tribal Treasures. Textiles would add color and enhance this display. Native flags or area maps could also be incorporated as an eye-catching backdrop.

Take care to coordinate the background colors with the predominant color of the collection that you are showcasing. Don't overload the display. Remember to leave room around the object so that each unique item can be viewed on its own merits.

ART BY PONDER GOEMBEL

The cast of characters includes a wisecracking marmalade tom, an angora diva, and a tough alley cat with a heart of gold. Goembel's illustrations, done in acrylic and ink, are fantastic and provide wonderful insight into the side stories developing as the book progresses. This animated witty book is a wonderful selection to read aloud or for one-on-one appreciation of the marvelous art.
—Kara Schaff Dean, Needham Public Library,
Book Pick-*Castaway Cats*,
School Library Journal,
June 2006

The art of illustrating juvenile literature has recently received an increased amount of respect and scrutiny. Since pictures in books are often the first means children have to decipher the world unfolding before them, it was about time this creative endeavor earned the attention it deserves. Consequently, artists illustrating for youngsters are charged with a formidable obligation. The graphics they create are one of the first tools a child draws upon to relate to the world in which he lives. Children's illustrators help to define a world the child has not yet experienced.

Historically, illustrations in books were reliant on the technology available for reproduction. The vision of early illustrators frequently exceeded the capabilities of the existing printers. Today's artists can be assured that their work will be electronically scanned and printed and can be saved for posterity.

With the possible exceptions of William Blake, Beatrix Potter and N. C. Wyeth, the work of book illustrators isn't often showcased in galleries, framed and waiting for public acknowledgment. Instead, their work is discovered and re-discovered as tiny fingers extract slender volumes from library book shelves. When the pages are opened, the magic unfolds.

A Baltimore native and award winning illustrator, Ponder Goembel grew up in a city which nurtured its artists and celebrated many diverse cultures. Her childhood memories were of block parties, crab feasts, musical concerts and art festivals.

While in elementary school, Ponder followed in her parents' footsteps and enrolled in a summer class at the nearby Maryland Institute of Art. Here her artistic abilities became apparent. A visit by a professional illustrator during Ponder's grade school years piqued her interest in this area of art. As a high school student, Ponder used her talent to design silkscreened brochures and posters promoting school sponsored activities. Prior to stage productions, the artist could be found assisting with the painting of theatrical sets.

Ponder sought a new and different urban experience for higher education. She found it at the Philadelphia College of Art, now part of the University of the Arts, located in the heart of the city. Ponder majored in illustration, but enjoyed the exposure to a variety of mediums. After graduation, she worked as a freelance illustrator. Ponder created drawings designed for advertisements, magazines, greeting cards, record albums and book covers.

Art by Ponder Goembel—*Castaway Cats*, **illustrated by Ponder Goembel, tells the tale of fifteen shipwrecked cats trying to survive on a deserted island. Palm trees, rocks, shells, sand and starfish combine to create a tropical paradise fit for felines.**

Ponder's black and white illustrations could be found in *Hear the Wind Blow: American Folk Songs Retold,* written by Scott R. Sanders, in 1985. Her first venture into professional picture book illustration using color came soon after the birth of her child. *A Basket Full of White Eggs* by Brian Swann was published in 1988. This project provided Ponder both a challenge and an opportunity. Sharing this experience with her young daughter reinforced her desire to continue to create meaningful artwork for children's narratives.

Other picture books followed: *Old Cricket* (*School Library Journal's* Best Book of the Year) and *Sailor Moo: Cow at Sea,* both by Lisa Wheeler, *Hi Pizza Man* by Virginia Walter, *The Night the Iguana Left Home* by Megan McDonald, and *Dinosnores* by Kelly DiPucchio. Her most recent work, *Castaway Cats,* also by Lisa Wheeler, is featured in the display.

Ponder summarizes her process for illustrating children's books:

1. Thumbnail sketches are created on tracing paper; these are small page-by-page mock-ups (like a story board) that show basic arrangements of images and words.

2. Final sketches are drawn from the thumbnails, enlarged to the same size as the book will be. Completed sketches are submitted to the editor, who suggests changes to be made by the artist.

3. The final art begins after all changes in the sketches have been accepted. Sketches are transferred to the painting surface, drawn with colored inks and painted with an acrylic wash. Touch-ups are made with opaque acrylics to create depth.

The artist decides how the words are divided over the pages, but the choice and arrangement of the typography and flap design is done by the publisher's design department.

For information about the artist Ponder Goembel, or to make arrangements for her to visit your school, library or book store to present a slide show and explain her creative process, please visit http://www.pondergoembel.com

CREDITS

I first met Ponder Goembel in the summer of 2005, at a book signing in one of Bethlehem's charming Main Street destinations, the Moravian Book Shop. At that time, her most recent publication was *Dinosnores,* written by Kelly DiPucchio. I was impressed by her obvious talent and amazingly detailed depictions of dozing dinosaurs emitting grunts and snorts amidst their slumber.

Ponder graciously agreed to meet with me to discuss her method of illustration the following spring. Shortly after that visit the positive reviews began to surface for her latest publication, *Castaway Cats.* At the time she was deeply involved in the thumbnail sketches for an upcoming publication, *Come Back Farm* by Rita Gray, to be published by E. P. Dutton in 2008. Ponder's home is located in Pennsylvania's picturesque Bucks County. Located above the family's antique store, Ponder's well organized studio houses an impressive professional portfolio and a comprehensive library for ready reference.

ASSEMBLING THE DISPLAY

1. A background of light blue felt created the illusion of the sky for this display. Palm trees previously created for Hot Nights, Cool Reads, were attached with straight pins flanking the life preserver, which was hung in the same manner. Letters for the book title, *Castaway Cats*, were created using the font Shruti sized at 250. These were printed on cardstock, cut and glued to the surface of the flotation device.

The image from *Castaway Cats* was copied and glued to black poster board. A border of black was left around the perimeter of the image. This was pinned to the life preserver. Miniature cut outs of fish hanging from twine and an anchor flanked the word *Cats*. Ocean waves were created from poster board in varying shades of blue and green. Fish, found through a Google image search, were printed on off-white card-stock cut and attached with pins throughout the waves.

An oar was cut from an old piece of corrugated cardboard. A Google image search helped to give ideas for the correct shape. Plastic letters (Helvetica 1½") purchased at an office supply store were affixed to the paddle area of the oar. The words *Art by* were created using the font Trebuchet MS sized at 90. This was printed on cardstock and glued to the handle of the oar. The oar was pinned to the clouds cut from cloud design poster board available at craft and office supply stores.

2. On the left of the display was a copy of the thumbnail sketches drawn for this book, which were provided by the artist. The font Curly MT sized at 110 was used for the heading *Thumbnails*. Although the original thumbnails were drawn on tracing paper, the ones shown are photocopies, which had better contrast for the purposes of photographing the display. Approximately two thirds of the total thumbnails were shown.

3. On the top right was a biography of the artist available on her Web site. This was mounted on green and black poster board and attached with double-sided tape.

The review of *Castaway Cats* from *School Library Journal*, June, 2006 (also available on their Web site), was enhanced with clip art of palm trees. This was mounted on black poster board and taped to the side of the case.

4. A starfish, rocks and shells lined the base of the display. A miniature rowboat was placed on end with tiny oars and a ship's wheel. This was supported by a Plexiglas box. A description of the illustration process was printed on off-white cardstock and glued to green poster board. The font Curly MT sized at 80 was used for the heading *Ponder This...* Books illustrated by Ponder Goembel featured in the display were *Dinosnores* by Kelly DePucchio, *Sailor Moo: Cow at Sea, Castaway Cats* and *Old Cricket* by Lisa Wheeler, and *Hi, Pizza Man* by Virginia Walter. A red floral lei was positioned under *Hi, Pizza Man.*

BIGGER AND BETTER

Should you feature *Castaway Cats* in your display case you could create a bonfire and add a wooden raft wrapped with cord. There could also be a message in a bottle, straw hat, ragged umbrella and fishing poles included in the display.

You could focus on any of Ponder Goembel's other works in your display. Feature a large pizza box if you choose *Hi, Pizza Man.* Since all of the characters are featured in a doorway, you could create that as the primary graphic for your background.

Mountains could enhance the background, and model dinosaurs along with vegetation could be scattered throughout a display featuring *Dinosnores.* Tiny pillows crafted from fiberfill could be included. Scatter "Zs" throughout the display to represent sleep.

Sailor Moo: Cow at Sea could include many props such as ocean waves, a chef's hat, cats and pirate memorabilia. Page through the book for additional ideas.

Check your area for local artists willing to show their work in your display space. You will be surprised at the number of talented individuals who live and work in your midst!

AMERICAN FOLK ART

One may look for and find, originality of concept, creativity of design, craftsmanly use of the medium, and flashes of inspiration even genius. Folk art makes its appeal directly and intimately, even to people quite uninitiated into the mysteries of art.

—Alice Winchester, 1974

Holger Cahill wrote in 1931,

Folk art is an expression of the common people and not an expression of a small cultured class. Folk art usually has not much to do with the fashionable art of its period. It is never the product of art movements, but comes out of craft traditions, plus that personal something of the rare craftsman who is an artist by nature if not by training. This art is based not on measurements or calculations but on feeling, and it rarely fits the standards of realism. It goes straight to the fundamentals of art—rhythm, design, balance, proportion, which the folk artist feels instinctively.

One of the reasons that there has been a sustained interest in American folk painting is that it touches the heart. The focal point is frequently the common man. The settings—farms, towns and American cities—reflect a simpler time that preceded the Industrial Revolution. The artist's failure to adhere to conventional rules of perspective, proportion, and color blending result in an abstract style which may seem quite contemporary to our twenty-first century eyes.

The body of work that is the legacy of the folk painter can be divided into two basic categories: pictures that chronicled the people and places of a bygone era, and paintings that enhanced everyday objects such as mantels, signs, fireboards, floor cloths and floors, wall and ceiling surfaces and furniture.

The primitive painter created portraits, landscapes and seascapes which were framed, proudly displayed and cherished. Even citizens of modest means could find a way to enhance their surroundings with art. Although folk artists weren't formally trained, they worked for a fee and therefore were considered professionals. Legend has it that many of these itinerant artists would paint the bodies and backgrounds of their portraits before going on the road. When they reached their destination, the painters would arrange for a sitting and then add the head of the subject. This theory came about after studying many portraits in which it was noted that the subjects were dressed identically. They were wearing the same jewelry and wardrobe and were sitting in stereotypical poses.

Religion served as an inspiration to the folk painter. Vividly colored angels and other religious symbols were easily identified in Fraktur embellished documents, drawings and watercolor paintings found in communities located in the isolated German settlements in rural Pennsylvania.

In the mid-eighteenth century, as the country moved in a direction that would ultimately permit political and economic freedom, a new focus emerged. Pictures depicting historical events with overtly patriotic themes flourished.

In the early nineteenth century, genre pictures became the vogue. A spirit of nationalism permeated many aspects of colonial life. The rustic farm with its family and livestock, the thriving town with burgeoning new factories, and the energetic city complete with bustling harbor were all captured on canvas at some point by the American folk artist.

During the 1800s, awareness of the Romantic movement and its effect upon English and European art made its way to America. The value of an education, even for females, became apparent. Young girls from prominent families were sent to seminary schools, where painting was a highly regarded discipline within the curriculum. Theorem and mourning pictures, tinsel pictures, reverse paintings on glass, and sandpaper pictures flourished at this time.

American Folk—This collection of American folk art makes a warm and welcoming display. Simple lettering, homespun fabric and carved figures are combined with redware, metal *objets d'art* and painted signs.

As the twentieth century approached, waves of immigrants arrived in America. They brought the diverse cultural traditions they held dear with them. Many of these newcomers migrated across the nation and recorded their homeland through paintings. Although it was widely believed that folk painting waned at the close of the nineteenth century, the art of the people is still apparent in many of the arts and crafts being created today.

CREDITS

Folk art has been a passion of this collector for many years. The warm wooden tones, homespun fabrics and simple themes combine to create a welcome environment in our home. Since Pennsylvania has a rich and colorful German heritage, folk art, both new and old, can be found in abundance throughout the state.

Although the focus of my collection has been wooden signs, figures, bowls, and portraits are also included. Some of the items on display are from my personal collection, and many are reproductions. It is with pleasure that I share these simple American Folk treasures with you.

ASSEMBLING THE DISPLAY

1. The camel felt background was chosen to provide a contrast to the dark tones prevalent in the major pieces of the display. Above the large rectangular sign were five stems of red berries available at a local craft store. Below and to the left was a Horseshoe Inn sign created by Warren Kimble and available in specialty shops. The framed print *Portrait of a Baby* (artist unknown) was found at a local country store. The title of this work was printed on off-white cardstock and mounted on black poster board then affixed to the felt with double sided tape. The reproduction game board was purchased at the Philadelphia Museum of Art store. A resin gingerbread mold and a wooden cookie mold were hung under the print of the baby and the game board.

2. On the top left was a photograph of a hollow cut silhouette of a man, circa 1830, artist unknown. This was found in *American Folk Art* (Ketchum 16).

Next was the Cahill quotation from the opening of this chapter.

Last was an unsigned work of art depicting a painted wood carving of a horse and sleigh, circa 1850 (artist unknown). This was found in *Young America: A Folk Art History* (Lipman, Warren and Bishop 89).

Items on the left were printed on off-white cardstock and mounted on black poster board.

3. On the top right of the display was a photograph of a watercolor painting titled *Mrs. Keyser*, artist unknown, circa 1834. This was found in *Folk Art in American Life* (Bishop 15).

The unsigned weathervane photograph was found in the same text (Bishop 161). Entitled *Saint Tammany,* it hangs beneath the watercolor. This mid-nineteenth century work was made of molded and painted copper and is unique both for its size (102½" × 103" × 12") and workmanship.

Last was the quotation introducing this chapter. All items were printed and mounted like the items on the left.

4. On the base of the display were stuffed country sheep, a sailor rowing balance toy, a carved leprechaun, an upside down basket which provided a base for the hand-made doll, a "Revere" punched tin lantern, a redware plate, a miniature stuffed rabbit with flag, a carved wooden star and a blue figurine of a woman.

The shiny black 2" letters were found at an office supply store and glued on camel colored poster board which was framed in black poster board. Tiny black hearts were cut from the extra vinyl adhesive which surrounded the letters. A book stand held the sign in place. More wine colored berry stems were placed over and around the words *American Folk*.

Books featured in this display were *American Folk Art* by William Ketchum, *Contemporary American Folk Art: A Collector's Guide* by Chuck and Jan Rosenak, and *Folk Art in American Life* by Robert Bishop.

Bigger and Better

This display could have easily been transformed into an appropriate holiday tableau. To accomplish this add some carved Santas, angels, or snowman figures, along with greens, a wreath, folk art ornaments, rustic bells and stars, grapevines, stockings, pinecones, or a miniature fir tree. Call it A Country Christmas or Homespun Holiday.

A patchwork quilt could serve as a backdrop or could line the base of your folk art display. Add stacked wooden boxes, homespun fabric, a weather vane, stoneware, hand-carved toys or a period flag to personalize this theme.

An excellent print resource for your display would be *Drawing on America's Past: Folk Art, Modernism, and the Index of American Design* by Virginia Tuttle Clayton, Elizabeth Stillinger, Erika Doss, Deborah Chotner.

Manhattan Skyscrapers

There is nothing more poetic and terrible than the skyscrapers' battle with the heavens that cover them. Snow, rain, and mist highlight, drench, or conceal the vast towers, but those towers, hostile to mystery and blind to any sort of play, shear off the rain's tresses and shine their three thousand swords through the soft swan of the fog.
—Federico García Lorca (1898–1936), Spanish poet, playwright

Many of us are familiar with the famous image of New York construction workers lunching on a crossbeam above the building site of the RCA Building in Rockefeller Center in the heart of Manhattan. This photograph, titled *Lunch Atop a*

Manhattan Skyscrapers—*Lunch Atop a Skyscraper* **by Charles C. Ebbets is the focal point of this tribute to the steelworkers who built the skyscrapers of Manhattan. Measuring accoutrements, electrical devices, plumbing material and building supplies are interspersed among the books on this topic.**

Skyscraper, was taken on September 29, 1932, by Charles C. Ebbets. The steelworkers, shown dangling hundreds of feet in the air, appeared relaxed as they fueled their bodies for the remaining hours of their shift. They are untroubled by their precarious situation, and not at all concerned about the prospect of falling to their death. Their bravery, in spite of the inherent risk, resulted in the evolution of the skyscrapers of New York City.

Although Manhattan boasts many of the United States' most familiar tall buildings, it can't claim the distinction of having the first of these structures. The earliest certified skyscraper was the Home Insurance Building located in downtown Chicago. Nine stories and one basement were completed in 1885. Six years later two additional stories were added. The architect, Major William Le Baron Jenney, created the first load-carrying structural frame. This development led to the "Chicago skeleton" form of construction and the tall skyscrapers of the future. In this type of construction, a steel frame supported the entire weight of the walls, instead of the walls themselves carrying the weight of the building. This engineering breakthrough was far superior to the previous standard.

Of the buildings worldwide that meet the criteria of "skyscraper," two-thirds are located in the vertical metropolis of New York City. The Skyscraper Museum in Battery Park documents these architectural wonders and examines the historical forces as well as the people who were responsible for shaping the shifting skylines. Visit the museum's Web site for more information: http://www.skyscraper.org/home_flash.htm

Rockefeller Center is a fascinating combination of linked indoor and outdoor spaces. The main axis of Rockefeller Center, a gently sloping promenade, invites Fifth Avenue pedestrians toward the outdoor plaza. Rockefeller and his architects felt that an abundance of greenery would relieve the austerity created by the center's primary building materials, which were stone and concrete. The roof gardens provide office workers in neighboring skyscrapers with an elevated green oasis in the heart of the city.

The Chrysler Building fulfilled the wishes of its owner, Walter P. Chrysler. He desired a provocative building which would not merely scrape the sky, but literally extend into the clouds. Built in 1930, its 77 floors briefly made it the highest building in the world, totaling 1,046 ft. The completion of the Empire State Building, the following year, removed that distinction so briefly held by the Chrysler Building.

Designed by William Van Alen, the Chrysler Building is often praised as the greatest example of Art Deco style skyscrapers, and the perfect tribute to American capitalism. The spire, a series of sunbursts punctuated by triangular windows, is the building's most striking feature. Like the setbacks emblazoned with winged radiator caps, wheels, and stylized cars, the inspiration for this design came from the automobile.

The architect, Van Alen, opted for some drama at the completion of the building project. He planned an unexpected finale for the introduction of now famous top design of the building. The entire seven-storey pinnacle, complete with special-steel facing, was first assembled inside the building, and then hoisted into position through the roof opening and anchored on top. The process took an amazing one and a half hours. The gleaming chrome-nickel-steel spire had a unique and dramatic debut.

The Empire State Building was the brainchild of John J. Raskob, the vice-president of General Motors at that time. He wanted the new building to exceed the height of the Chrysler Building, which was then under construction. The Empire State Building reached a height of 1,250 feet and established a new record for skyscrapers in Manhattan. Designed by the firm of Richard H. Shreve, William Lamb and Arthur Loomis Harmon, construction began in 1930 and was completed a year later. The phenomenal speed of construction saw four and a half stories rise in a week. This was made possible by effective logistics combined with a skilled and organized workforce. Though designed at the end of the Art Deco period, its exterior shows little of the decorative characteristics of that period. It remained the tallest building until the World Trade Center was completed in 1975.

Considered the oldest remaining skyscraper, the Flatiron Building is 285 feet tall. Designed by Daniel Burnham of Chicago, this structure was one of the first buildings in the city to employ a steel frame to support its façade. Sometimes referred to as

"Burnham's Folly," critics felt that its shape, like a flatiron, was less artistic and actually more dangerous. They thought it might fall over! The apex of the building is just six feet wide. It expands into a limestone wedge adorned with Gothic and Renaissance details of Greek faces and terra cotta flowers.

The Citicorp Center brought new life to a downtown Manhattan city block that had been largely filled by a large Lutheran church. It created an exciting new internal plaza for people with shops, restaurants and performance spaces on a number of levels.

The twin towers of the World Trade Center were proof of New York's belief in itself. Built during a period when the future of the city seemed uncertain, the towers served to invigorate the city and halt the decline which lower Manhattan was experiencing. Chase Manhattan Bank chairman David Rockefeller and his brother New York governor Nelson Rockefeller were the catalysts behind the project, believing it would be of great benefit to the city.

Hired to design the World Trade Center project was Minoru Yamasaki and Associates of Michigan. Critics of the two-towers design felt that these structures would challenge the existing skyline, interrupt TV reception and strain the city's services. Despite these faultfinders, building began in 1966. Construction required the excavation of more than 1.2 cubic yards of earth, which was transferred to the banks of the Hudson River, where over 23 acres were created in the Battery Park area of the city. A total of 10,000 workers were involved in the construction of this project. 60 lost their lives in the process.

During the construction heyday of the 1930s and 1940s, skyscrapers were being built at a record rate in New York City. Many Native Americans, particularly Iroquois, worked weekdays building skyscrapers in the city. They commuted weekends to their hometowns in northern New York state or Canada. Brooklyn became home to those preferring to establish a community closer to work. These Americans took pride in being a part of the construction process for most of the buildings aforementioned, as well as the UN Assembly Building. After the 9/11 attack, descendants of the original laborers traveled to the site of the tragedy and helped cut and remove steel.

CREDITS

For several years, our son, Dennis, lived in a high-rise in mid–Manhattan. From his rooftop deck there was a clear view of the skyscrapers of Manhattan, including the Empire State Building. From that vantage point, the nighttime panorama was surreal, magical.

We relish time spent in the city partaking of the amenities it has to offer. However, we are dwarfed and awed by its architecture. Time spent atop the roof, among the towering structures of the city, ultimately led to the inspiration for the display Manhattan Skyscrapers.

Our son, Brian, is an architect in Philadelphia. An innovative, young and energetic professional, he is making his mark on that city. Although designing a skyscraper is not his focus, Brian's work keeps us interested and involved in the profession of architecture.

ASSEMBLING THE DISPLAY

1. The poster of the construction workers lunching atop a skyscraper was mounted on yellow poster board and attached to the display case lined with black felt. This artwork can be purchased at http://www.allposters.com/-sp/Lunch-Atop-a-Skyscraper-1932_i918974_.htm

A short description of the photo was hung on the top right of the poster. The following quote was centered over the poster:

> New York ... is a city of geometric heights, a petrified desert of grids and lattices, an inferno of greenish abstraction under a flat sky, a real Metropolis from which man is absent by his very accumulation.
>
> —Roland Barthes

Centered at the bottom of the poster was this quotation:

> I'm about four skyscrapers behind.
>
> —Philip Johnson, architect

There was a paragraph about the role the Iroquois played in building many of the skyscrapers of New York. Also noted were the volunteer efforts of their descendants at the World Trade Center after the 9/11 tragedy. This information was found in *Sky Dancers,* by Connie Ann Kirk.

All of the items included on the center background were printed on white cardstock and mounted on yellow and/or black poster board.

The title *Manhattan* was actually a metal sign originally made for a home theatre. It was affixed to the felt with double sided tape and secured with pins.

2. On the top left of the display case was information about the design and building process of the Chrysler Building. This can be found if you visit http://www.great buildings.com/buildings/Chrysler Building.html

A photograph of the Chrysler Building was next. Under that was background information about the building's architect.

This information was printed on white card stock and double mounted in yellow and black.

3. A photograph of the Rockefeller Center as it appears today was attached to the right side of the display case along with information about the building. Two quotes flanked this image:

> Anon, out of the earth a fabric huge, rose, like an exhalation.
>
> —John Milton, *Paradise Lost*

> The poetry of bricks and mortar.
>
> —Horace Greeley

4. Strewn throughout the bottom of the display case under a fully extended measuring stick were a hammer, some galvanized pipes and fittings, a plumber's wrench, a paint can, two paint brushes, and a paint stick (these were placed on and around 2

horizontal bricks), and 10" nails, nuts and bolts, weather stripping, and an architectural star.

An image of the Empire State Building was glued to poster board, cut to shape, and placed just off center at the base of the case. Sitting atop a vertical brick, and printed on white card stock, was text of the history of the first skyscraper located in the city of Chicago. This information was available at http://www.chipublib.org/004 chicago/timeline/skyscraper1.html

Small triangles of poster board were taped to the verso of the Empire State Building and the text regarding the first skyscraper, which permitted them to stand upright.

Books featured in the display were *Manhattan Skyscrapers* by Eric P. Nash, which was elevated on a horizontal brick, *Skyscraper* by Eric Howeler, *Sky Scrapers* by Andres Lepik, *Skyscraper Architects* by Ariadna Alverez Garreta, and *Skyscraper: The Search for an American Style 1891–1941* edited by Roger Shepherd.

BIGGER AND BETTER

Should your display space be larger, you could include additional information on the architects who designed these tall buildings. Add a hard hat, a wooden level, additional freestanding cut-outs of skyscraper images, a period lunch box or thermos, work boots, books and text relative to the formation of labor unions, old city maps and period postcards, heavy duty extension cords, vintage doorknobs, and tin ceiling tiles.

You may decide to focus on skyscrapers in your local area or the nearest large city. Perhaps some local photographers can supply you with the necessary photographs. Architectural firms may be willing to lend models from previously designed buildings, which could be a great focal point.

Cultures

ITALIA

You may have the universe if I may have Italy.

—Giuseppe Verdi

From the snow capped Alps at the northern end to sunlit Sicily down south, Italy, proud country of fifty-eight million citizens, attracts forty million visitors each year to its shores. Surrounded by the Mediterranean to the west, and the Adriatic Sea and Dalmatic Coast to the east, Italy's natural beauty is unrivaled.

Each Italian city is unique in its own right: Naples—the home of thin crust pizza and the birthplace of famed tenor Enrico Caruso; Sicily—separated from the mainland by the Strait of Messina and born of volcanic ash; Bologna—culinary center and home to the oldest university in all of Europe; Venice—comprising 118 islands and 400 bridges, known as the city of waterways; Milan—industrial and financial capital as well as fashionable design center; Verona—a city of monuments and the setting for Shakespeare's *Romeo and Juliet*; Genoa—birthplace of Christopher Columbus; Pompeii—sitting in the shadows of Mt. Vesuvius, once a luxurious resort where Romans escaped from the capital; Florence—home to priceless Renaissance works of art; and Rome—the ancient city which was home to conquerors and an advanced civilization.

The cities of Florence and Rome were selected as the focus of this display as they are popular destinations for throngs of tourists, especially art enthusiasts, and have special meaning to the author.

Rome

Since its founding 2,700 years ago on seven hills, near the banks of the Tiber River, Rome has grown into a city of three million people covering 580 square miles located in central Italy. Within this geographic area is the independent State of the Vatican City, home of the Roman Catholic Church. In 1870 Rome was made the capital of the newly united Italy. The city lies a distance of 17 miles from the sea and has excellent links to numerous historic cities and towns.

Tourists flock to the Coliseum, an old amphitheater which is situated in the center of Rome. Construction began in the year 72, under the Emperor Vespasianus, and was completed eight years later during the reign of Titus. The Coliseum is 165 feet high, and the ellipse has axes which measure 610 and 515 feet. The stalls, consisting of steps rising from the oval of the arena to the balcony, could seat almost 50,000 spectators.

The games in the amphitheatre consisted of gladiatorial combats (fights between men), venations (men against the wild beast) and even naumachiae (naval battles). The gladiators were recruited from slaves, condemned criminals, Roman citizens and freed men. They were trained in special schools and divided into various categories which used different types of arms, armor, and combat according to their physical attributes, or racial background. The fallen gladiators asked for mercy from the emperor who would look to the crowd before deciding thumbs up for life, or thumbs down for death!

The museums of Rome house some of the great treasures of Egypt, Greece, Rome, and artifacts from the early Christians. They own frescoes by Raphael and Michelangelo as well as priceless manuscripts and jewels. Rome's museums and galleries are recognized as having two major strengths: Greek and Roman archeological treasures and paintings, and sculpture from the Renaissance and the Baroque period. The Vatican museums have superb collections of artwork from both of these eras. The renowned Borghese Gallery, with its splendid gardens, houses exquisite sculptures created by Gian Lorenzo Bernini.

Italia—A faux marble column anchors the title of this display which features a scene from the Sistine Chapel and photographs of Florence and Rome. Colorful fruits surround a gold plaster of Paris cross, and grapes dangle from the vine.

Florence

The beautiful and ancient Italian city of Florence, the capital of the Grandy Duchy of Tuscany, is located quite near the Apennines. It is situated in a plain, surrounded by rolling hills which house villas and castles. The Arno River divides Florence into two equal parts. Four bridges cross the river.

Florence is the home of the grand duke and the royal family, who reside in the Pitti Palace, named after the wealthy citizen who arranged for it to be built, Luca Pitti.

The enchanting Ponte Vecchio ("old bridge") houses the jewelry vendors and is a major attraction atop the River Arno. Florence is also known for its fine Tuscan food, ceramics, marble, pottery and terracotta, and a wide assortment of leather products.

The Ufizzi Gallery is home to priceless works of art. The nucleus of the gallery comprises works of the Medici collections, which were assembled during the fifteenth and sixteenth centuries. The core of its original collection included statues, paintings, drawings, miniatures, scientific instruments, tapestries, weapons and armors. Some of the great Italian artists represented in this gallery are Giotto, Botticelli, Leonardo, Michelangelo, Bellini, Raphael, Titian, and Caravaggio.

Leaving Italy, a visitor realizes that they have experienced the most beautiful expression of art and architecture to have survived the centuries.

Credits

A longtime dream became a reality when my husband Dennis and I visited Rome and Florence in March of 2006. His photographic efforts of both cities are featured in this display. We found the art and antiquity of Rome astounding. Images of colorful Florence and its magnificent treasures will remain a cherished memory.

The poster art of Michelangelo featured in this display is readily available at the Vatican Museum as well as other tourist shops throughout Rome and Florence. If a trip isn't possible, take a virtual tour of the Vatican museums and the Sistine Chapel located at this site: http://mv.vatican.va/3_EN/pages/MV_Home.html

For additional poster art related to the Vatican, visit http://www.allposters.com (search using the term "Vatican Museums")

Assembling the Display

1. Black, yellow and blue watercolors were applied to white poster board to create a Roman column and a slab of marble. This was pinned to a rectangle of gold poster board which was placed on the upper left side over black felt. Another gold rectangle was placed on the lower right. The font Castellar, sized at 400, was used for the title *Italia*. The letters were printed with gray ink on white cardstock, cut out and accented with a silver Sharpie, then glued to the faux marble slab.

The font Castellar can be obtained if you visit http://www.1001freefonts.com

The poster by Michelangelo, of a scene from the ceiling of the Sistine Chapel, was glued to gold poster board and pulled forward on pins. Flanking this poster were photographs of Florence (the Ponte Vecchio and the Ufizzi Gallery) and Rome (the Coliseum and a view from Palatine Hill).

The quote introducing this display was printed on off-white cardstock and glued to gold poster board. This was placed in the top center of the display. Grapes made from resin flank the Verdi quotation. These were pinned to the felt.

2. On the top left was information about the city of Florence which is available if you visit http://www.thais.it/citta_italiane/firenze/introduzione/pag_01.htm

Under that were postcards from the Galleria Borghese of sculptures by Gian Lorenzo Bernini.

Under that was this quote:

> There on that scaffolding reclines
> Michael Angelo.
> With no more sound than the mice make
> His hand moves to and fro.
> Like a long-legged fly upon the stream
> His mind moves upon silence.
>
> —W. B. Yeats

All items on the left were printed on off-white cardstock and glued to black and/or gold poster board.

3. On the top right was a description of the Coliseum which can be found if you visit http://www.the-colosseum.net/idx-en.htm

Below that were additional postcards from the Gallery Borghese of sculptures by Bernini.

A history of Rome was next and can be found if you visit http://www.italy1.com/history/

Items on the right were printed and mounted as those on the left.

4. On the base of the display was a papier-mâché gold cross purchased at a local discount store. This was elevated on Styrofoam which was covered in black velvet. Resin fruit was placed around base of the cross.

A bookmark of a religious triptych was centered in front of the fruit.

Books featured in the display were *Venetian Painting in the 15th Century* by Otto Pächt, *Art and Archaeology of Rome: From Ancient Times to the Baroque* edited by Andrea Augenti, *The Birth of Venus* by Sarah Dunant, *Michelangelo: A Biography* by George Bull, *One Hundred and One Beautiful Small Towns in Italy* by Paolo Lazzarin, *Venice Triumphant* by Elisabeth Crouzet-Pavan, *Guide with Reconstructions, Ancient Rome, Past and Present* by Romolo Augusto Staccioli, and *Complete Guide to Florence and Its Hills* by Roberto Bartolini.

BIGGER AND BETTER

There are countless themes you could choose for your display on Italy. Here are some possibilities: wines, foods, museums, gardens, obelisks, basilicas, regions, crafts, inventors, art of specific eras, and specific artists or sculptors. You could zero in on fashion, the automotive industry, or tourism. Most of the attractions, such as the Coliseum, or the Vatican, could be display topics on their own.

How about following Dan Brown's lead and do an *Angels and Demons* tour through Rome? You could map out the route his characters took throughout the best-selling novel set in Rome.

Ask staff and patrons about their travels. You will find amazing treasures and photos that you can incorporate into eye catching displays. Your display could also be tied into community programming that your library may be offering.

CHINESE CALLIGRAPHY: THE ART OF EXPRESSION

Everything has its beauty, but not everyone sees it.

Confucius, 551 BC–479 BC

The origins of brush writing in China, like the origins of all the arts in that ancient culture, are somewhat vague. The earliest known symbols were pictographs found on bones, stones, shells, and metal. As early as the Shang dynasty (1523–1028 BC), an abstract script had evolved from such pictographs, and by the time of the Han dynasty (202 BC–220 AD) the written language had become formalized. Although the early Chinese were using written language, there was little flexibility of form in the inscriptions made to solid surfaces. When bamboo and paper came into use, the brush became the instrument that converted the physical act of writing to the ultimate means of self–expression (Froncek 112).

The techniques for the calligrapher are relatively simple, with some refinements. The artist usually begins the training with the flexible yet flabby goat hair brush. This instrument is harder to use than a tool made of the more rigid weasel-hair. The principle of holding a brush is usually referred to as "solid fingers and empty palms." Normally, the brush is fully loaded with high-intensity ink. Brushstrokes can then be layered to create texture and vary tone. The choice of paper or silk defines the style and technique that the artist will employ (Weng xii–xiii).

To do justice to the study of the art of calligraphy, one must recognize its relationship to painting. All of the literature on this subject references both of these arts. "Calligraphy and painting," according to an old Chinese saying, "serve a single aim, the revelation of inner goodness." The materials for both the pictorial and calligraphic arts are identical: silk or paper as a support, the brush as a tool, and ink as a medium. The only difference is that paintings may also use colors.

Calligraphic expressions are highly individualistic. Most Chinese are able to distinguish the works of a master calligrapher as easily as Westerners could recognize the difference between a Monet and a Vermeer.

Chinese Calligraphy—This dynamic Chinese symbol means "book" or "written word." Decorative chopsticks, fans and delicately embossed china are among the objects featured.

Featured in this display is the painting entitled "Admonitions" by Ku K'ai-chih (AD 341–402) which is a portion of a large scroll painted on silk. One of the most valuable items in the history of Chinese art, this painting is now in the collection of the British Museum (Ting 44).

The discovery of the oracle bones in China goes back to the end of the nineteenth century, when a Peking scholar was prescribed a compound which included "dragon bones" to treat his illness. The scholar noticed some carvings resembling writing on the bones that he had received from the pharmacy. This led to the discovery of Anyang, the last capital of the Shang dynasty, where archeologists have found enormous amounts of these carved bones. Oracle bone writing was viewed as a divine link between a human ruler and the world of the supernatural.

CREDITS

The impetus for this exhibit was a visit to the Princeton University Art Museum. This institution, located in Princeton, New Jersey, has a significant collection of Asian art and artifacts. While browsing the museum gift shop, I discovered a poster featuring the Chinese symbol for *book* or *written word*. I thought this symbol was very powerful, and that the size of this graphic would fill the library display case nicely. The exhibit for which this poster was created dated back to 1989, but this item is standard inventory and should be available if you visit www.princetonart-museum.org

There were a host of books available for purchase on the art of calligraphy at the museum. *The Embodied Image: Chinese Calligraphy from the John B. Elliot Collection* by Robert E. Harrist proved to be an excellent resource.

I had planned to title the display *The Art of Expression.* But after hanging the large poster, it was apparent that other signage would be redundant.

ASSEMBLING THE DISPLAY

1. The poster was mounted on black poster board to give it some structure. The background was black felt, which provided a good contrast to the white which surrounds the image.

Hanging above the poster and at the top left and right of the display were framed calligraphy prints of the symbols for the words *wisdom, love, tranquility,* and *prosperity.* A bamboo fan and chopsticks were placed above and to the left and right of the symbol. A sentence which explained the large symbol was printed on white cardstock and mounted on black poster board, then attached beneath the poster. Below that was a color reproduction of a section of *Admonitions,* referred to above, which was mounted on black poster board. A jade pendant was hung at the top of the color print.

2. On the top left, under the framed print, were two documents on calligraphy and painting largely found in the Harrist monograph. Below this were scanned images of bamboo created using both the painted image and calligraphy. All of these were printed on white cardstock and mounted on red or black poster board.

3. On the top right of the display was information about Chinese script which is available at http://www.crystalinks.com/chinascript.html

Next was the quote by Confucius that introduced the display. Many such quotations are available at this site: http://www,quotationspage.com/quotes/Confucius

Below that was material on the pictographs carved into the oracle bones, plus a color photograph depicting them. This information includes references to inscriptions cast on ritual bronze vessels, as well as manmade objects, and can be found if you visit http://www.logoi.com/note/chinese_origins

All of the items in this section were printed on white cardstock and mounted on red or black poster board.

4. The Asian objects within the display have all been enhanced with either calligraphy or painting. A tray, a tea set, chopsticks and miniature dishes, were included on the base of the display. The main colors used were black, red, and gold with touches of pink and grey.

The books featured were *Chinese and Japanese Calligraphy: Spanning Two Thousand Years* by Heinz Götze and *Chinese Art Treasures: A Selected Group of Objects from the Chinese National Palace Museum and the Chinese National Central Museum, Taichung, Taiwan.*

BIGGER AND BETTER

Should your display area be larger than the one shown, you may want to include some calligraphy brushes and paints, or additional books on the Chinese culture and related literature such as *The Bonesetter's Daughter*. Written by Amy Tan, this book chronicles the LuLing family, who were ink makers believed to be cursed by their connection to a local doctor who cooks up potions and remedies from human bones.

Calligraphy prints similar to those featured in this display would be available at local specialty shops, as well as Web sites such as www.wavedancing.net/gallery and www.artisticchinesecreations.com/calligraphy

Stencils of Chinese calligraphy are available in area craft stores, should you want to create some for your display.

PARIS, CITY OF LIGHTS

Everything ends this way in France—everything. Weddings, christenings, duels, burials, swindlings, diplomatic affairs—everything is a pretext for a good dinner.

—Jean Anouilh

Dubbed the City of Lights since the 19th century, Paris has long been known as the city of romance as well. The capital of and largest city in France, Paris is a leading cultural, business and political center. Its neoclassical architecture draws thirty million tourists annually. Paris is also a major hub of the arts, haute couture, and fine cuisine.

A charming characteristic of the French capital is the tree-lined quays along the River Seine. That section, known as the Left Bank, boasts open-air bookstalls, historic bridges, and beautifully landscaped boulevards, such as the Champs-Elysées. This boulevard is also known as *La plus belle avenue du monde* in French (the most beautiful avenue in the world). It stretches from the Concorde Square to the Arc de Triomphe. Paris is home to some of the finest shops and hotels in the whole of Europe.

Writers like Henry Miller, T. S. Eliot, John Dos Passos, Ernest Hemingway and F. Scott Fitzgerald lived in Paris during the period following World War I, and prior to the Depression. Composer and song writer Cole Porter, photographer Man Ray, and Modernist poet Ezra Pound all called Paris home during this period.

The collapse of Wall Street would serve as the catalyst for the return of many of the expatriates back to their homes in the States. This so-called lost generation included American expatriates Gertrude Stein and Alice B. Toklas. They led the list of celebrities who "occupied" Paris after World War I and ushered in one of its most glamorous eras. The appeal that drew these expatriates was the low cost of living and the fact that Paris was widely viewed as the cultural capital of the Western world. Like the thousands of tourists who flocked to Paris, these Americans were stirred by the city's physical beauty, its sense of history, its exquisite restaurants and open-air cafés, and its lively and sometimes even infamous nightlife. They were drawn to Paris by the reputed vitality of its artistic and intellectual scene. The city tolerated innovation and experimentation, held its artists in high esteem and allowed for individual freedom.

History was made in Annonay, France, in 1783. This was the site of the first hot air balloon flight. The initial passengers, a sheep, a duck, and a rooster, made history on September 19th of that year. Two months later a manned flight, piloted by the Montgolfier brothers, embarked from Paris and remained airborne for a record-setting twenty-two minutes. They ascended 500 feet before finally landing in a vineyard, miles away. The pilots had stowed a bottle of champagne on board, and toasted the wary local farmers who had gathered as the balloon made its descent. Even today, shared champagne toasts remain a landing tradition among modern balloonists.

The Eiffel Tower was built for the International Exhibition of Paris of 1889, commemorating the centenary of the French Revolution. Seven hundred proposals were submitted in a well publicized design competition. Gustave Eiffel's rendering was chosen by unanimous decision. He was assisted in the creative process by engineers Maurice Koechlin and Emile Nouguier, as well as architect Stephen Sauvestre. There was some initial controversy regarding the usefulness of the structure. Nonetheless, construction commenced in 1887.

Paris, City of Lights—A hot air balloon and the Eiffel Tower soar into fiberfill clouds. Included among the French accessories are a floral hatbox, a string of pearls, perfume, a decorative plate and a small rooster. A large gold fleur-de-lis plaque anchors the tableau on the display base.

Eiffel's innovative design was comprised of two sections: a base composed of a platform resting on four pylons and, above this, a tapering tower which rose atop a second platform to meld into one simple column. It took 300 steel workers with 18,000 iron pieces a span of two years to construct. Upon completion, the tower soared to 300 meters in height, and weighed seven thousand tons. It remained the tallest structure in the world until 1931, the year the Empire State Building was built.

Perhaps the best known monument in the world, the Eiffel Tower attracts six million visitors each year and has had an enormous impact on both the economy and the skyline of the City of Lights.

CREDITS

French is the native tongue of the newest member of our family. Born in Quebec, Chloe has brought an international flavor and a fresh point of view to the members of her new American family. We have endeavored, of course, to acquaint ourselves with her native tongue, as a gesture of good will. However, our multi–lingual daughter-in-law can more than hold her own in the language department. Chloe's enthusiasm for the city of Paris and all things French was the inspiration for this display.

The Main Gallery, Firestone Library, Princeton University, mounted an exhibit titled Portraits of the Lost Generation in the spring of 2005. It was comprised of photographs by Man Ray and other expatriates living in Paris between the years 1920 and 1939, and from the papers and library of Sylvia Beach. I saved the pamphlet from that exhibit and was able to incorporate this dimension of Parisian history into Paris, City of Lights. Hopefully, a trip to Paris is on the travel agenda for the near future. This display has helped to prepare for the journey which I know will be an incredible and unforgettable experience.

ASSEMBLING THE DISPLAY

1. The font Dumbledore 1 3D sized at 620 was used to create the word *Paris*. To download this free font, visit http://www.grsites.com/fonts/d018.shtml

The font Christmas Lights, sized at 250, was chosen for the subtitle *City of Lights*. The title and subtitle were printed on white cardstock, attached with pins and pulled forward.

The latter font can be downloaded from this site: http://www.fontfreak.com

The illustration of the Eiffel Tower was found through a Google image search. See Resources, in techniques, for instructions for creating the tower. The balloon and basket were drawn freehand with help from an image found through Google. Both were made from cranberry and white poster board with charcoal yarn serving as the ropes.

Polyurethane filling was placed throughout the display to give the illusion of clouds.

2. On the top left of the display was information regarding the history of the hot air balloon. This was created in Power Point using Word Art for the title. The chronology of ballooning can be found at http://www.balloonzone.com/history.html

Next came this quote by the novelist Henry Miller, during his Paris years. It was printed and mounted as above:

> I have no money, no resources, no hopes. I am the happiest man alive.

Below that was a Power Point creation titled "Sight Seeing in Paris." This information was readily available in travel guides for the city, as well as at this site: http://www.pariserve.tm.fr/English/paris/index.htm

All items on this side of the display were printed on white cardstock and mounted on cranberry and silver poster board.

3. On the top right of the case was a fact sheet about Paris which included data on geographic size, population and characteristics of the city. Also included were such famous landmarks as the Louvre, the Arc de Triomphe, the Luxembourg Gardens, and Notre Dame Cathedral.

Below that was the quote introducing this chapter.

Under that was a description of the Eiffel Tower and its architect, and facts relating to the erection. It was created using Power Point with a watermark of the tower, found in Clip Art, centered on the page.

All of the items were printed and mounted as those on the left side.

4. The base of the display was covered in cranberry and ecru toile fabric. Varying sizes of Styrofoam blocks were placed under the fabric to provide both different elevations and a support for the plaster of Paris plaque of gold leaf fleur-de-lis. A souvenir map of Paris was placed in front of this plaque. Old French francs and a miniature Eiffel Tower were positioned atop the map.

Interspersed throughout the base of the display were pearls draped on an off-white iron fleur-de-lis, a bottle of bath oil, a candle, a small floral and striped hatbox, a plate with a French cheese motif and a painted plaster rooster.

Books featured in the display were *La belle France: A Short History* by Alistair Horne, *Capturing Paris* by Katharine Davis, *Authentic Bistros of Paris* by Francois Thomazeau, *Au Contraire! Figuring Out the French* by Giles Asselin and Ruth Mastron, *Paris Tales* by Helen Constantine, *Americans in Paris: A Literary Anthology* by Adam Gopnik, *Paris Then and Now* by Peter and Orel Caine, *Paris: The Biography of a City* by Colin Jones, and *Into a Paris Quarter: Reine Margot's Chapel and Other Haunts of St.-Germain* by Diane Johnson.

BIGGER AND BETTER

Your display might focus primarily on the south of France. Call it Provence! and include provincial fabrics, bright colors, sunflowers and other flora native to that region. Add grapevines and photos of the Alps to create a colorful display. Focus on the Basque section of the country, and call it Basque in the Sun.

Choose among the following topics: museums, cathedrals, the Left Bank, French artists and writers, French couture or cuisine. "The Lost Generation" of Americans would make an interesting topic for display.

WOMEN WORLDWIDE

As a woman I have no country. As a woman my country is the whole world.
—Virginia Woolf

The quest for equality for females has been a long and valiant struggle for women worldwide. Happily, in some areas of the globe, great strides have been made. However, barriers still exist within many cultures, so parity and justice remain primary goals for millions of women.

Women have traditionally provided the leadership on the homefront, securing the family as well as the community in times of crisis. Women have stretched their personal budgets to feed and clothe their families during trying economic times. However, the authority often granted women on the local level seldom rises up the ladder to state, national and international ranks. Despite the fact that women constitute fifty percent of the world population, women's voices often go unheard.

The twenty-first century has been a time of steady transition for women. Their roles in leadership, in areas of health and commerce, and in communication are constantly evolving. These global changes have provided an opportunity for women to offer new and creative solutions to the challenges before them.

Women's equal participation in decision-making is necessary for both democracy and justice. If women's perspectives are not being considered at all levels of the

Women Worldwide—The poster features the faces of diverse women worldwide. The carved wooden dolls were crafted in Bali and the other artifacts are from the Far East.

decision-making process, the goals of parity, economic development, and global peace cannot be attained.

The implementation of quota systems in third world nations has been effective in achieving a better proportion of women in government. It was interesting to note that Rwanda is ranked number one in the world with over 48 percent women in the Lower House, and over 34 percent representation in the Senate. Sweden was a close second, followed by Norway. For this data, please visit http://www.ipu.org/wmn-e/classif.htm

There are many women who have overcome the gender barrier and recently achieved positions as heads of state. Some of the more noteworthy are Angela Merkel, federal chancellor of Germany; Michelle Jeria, president of Chile; Tarja Halonen, president of Finland; Yuliya Tymonshenko, prime minister of the Ukraine; Helen Elizabeth Clark, prime minister of New Zealand; and Luisa Dias Diogo, prime minister of Mozambique. This distinguished group of women represent but a small fraction of leaders compared to the male dominated governance worldwide.

For additional information on the topic of women leaders in politics, and women, war, and elections, visit http://www.idea.int/gender/activities.cfm?renderforprint=1& or http://www.terra.es/personal2/monolith/00women.htm

CREDITS

Librarians hungry for display material relish the American Library Association's annual conference. Here, vendors have the opportunity to display state of the art technology. Writers and illustrators are available to sign their latest works. Notable authors are featured speakers. Publishers exhibit their most recent publications, along with colorful posters, most free for the taking. Several years ago, this poster on women was offered by the Greenwood Publishing Group. It was clear it would make a striking centerpiece for a display on various aspects of women's issues worldwide.

Artifacts featured in the display were part of an exhibit in the Cressman Library. These items are from the collection of Marjorie Wright Miller, Cedar Crest College, class of 1930. Marjorie traveled around the globe throughout her life and our library was the recipient of many of her art treasures.

ASSEMBLING THE DISPLAY

1. The poster from Greenwood Publishing Group was attached to gold poster board for support and pinned to the black felt background. The title lettering was created by using the font Shangrila in all capital letters, with the large Ws sized at 600, and the other letters sized at 450. This was printed on white cardstock, cut and traced on gold poster board. The letters were attached with glue. The Shangrila font was available at http://www.1001freefonts.com

The quote by Marie Curie was printed on white cardstock and glued on gold poster board then attached with pins. The font Arial was selected. It was sized at 48 bold. A small wine colored rosebud was affixed to the top left. For this and other quotes by women, visit http://www.wendy.com/women/quotations.html

2. On the top left of the display was a chart which was edited to include the percentages of women in both houses of government in forty countries throughout the world. A table which included all countries can be found at this site: http://www.ipu.org/wmn-e/classif.htm

Next was the quote by Virginia Woolf, which introduced this chapter.

On the bottom left was a fact sheet on women's elections worldwide. This information can be found if you visit http://www.WomenWarPeace.org

All items on the left were printed on white cardstock which was mounted to cranberry and/or gold poster board then attached with double sided tape.

3. On the top right were some sentiments found at the above mentioned Web site in the section "Women, War, Peace and Elections."

Next was the following quote:

> Women must refuse narrow definitions and say that there can be diverse cultures and ethnic identities living together, that there can be tolerant religions that don't have to be in opposition to the other, that we can live in solidarity and respect with those who are different. If women do this, we can be the key to denying narrow fundamentalist movements their source of power and source of regeneration.
> —Charlotte Bunch, 1995

Below that was a summary of the election in Afghanistan in 2004 which permitted women the right to vote. This information could be found at www.un.org/womenwatch/osagi/ resources/faces/1-Elections_faces_en.pdf

A watermark, "First Election," was inserted in MS Word and centered horizontally on the page.

All items on the right were printed and mounted like those on the left.

4. On the base of the display, figures from Indonesia were elevated on Styrofoam which was covered with black velvet. A porcelain fan was flanked by a carving of a Garuda from Djakarta, Java, on the left, and a small figure of a South American native, with papoose, on the right. This figure was elevated on Styrofoam covered in black felt.

A heart, trimmed with lace and filled with potpourri, was elevated on a book stand and placed on the left of the books. A miniature brass gong was placed among the books on the right. Sheer wired mesh gold ribbon was arranged in the front of the display.

Books used in the display were *Women and Politics Worldwide* edited by Barbara J. Nelson and Najma Chowdhury, *Women's Lives: Multicultural Perspectives* by Gwyn Kirk and Margo Okazawa-Rey, *Chronology of Women Worldwide: People, Places and Events That Changed Women's History* edited by Lynne Brakeman and Susan Gall, *Women's America: Refocusing the Past* by Linda K. Kerber and Jane Sherron DeHart, and *Women and Gender: A Feminist Psychology* by Mary Crawford and Rhoda Unger.

BIGGER AND BETTER

Your display could focus on women in education, women in crisis, women in the arts, or women's employment. You could select a country or a continent and focus on the issues in just that region of the world.

Women's health concerns, such as AIDS, would make a compelling display. Much information is available on that topic. For one comprehensive site, visit http://www. iwhc.org/withwomenworldwide

If you have access to artifacts from a particular area of the world, you could include them and limit the scope of your display to that particular region.

You may decide to select newly emerging societies, or highlight just those countries that have established quotas for women in government, for your exhibit.

Focus on America. The US Senate boasts the largest number of female senators in our nation's history. Feature those elected officials in your display on women. The United States may possibly see a woman elevated to the presidency before the end of this decade. Your display could develop and expand that concept. Tie it into the upcoming elections.

INDIAN ARTS

India ... always knew how to laugh, observe, love, and suffer with the same intensity as any other people. Her anonymous artists transfused their ever-fresh enthusiasm to stone and bronze, murals, and lacelike marble in different styles but with unabated appreciation of unfathomable beauty.

Mario Bussagli,
professor of the history of art in India
and Central Asia, University of Rome

The basic foundation of Indian culture has remained unchanged for thousands of years. Consequently, historians consider India to be the oldest civilization. Scientific research indicates that Indic tradition has a cultural continuance that can be traced for a period of more than ten thousand years.

The Indian subcontinent encompasses an area as large and culturally varied as Europe. It has produced through its village artisans, its centers of specialist production and its imperial workshops, a large and varied body of art. The artists of India have drawn both from the roots of their indigenous traditions as well as the external influences of foreign patrons and prior rulers.

The arts of India are among the greatest aesthetic achievements of mankind, but the recognition of their significance in Western culture didn't come about until the end of the 20th century. However, Indian art has always met with mixed reactions in the West. During the 19th century, appreciation of Indian artistic endeavors was limited to the applied arts, and most writers did not consider Indian sculpture and paintings worthy of acknowledgement. In the early 20th century, India's standing in relation to the art of similar great cultural traditions began to be re–examined, largely due the influence of E. B. Havell. Havell had been a principal of the Madras and the Calcutta schools of art and was an enthusiastic patron of the arts.

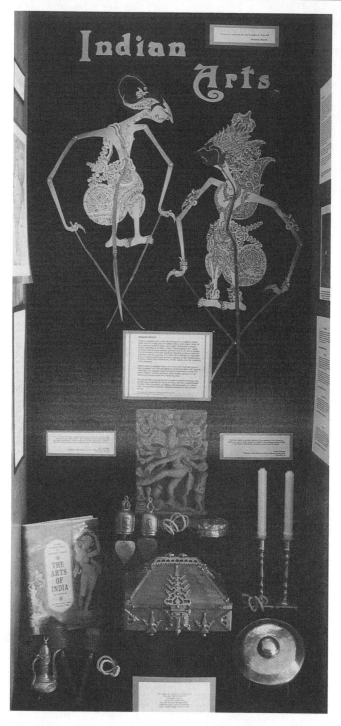

Indian Arts—These exquisite puppets are made from buffalo hide. Shows are performed to male only audiences. The women, segregated behind the theater curtain, see the show only in shadow—thus the name "shadow puppets."

The architecture of India is renowned for its forts, tombs and temples. The most famous structure, the Taj Mahal, was begun in 1631 and continued through 1648 in Agra, seat of the Mughal Empire. The tomb is raised on a terrace, and sheathed in marble. The mosque and counter-mosque on the transverse axis were built with red sandstone. The four minarets are scaled down to heighten the effect of the dominant, bulbous dome. This unique Mughal style combines elements of Persian, Central Asian, and Islamic architecture. The tomb was built by Shah Jehan for his beloved wife, Arjuman Banu Begum, who died giving birth to their fourteenth child. He wanted the most beautiful mausoleum on Earth to be dedicated to her memory.

Prayer wheels are commonly found in India and throughout the Far East. Whether wall mounted or hand held, these wheels are filled with long strips of paper containing prayers for the happiness, and relief from suffering, for people everywhere. Turning the wheel is believed to release these prayers into the atmosphere and send the blessings out where they are needed. The wheels are turned in unison as prayers are chanted.

Other objects selected for display include a pair of intricately designed shadow puppets. These imaginative creations hold a long standing place of tradition within India, and are a large part of the

Indian culture even today. Some of the largest puppets in India were called Tholumatte puppets, which originated in southern India. These puppets were made from the hide of large animals and were five to six feet in height. The front paws of the hide would be attached to sticks while the legs were left to hang free. The hides were painted in a beautiful array of colors.

The puppet shows would be performed in front of a sheet of fabric hung on bamboo, with candles placed in a row behind the sheet to give off a flickering glow. Only the men were permitted to sit in the audience facing the puppets during a production. The women were forced to watch backstage from behind the curtain, seeing only the shadows of the puppets. The shows often performed the narratives behind paintings and scrolls, and could last for up to six hours.

Others types of puppets were only a foot and a half tall. Each of these puppets had intricate designs with specific meanings carved into them. Today's shadow puppet shows often comment on religion and philosophy, yet follow many of the same ritualistic religious traditions of the ancient shows. For more information on this unique form of entertainment, visit http://www.pride-net.com/1997/october/puppetry/history.htm and http://www.puppetindia.com/shadow.htm

Many of the works of art in India reflect the rich mythology which prevails. The wood carving featured in the display is of the black goddess Kali who was frequently regarded as a sex goddess, a courtesan or divine harlot. She was also perceived as a devoted spouse or even the spotless virgin. Kali is seen as the essence of Blackness personified, who ruled over all the dark elements of nature.

The prevalent use of metal in Indian art symbolized man's understanding of his mortality and his desire to leave his creations for posterity. This would guarantee his legacy on Earth. Featured in the display are several brass items: a pair of candle holders, two bells adorned with elephant heads with bell shapes dangling, a brass vessel, a wooden box adorned with brass hardware, and a gong.

The craftsmen of Kashmir, India, are known for their fabulous decorative pieces made out of papier-mâché. The rose toned floral box in the shape of an oval adds a splash of color to the display.

CREDITS

Our youngest son spent many months in Hyderabad, India, setting up an office for the international accounting firm for whom he works. Dennis kept an online journal and attached photos so that his family and friends could share in this incredible experience a world away. His photo of the tombs at Qutb Shahi is featured in the display.

The items featured in Indian Arts are largely from the Marjorie Wright Miller, class of 1930, collection.

ASSEMBLING THE DISPLAY

1. The shadow puppets were attached with straight pins to the background of black felt. The font for *Indian Arts* was found at http://www.surreyindiaartsclub.com/.

The font was enlarged on the photocopier, cut and traced onto gold poster board.
   Over the title was this quote:

> All true art must help the soul to realize its inner self.
>
> —Mahatma Gandhi

Under the puppets was a document titled "Shadow Puppets." Information on them can be found if you visit http://www.pride-net.com/1997/october/puppetry/history.htm or http://www.puppetindia.com/shadow.htm

Below and to the left was the quote introducing the display. To the right was this quotation:

> The Art of India is an exact reflection of the essence of its civilization, which is so hard to define despite its marked characteristics and so fruitful in the fields of philosophy, linguistics poetry, and the theater.
>
> —Mario Bussagli,
> professor of the history of art in India
> and Central Asia, University of Rome

2. On the top left side of the display was the following quote:

> India is: the cradle of the human race, the birthplace of human speech, the mother of history, the grandmother of legend, and the great grandmother of tradition. Our most valuable and most astrictive materials in the history of man are treasured up in India only.
>
> —Mark Twain

Under this was a colorful map of India found through an online image search. Next was a poem titled "A Modern-Day Meditation," by Nitin Mehta. This can be found if you visit http://india.poetryinternational.org/cwolk/view/24278

Items on the left were printed on white cardstock and mounted on black and/or gold poster board.

3. On the top right was a history of India's majority religion, Hinduism. Information on this can be found if you visit http://www.mnsu.edu/emuseum/cultural/religion/hinduism/history.html

Under that was a photo of the archway surrounding one of the tombs at Qutb Shahi, located twelve kilometers from Hyderabad. Information about the unique architecture of these structures can be found at this site: http://www.explohyd.com/qutb.html

Last was a description of the items featured in the display.

Information on prayer wheels can be found if you visit http://www.michaelolaf.nte/templewheels.html

For information about the gong, see http://www.carousel-music.com/nf/gongsnf.html

Description of carved wooden boxes are available at http://www.easy2source.com/products/sandook.html

The process of the craft of papier-mâché can be located at this site: http://www.handicraft.indiamart.com/materials/paper-mach-crafts.html

Items on the right were printed on white cardstock and mounted on gold and/or black poster board.

4. The black velvet fabric was draped over Styrofoam forms to create various levels for displaying the objects. The wooden carving of Kali sits atop the tableau. Two brass bells and the papier-mâché box flank the carving. On the lower shelf is a carved wood and brass box. Below that is an acknowledgment of the donor of the artifacts. On the bottom left is a set of prayer wheels and a brass vessel. On the top right is a pair of brass candlesticks and below that a brass gong. Gold wire cording was coiled and cut into 3 inch sections and placed at intervals throughout the arrangement.

The book featured in the display was *The Arts of India* by Ajit Mookerjee.

BIGGER AND BETTER

There are some colorful and comprehensive books that could be added should your space allow. *Arts of India 1550–1900* edited by John Guy and Deborah Swallow, and *India Unveiled* by Robert Arnett both have excellent covers for display. The subject of Indian mythology is so vast, it could be a theme unto itself.

An Indian rug could serve as a backdrop or be placed over Styrofoam steps where display items could be placed. An Indian sari could be hung or draped in the design. Jewelry would add additional color and richness. The Taj Mahal would be a great topic for a display on India.

People

THE LEGEND OF BLACKBEARD

Come all you jolly sailors
You all so stout and brave;
Come hearken and I'll tell you
What happen'd on the wave.
Oh! tis of that bloody Blackbeard
I'm going now for to tell;
And as how by gallant Maynard
He soon was sent to hell.
—Benjamin Franklin (attributed)

Blackbeard is perhaps the most notorious of the sea rovers who ambushed ships on the Atlantic Ocean and Caribbean Sea from 1717 through 1718—an era commonly referred to as the Golden Age of Piracy. Despite his legendary reputation, his origin is obscure. His name may have been Edward Drummond, although there is some dispute among historians regarding that. He began his career as an honest seaman, sailing out of the port of Bristol, England. Following service as a privateer in the Queen Anne's War, he abandoned his roots and moral code.

By 1717 Blackbeard was operating off the Delaware and Chesapeake bays along with two other pirate captains, his mentor Benjamin Hornigold and Stede Bonnet. Late in the fall of that year, the band of pirates sailed to Martinique and captured the French slaveship *La Concorde*. This vessel would be renamed *Queen Anne's Revenge,* and eventually become Blackbeard's flagship. He armed the vessel with cannons and reinforced the ship's sides. The rearmed craft proved swift and easy to manipulate, and was capable of carrying a crew of 250.

Blackbeard's reputation for cruelty was well founded. His capricious personality craved excitement tinged with both cruelty and terror. He believed that spontaneous barbarous outbreaks were necessary in order to maintain control and discourage mutiny. It is rumored that during a meeting on the ship's deck, he extinguished the lantern and randomly fired his pistol beneath a table, thus crippling a member of the crew. On another occasion he closeted himself in the hold with several others and commanded that pots of sulfur be lit. This created clouds of smoke that forced the others to flee. Blackbeard held out the longest.

As Blackbeard's reputation as a villain grew, so did his beard and hair. He braided his dark beard with black ribbons and stuffed burning rope under his hat to create the ferocious look that artists have captured and which has become his trademark.

Blackbeard's day of infamy came in the Charleston harbor when he blockaded the port, seized eight cargo ships, captured a number of prominent citizens and locked them in the dark hold of the ship. He threatened to kill them if the townspeople didn't meet his demands, which included a chest of medical supplies. These he required, as it was rumored that he had contracted a venereal disease. When the ransom was delivered, the hostages, relieved of their clothing and jewelry, were released.

In 1718, Blackbeard sailed to North Carolina and established a refuge on Ocracoke Island, near the settlement of Bathe Town. This location provided a lucrative outlet for his booty. A bribe to the colony's governor proved good insurance for this enterprise, as well as safety from prosecution. Although local townspeople eagerly took advantage of the discounted prices of pirated goods, resentment was growing over the outlaws' brash display of lawlessness.

Virginia governor Alexander Spotswood, weary of the wanton behavior and disregard for human life, decided to retaliate. On November 22, 1718, Lieutenant Robert Maynard of the Royal Navy arrived at Ocracoke. Although outnumbered, Blackbeard managed to escape through an unmarked channel, while the sloops ran aground. When the

Legend of Blackbeard—Pirate booty sits at the base of the display on the infamous Blackbeard, who dominated the sea during the Golden Age of Piracy.

tide rose, the pursuit continued. A bloody battle ensued until Blackbeard boarded Maynard's seemingly deserted ship. The trap worked and the concealed crew emerged.

Blackbeard and Maynard engaged in hand-to-hand combat. The pirate was first wounded, then finally killed by a navy seaman. The remaining pirates were either killed or captured. The heroic Lieutenant Maynard returned to Williamsburg with Blackbeard's decapitated head dangling from the bow of the ship. The surviving pirates were tried in March of 1719. The verdict was guilty and the sentence deemed that the thirteen rogues would be killed by hanging in Williamsburg, Virginia.

Blackbeard's skull hung for many years from a pole at the point where the Hampton River meets the James River. The site is still referred to as Blackbeard's Point.

Legend and truth about Blackbeard's personal life have melded together over the years. He is said to have had 14 wives, the last a mere teenager completely unaware of his notoriety and his marrying ways!

There has been a resurgence of interest in Blackbeard over the past decade due to the 1996 discovery of the *Queen Anne's Revenge* and the formation of the QAR Project. Over 2,000 artifacts have been recovered and conserved, while thousands more await removal, processing, and treatment. Studying the artifacts retrieved from this vessel provides archeologists with valuable insight into the period's naval technology, colonial provisioning, slave trade, life aboard a ship, and the material culture of piracy.

Excellent resources for this display were *The History of Pirates* by Angus Konstam, *Blackbeard the Pirate: A Reappraisal of His Life and Times* by Robert E. Lee, and *Pirate* by Richard Platt.

For online information, visit http://www.history.org/foundation/journal/blackbea.cfm

CREDITS

A trip to the southern Outer Banks of North Carolina sparked interest in the infamous buccaneer Blackbeard, aka Edward Teach. A home in which he lived lies in the charming town of Beaufort, North Carolina, and is a point of interest on sightseeing tours through and around the waters of the Crystal Coast. The seafaring heritage and rich colonial history of this area makes it a fascinating tourist destination.

If you get to the southern Outer Banks, check out the North Carolina Maritime Museum in Beaufort. Their collection of books, maps and maritime items are effectively displayed and the information is artfully arranged.

The shops in Beaufort offer a wide variety of pirate memorabilia. Purchasing a few of these items, such as the poster and pirate flag, made the creation and installation of this display a relatively easy one.

ASSEMBLING THE DISPLAY

1. The featured poster of Blackbeard was mounted on red poster board on a background of black felt, and affixed just off center in the top of the display space. This

graphic is available online through the North Carolina Maritime Museum in Beaufort, along with other pirate and maritime items.

For more information, visit http://www.ah.dcr.state.nc.us/sections/maritime/main/mission.htm

The words *Legend of* were cut from red poster board, mounted on a strip of black poster board and attached to the left side of the poster along with a toy cutlass. The Jolly Roger flag was centered over the poster and attached with pins. At the bottom left of the poster was a parrot which was drawn freehand. Beneath the parrot, an 18th century maritime map of the southeastern United States and the Caribbean was positioned between two compass dials which were taken from the map, then enlarged and printed on cardstock. All of these graphics were available through an online image search.

2. On the top left was a paragraph about a pirate's attire to which an eyepatch was attached. This can be found if you visit http://www.elizabethan-era.org.uk/pirate-clothing.htm

Next was a biography of Blackbeard which can be found at this site: http://www.ah.dcr.state.nc.us/sections/maritime/blackbeard/default.htm.

A painting of Blackbeard, found on a Yahoo image search, was cut in the shape of a circle and positioned between the top two items.

A list of pirate's rules was next. This can be found if you visit http://www.piratesinfo.com/fact/facts/conduct.htm

A ship's manifest found through a Google image search was last.

All of these documents were printed on white cardstock and mounted on red and/or black poster board.

3. On the right was information about the *Queen Anne's Revenge* and Blackbeard's demise at Ocracoke Inlet. For that information visit http://www.ah.dcr.state.nc.us/qar/history/history.htm

An illustration of the *Queen Anne's Revenge*, found on a Google image search, was next followed by a document which provided an overview of the history of the pirate flag, the Jolly Roger. This information was found in *The History of Pirates* by Angus Konstam.

The quotes included on the right were the one introducing this chapter, and this one:

> Such a day, rum all out;—
> Our company somewhat sober:—
> A damned confusion amongst us!—
> Rogues a-plotting:—
> Great talk of separation—
> so I looked sharp for a prize:—
> Such a day found one with the
> great deal of liquor on board,
> So kept the company hot, damned hot;
> then all things went well again.
>
> —One of several memoranda, said to be in Blackbeard's
> own hand, found aboard the sloop *Adventure,*
> after the pirate was slain at Ocracoke Inlet in 1718.

This and other information about pirates can be found at the Web site cited regarding Blackbeard's biography.

4. The bottom of the case was draped with velvet over forms of Styrofoam. This provided the proper elevation for the treasure chest, which was lined with a red and gold metallic striped scarf. A silver goblet and piles of costume jewelry filled the chest. Another goblet and an exotic lamp flank the chest. Strands of jewels and broaches fill and surround these items. Gold and silver coins, cut from poster board, were interspersed with real coins.

Books featured in the display were *Blackbeard: A Tale of Villainy and Murder in Colonial America* by Margaret Hoffman, *Under the Black Flag: The Romance and the Reality of Life Among the Pirates* by David Cordingly and *The History of Pirates* by Angus Konstam.

BIGGER AND BETTER

If your exhibit space permits, you could include some palm fronds native to the region, a pirate hat, ruffled shirt, or scarf. A collection of pirate flags strung on a large rope would make a great visual for your display.

Booty such as pewter plates, bolts of vintage fabrics, sacks of flour or sugar, ropes or a rope ladder, and an anchor could be added. Artificial flora and fauna peculiar to the area would also add interest. Many of the resources on pirates include information on women pirates. That would be a novel idea for your space!

C. S. LEWIS: INTO THE WARDROBE

Don't use words too big for the subject. Don't say "infinitely" when you mean "very"; otherwise you'll have no word left when you want to talk about something really infinite.

—C. S. Lewis

The second son of Albert and Flora Lewis was born in Belfast, Northern Ireland, on November 29, 1898. Christened Clive Staples Lewis, the family soon nicknamed him "Jack." Lewis's early childhood was relatively happy. Northern Ireland was not experiencing civil strife at that time, and the family was considered affluent.

At the age of 7, the Lewis family moved to the outskirts of Belfast to a large gabled home known as Little Lea. The house had dark, narrow passages and an overgrown garden which the Lewis brothers played in and explored together. The library at Little Lea had an impressive number of volumes. Two of Jack's favorites were *Treasure Island* by Robert Louis Stevenson and *The Secret Garden* by Frances Hodgson Burnett.

When Lewis reached the age of 10, his carefree days of childhood came to an abrupt end. His mother lost her battle with cancer, and Jack was sent to join his brother Warren at the Wynyard School in England. Lewis despised the strict rules and callous headmaster at Wynyard and was delighted when it closed in 1910.

After a year in Belfast, Lewis returned to England to study at the Cherbourg School in Malvern. This time, however, the educational environment was a positive one. It was during these years that Lewis developed a love of poetry, particularly the writings of Virgil and Homer. He also gained a mastery of several languages which included French, German and Italian.

Shortly after Lewis entered Oxford University in 1916, he decided to support the war effort and enlisted in the British Army. He was commissioned an officer in the 3rd Battalion, Somerset Light Infantry, and was deployed to the Somme Valley in northern France. Lewis was wounded in April of 1918 during the Battle of Arras. After a

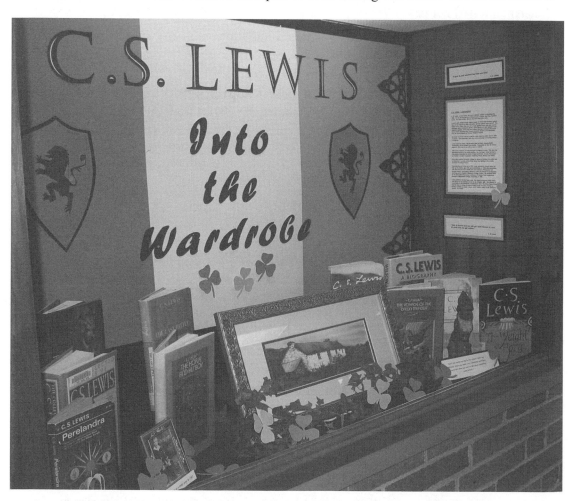

C.S. Lewis: Into the Wardrobe—The flag of Ireland provides a colorful backdrop to showcase the work of prolific Irish writer C. S. Lewis. The coat or arms features a lion which represents a main character in his series *The Chronicles of Narnia.*

period of recuperation, he was assigned to Ludgerhall, Andover, England, in October 1918 and discharged two months later.

Lewis suffered a personal loss during World War I. His dear friend, Paddy Moore, was killed in battle and buried near Peronne, France. Lewis paid tribute to the memory of Paddy Moore in a poem titled "Death in Battle." It was the first poem Lewis had published outside of a school magazine.

In 1925, after graduating with high honors in Greek, English and Latin literature, and philosophy and ancient history, Lewis was offered a prestigious teaching position in the English department of Magdalen College, Oxford. He remained at Oxford for almost 30 years before becoming a professor of medieval and Renaissance literature at Magdalen College, Cambridge.

While at Magdalen, Lewis published his first major work, *The Pilgrim's Regress* (1933), which was about his spiritual journey to the Christian faith. His friend, J. R. R. Tolkien, a colleague and a devout Roman Catholic, was responsible in large measure for Lewis's spiritual awakening and religious conversion. Other works followed, such as *Allegory of Love,* and *Out of the Silent Planet,* the first of a trilogy of science fiction novels. The main character in that series was based on his good friend, Tolkien.

When Lewis first considered writing children's books, his publisher and some of his friends tried to dissuade him. They felt that it would affect his reputation as a serious writer. Tolkien was a particularly vocal critic of the first Narnia book, *The Lion, the Witch and the Wardrobe.* He felt that there were too many conflicting elements. If there was a Father Christmas, should there also be a wicked witch? If talking animals are included, are children really necessary? Lewis dismissed much of the criticism and went on to write six more books in this series.

The kingdom of Narnia C. S. Lewis created is a fantasy world where magic is common and good battles evil. Throughout most of the series, the English children find themselves confronted with wrongs that must be righted. This becomes possible through the assistance of Aslan, the lion they have grown to love.

Although there are many obvious elements of Christianity present in the series, the books can be read simply for their imaginative adventures. Lewis drew on characters from both Greek and Roman mythology as well as those found in British and Irish fairy tales. *The Chronicles of Narnia* appeal to a wide audience including children, Christians and non–Christians. For background on the development of this series and a comprehensive biography of C. S. Lewis, visit http://www.factmonster.com/spot/narnia-lewis.html

Lewis married divorcee Joy Davidman Gresham, who had converted to Christianity partially due to the influence of his writings. They wed secretly in 1956 in a civil ceremony, and repeated their vows in a church ceremony at her hospital bed the following year. After an arduous fight that included several remissions, Joy's battle with bone cancer ended her life in 1960. *A Grief Observed,* a memoir of the suffering his wife's death had caused, was published under the pseudonym N. W. Clerk.

After Joy's death, Lewis's own health deteriorated and he resigned his position at Cambridge in the summer of 1963. Lewis's death at age 65 on November 22, 1963, was greatly overshadowed by the assassination of President John F. Kennedy, which took place a continent away on that same day.

The Chronicles of Narnia have sold over 100 million copies and have been translated into 41 languages. Adaptations have been made for radio, television, the stage and the cinema. C. S. Lewis's readers worldwide have been inspired by the extensive body of work left behind by this gifted and prolific writer.

CREDITS

Many years ago a neighbor invited my family on a ride aboard the sailboat he had named *Narnia.* At the time, I was unaware of the significance of that name and the magical place it represented. Soon after our boating excursion, I made a point of researching the enchanted kingdom known as Narnia.

Our oldest son, Brian, who was about ten years old at the time, was at an ideal age to be introduced to the wondrous world that C. S. Lewis created for children, the one that existed just beyond the back of the wardrobe. Brian's interest in *The Chronicles of Narnia* lasted for many months and made him a great and loyal fan of the author.

Several years later, as a staff member in the Annapolis and Anne Arundel County Public Library system, I had the pleasure of introducing many young readers to the delightful works of C. S. Lewis.

ASSEMBLING THE DISPLAY

1. The flag of Ireland, made from green, orange and white poster board was mounted on a background of black felt. The title *C. S. Lewis* was created using the font Castellar sized at 400. *Into the Wardrobe* used the font Forte, sized at 300.

The coat of arms depicting a lion was found through a Google image search. It was printed, then enlarged on the photocopier, cut and glued to a shield of silver poster board mounted on black poster board. The coats of arms were glued to the poster board, flanking the title signage. For information regarding Irish heraldry, visit http://scripts.ireland.com/ancestor/magazine/heraldry/index.htm

The Celtic knots were found through a Google image search. They were printed on cardstock, traced onto black poster board, cut and glued to the background. Shamrocks, located in the same manner, were printed on cardstock and traced onto two shades of green poster board. They were glued to the bottom center of the flag and interspersed throughout the display.

2. On the top left was a quote by C. S. Lewis taken from the preface of *The Lion, the Witch and the Wardrobe*:

> Someday you will be old enough to start reading fairy tales again.

Under that was the poem "Death in Battle" which can be found if you visit http://poetry.poetryx.com/poems/7527/

Finally, there was information on the background of the conflict surrounding the author's decision to write *The Chronicles of Narnia*, intended for a juvenile audience. This information can be found if you visit http://www.narniafans.com/cslewis.php

All material was printed on white cardstock and mounted on orange or green and black poster board.

3. On the top right was this quotation:

> I gave in, and admitted that God was God.
>
> —C. S. Lewis

Under that was a biography of the author which can be found at the same site as the information on *Chronicles of Narnia*.

Lastly was another quote by Lewis:

> Aim at heaven and you will get earth thrown in. Aim at earth and you get neither.

Items on the right were printed and mounted as those on the left.

4. On the base of the display was a print of an Irish cottage with a thatched roof by Thomas Patrick Hanlon of Bath, Pennsylvania. This was surrounded by artificial ivy. A framed copy of a photograph of Lewis as a child, found through a Google image search, was set to the left of the print. A carved wooden leprechaun was placed to the right. The quote which introduced the display was printed on cardstock, mounted on black poster board and place in front of the wood carving.

Books by C. S. Lewis featured in the display were *The Screwtape Letters*; *Mere Christianity*; *Perelandra*; *Collected Works of C. S. Lewis: The Pilgrim's Regress, Christian Reflections, God in the Dock*; *The Last Battle, The Horse and His Boy, The Voyage of the Dawn Treader, The Weight of Glory* and *Miracle*.

Also included was *C. S. Lewis: A Biography* by A. N. Wilson.

BIGGER AND BETTER

Should you choose to do a display on C. S. Lewis, you could emphasize his faith and include Christian artifacts. Draw a door and have that be the focal point of your display. Add a lion and a witch, or a witch's hat, and place these items among the books. Other items that reflect the journey in the series would be a silver chair, a prince's crown, a horse, and a magician's hat or wand.

You could combine your display with one on J. R. R. Tolkien, since they were friends and fellow Christians. Use the book entitled *Tolkien and C. S. Lewis: The Gift of Friendship* by Colin Duriez for background information on their enduring friendship. Include images of Oxford where they were colleagues on the faculty. Feature Tolkien's *The Lord of the Rings* trilogy.

Your display on other Irish writers might focus on John Millington Synge, Brian Friel, William Butler Yeats, Sean O'Casey, Samuel Becket, James Joyce, Oscar Wilde or Iris Murdoch. All of these writers made major contributions to the field of literature.

Add bagpipes, a harp, clay pipes and a stone (representing the Blarney stone) to your display. A rainbow and a pot of gold could also be worked into your design.

For a comprehensive list of Irish writers with links to their works, visit http://www. irishwriters-online.com/listmn.html

Thomas Patrick Hanlon has a wonderful Web site for his Celtic art. Please visit him at http://www.thomashanlon.com/

MANET BY THE SEA

You're on very good terms with Renoir and take an interest in his future—do advise him to give up painting! You can see for yourself that it's not his métier at all.

—Manet to Monet

The Philadelphia Museum of Art, the Art Institute of Chicago, and the Van Gogh Museum in Amsterdam collaborated to organize the first museum retrospective devoted to the marine paintings of Edouard Manet. The 2004 traveling exhibit, titled Manet and the Sea, was the first to explore the nautical paintings and drawings of this visionary French Impressionist and his celebrated contemporaries.

Edouard Manet was born into the ranks of the Parisian bourgeoisies in 1832. His parents were Eugénie-Désirée Fournier, daughter of a diplomat, and Auguste Manet, magistrate and judge. His father had aspirations that his oldest son would follow him into the bureaucratic world. Destiny would prove otherwise.

Although he was afforded a privileged education, Manet did not excel as a student. Throughout his youth, however, he was highly influenced by his uncle, Charles Fournier, who introduced him and some of his friends to the art treasures housed in the Louvre.

There is extensive documentation of Manet's desire for a career in the French navy. His six month voyage from Le Havre to Rio, aboard a three-masted ship, was something of a floating cram session. The four instructors on board were obliged to instill the knowledge and expertise students would need to pass the entrance examination for officer's school. After a unsuccessful first attempt, an exception was made and Manet was permitted to take this exam a second time. Still, he was unable to meet the standard. Despite this disappointment, the experience at sea provided him with a wealth of visual impressions from which, as a mature artist, he would later draw.

Following his service in the merchant marines, where Manet first developed an affinity for the sea, he began a six year period of study in the studio of Thomas Couture. Although Couture's style was rather traditional, his innovative principles made him attractive to young artists. Manet was highly influenced by the works of the old

Manet by the Sea—The lighthouse, sand and shells add a nautical touch in keeping with the theme of these maritime paintings by Edouard Manet.

masters including Goya and Velazquez. However, he made a conscious decision not to follow past ideals, but rather to pursue contemporary realism.

Manet initially painted genre (everyday) subjects, such as old beggars, street urchins, café characters and Spanish bullfight scenes. He adopted a direct, bold brush technique in his treatment of realistic subject matters. Manet's ordinary subjects were endowed with radiant reality focusing on form as well as color. He was the first artist since the Renaissance to defy proportion and perspective and even omit inconvenient visual facts, if this resulted in a stronger picture.

In 1864, the official Salon des Refuses accepted two of his paintings, thus acknowledging his position in the art world. The following year this museum became involved in a storm of protests when they exhibited Manet's *Olympia*. The subject was a nude based on a Venus by Titian. His attempt to translate the reclining prostitute, lying in repose, into modern terms met with much fury among many of his contemporaries.

Manet began painting the sea when he was in his early thirties. His first real seascape was the *Battle of the Kearsarge and the Alabama*. Experts noted its historical accuracy and relevance, since the actual battle had taken place just several weeks prior. Subsequent paintings, which totaled around forty works, depicted family members at the beach in Trouville and tranquil interpretations of resorts such as Arcachon and Boulogne. By the time Manet began his artistic affair with the sea, it was clear that the Impressionists held him in very high regard.

CREDITS

The Philadelphia Museum of Art is located on the banks of the Schuykill River and overlooks the infamous Boater's Row, the popular venue for exciting university crew races and more than a few memorable college parties! Located just an hour from the Lehigh Valley, the museum is a wonderful destination point, and one which my husband and I frequent whenever possible.

Several years ago, the museum featured an exhibit entitled *Manet and the Sea*. It featured 33 of Manet's oil paintings, along with several drawings of seascapes. A recently discovered sketchbook offered a fresh look at the artist during his most spontaneous moments. The curators enhanced this exhibition with paintings by artists who inspired Manet, and others to whom he served as an inspiration. The list includes Courbet, Whistler, Monet, Morisot and Manet's only pupil, Eva Gonzales. These works of art were drawn from more than 60 public and private collections and provide a comprehensive overview of the artist and his peers.

ASSEMBLING THE DISPLAY

1. The font chosen for the title word was Bold Impact. It was sized to fit on an 8½" × 11" piece of white paper. Then it was magnified on the photocopier, printed on cardstock, glued to black poster board and pinned to the background of black felt.

Monotype Corsiva Italic was selected for the subtitle *By the Sea*. It was enlarged as above.

Above and to the left of the title was a biography of Manet. This information, along with a timeline, can be found if you visit http://www.allaboutartists.com/index.html

Above and to the right of the title was a paragraph titled "Summer on the Seine," which summarizes the relationship between Monet and Manet during the summer of 1874 when Renoir joined them. It was there that all three painted *The Monet Family in the Garden*. For background information visit http://www.wetcanvas.com/Museum/Artists/m/Edouard_Manet/index.html

The above information was printed on white cardstock and mounted on turquoise and black poster board.

The seascapes were taken from *Manet: A Visionary Impressionist* by Henry Lallemand and include a portrait of Manet, and copies of the following prints: *The Folkstone Boat-Boulogne* (1869), *The Grand Canal, Venice* (1875), *Moonlight Over Boulogne Harbor* (1869), *The Escape of Rochefort* (1880–1881), and *Argenteuil* (1874). These prints were double mounted on turquoise and black poster board and were labeled with the title and the year that the work was produced. They were hung on the right and left sides, as well as on the center portion of the display case. Shells were attached with pins above the title signage.

The following quotes by Antonin Proust, close friend and biographer, and Manet himself were included below the title:

> Of medium height, well muscled.... He was obviously a thoroughbred. Beneath a broad forehead, the frank, straight line of the nose. The eyes small, the glance lively.... There were few men so attractive.
>
> —Antonin Proust

> I paint what I see, and not what others like to see.
>
> —Edouard Manet

Both quotes were printed on white cardstock and mounted on black poster board.

2. On the top right was a critique of Manet's seascapes taken from a review on the *Maritime Celebration* by N. F. Karlins, a New York art historian and critic. This information can be found if you visit http://www.artnet.com/Magazine/reviews/karlins/karlins3-3-04.asp

3. A large black and white lighthouse was placed on the base of the display left. The Pierre Schneider monograph, titled *The World of Manet,* was opened to the page featuring the painting entitled *The Battle of the Kearsage and the Alabama*. Also included were shells of various sizes and shapes. Finally, a starfish was placed at the base of the lighthouse and a large snail shell on top of the opened book. Sand, readily available at the local dollar store, was lightly spread around the base of the unit.

The books featured in the display were *Manet: Olympia* by Theodore Reff, *Manet and the Modern Tradition* by Anne Coffin Hanson, and *Manet and the Sea* by Juliet Wilson-Bareau and David Degener.

BIGGER AND BETTER

If your display area permits, add an anchor, some old fishing lures, an artist's palette and brushes, some fish netting, a fishing pole, buoys, an old compass, or additional lighthouses.

Since Manet was a prolific painter, you might prefer having a different focus on the artist. Instead, choose his still lifes, portraits, children, nudes, or landscapes.

Nature

STAR BRIGHT

> The sun, with all those planets revolving around it and dependent on it, can
> still ripen a bunch of grapes as if it had nothing else in the universe to do.
> —Galileo Galilei

All of us are aware of the overwhelming importance of the Sun to our life on Planet Earth. Although an average star, with regard to size and temperature, the Sun is similar to millions of others in the universe. Many stars are much larger and hotter, others smaller and cooler. There are billions of stars in the universe like our Sun. It is special to us only because it is *our* Sun.

This star is the source of light, heat and energy vital to our well being. In fact, it is a colossal energy machine! If the total output of the Sun's energy was gathered for one second, it would provide our country with ample energy for the next 9,000,000 years.

Located 93 million miles away from Earth, the Sun appears bigger and brighter than other stars because of its distance. The next closest star is about twenty five million miles further away. Fueled by hydrogen, the Sun uses about 4 million tons of this element every second. Despite this energy use, the Sun has enough resources to shine for another five billion years.

The Sun has fascinated man since the beginning of time. Primitive peoples created numerous myths concerning the Sun. Some of those beliefs involved the moon, since the Sun and the moon were seen as interrelated. The Sun was perceived as both male and female. For example, among the aboriginal tribes, the Sun manifests itself as a woman who has a dead lover beneath the surface of the earth. Each night, she entered the nether world to be with him. Each morning she rose and dressed in a red kangaroo skin, a gift from her lover. Countless stories tell of the Sun descending into the underworld at the day's end and rising anew at the break of day. The Sun was perceived as having walked, ridden, or been carried from west to east.

Medical research suggests that although the Sun has some known harmful effects, it can also heal and prevent chronic health problems. Physicians who used sunlight as medicine therapy during the first half of the 20th century were unable to explain precisely why the therapy worked.

There is a dichotomy as to how the effects of the Sun are perceived in the medical community today. On the one hand physicians recommend that the Sun be avoided. However, studies show that melanoma tends to occur on parts of the body that are less exposed, such as the back of the legs, or the trunk of the body. In Europe, malignant melanoma is more likely to be developed by people living at higher latitudes, where there is less sunlight. Obviously, there needs to be further studies conducted to determine the action of sunlight on the human body, and the role it plays in the cause and/or prevention of disease.

Much has been written on the topic of solar power. This energy source is becoming more and more economical as costs associated with production decrease. Facilities can operate with relatively little maintenance or intervention following the preliminary setup. As with any technology, there are negatives. The best placed locations for solar power panels tend to be remotely located from the places of the highest energy demand. This is certainly a technology that is favorable to the environment and warrants continued study and experimentation.

Star Bright—The bold metal sun, set within the yin-yang shape, sits between a blue sky touched with clouds, and a brilliant and clear star studded night.

CREDITS

We recently did some research relevant to the selection of appropriate windows for the newly created sunroom in our home. All of this data led us to consider the power and effects of the rays of the Sun. Clearly we wanted to harness as much solar power as possible as this would assure maximum use of the space throughout the four seasons. However, we wanted to be assured that the UV rays that penetrated these windows would be minimal, and that glare would not be an issue.

This cursory study of solar power and UV rays heightened our awareness of that bright ball that travels across our sky each day. As a result, the idea for Star Bright was formed.

While shopping at a local craft store, I spotted some metallic images of the Sun on sale at great prices. The one I selected, which became the central image for the display, now graces a wall of our new sunroom.

Any sizeable sundial could effectively serve as the center of your display.

ASSEMBLING THE DISPLAY

1. A circle, two inches wider than the diameter of the sun, was cut from black poster board. A yin-yang shape, using only half of the design, was cut from the same material and pinned within the circle. Ovals (1¾" high) were cut from silver poster board and glued to the right side of the circle. Half ovals were glued to the left side. These shapes represented the cycle of the moon.

The yin-yang shape can be viewed using this search: http://images.google.com/images?q=yin+yang&hl=en

A metallic sun was attached to the corkboard with 2 pins. The background selected was of sky blue felt that had fiberfill attached to denote clouds. The bottom portion was black felt, which suggested the night sky. Stars of varying sizes, found through a Google image search, were scattered behind the Sun, on the right, and throughout the section of black felt.

The title was created using the font TwoforJuanNF sized at 300, which can be obtained if you visit http://www.1001freefonts.com

This font was printed on off-white cardstock and attached with pins.

2. On the top left of the display was a fact sheet about the Sun. A clip art image of the Sun was inserted into the document. This was mounted on blue and black poster board, and hung with double sided tape. For facts about the Sun, visit http://www.solarmovie.com/learn/educatorsguide/facts.html

Next was information titled "What Is Sun Damage." An image of the sun from clip art was inserted into the upper right corner. This site provided excellent material: http://www.sundamge.ca/sun_damage.html

This quote by Galileo that introduced the chapter was next.

The next piece, "Current Research in Solar Energy," included information gathered from the text *Got Sun? Go Solar*, as well as at this online location: http://www.history.rochester.edu/class/solar/current.htm

Mother Teresa's quotation was hung at the bottom:

> See how nature—trees, flowers, grass—grows in silence; see the stars, the moon and the sun, how they move in silence ... we need silence to be able to touch souls.

All of the items on the left were printed on off-white cardstock and mounted on blue and/or black poster board.

3. On the top right was a tarot card image found through a Google search. Information about tarot cards, and the Sun card, was hung next.

Man, Myth and Magic: The Illustrated Encyclopedia of Mythology, Religion and the Unknown, was a good source for information on the significance of the Sun in tarot cards. For online facts about tarot cards visit http://skepdic.com/tarot.html

This quote, by Copernicus, was next:

> Finally we shall place the Sun himself at the center of the Universe. All this is suggested by the systematic procession of events and the harmony of the whole Universe, if only we face the facts, as they say, "with both eyes open."

"Sunlight and Health in the 21st Century" consisted of information found in Richard Hobday's *The Healing Sun*. A clip art image of a sunbather was inserted into the bottom of the document.

A quote by Buddha was the last item on the right:

> Three things cannot be long hidden: the sun, the moon, and the truth.

All of these items were printed on off-white cardstock and mounted as those items on the left.

4. On the base of the display Styrofoam forms were positioned to provide different elevations for the books. The base was covered in black felt. Two different sun graphics, found in clip art, were printed on cardstock, cut out and placed among the monographs.

Books featured in the display were *The Sun* by Seymour Simon, *Children of the Sun* by Alfred W. Crosby, *Waiting for the Sun* by Barney Hoskyns, *Got Sun? Go Solar* by Rex Ewing, *Sun, Moon, and Earth* by Robin Heath, *The UV Advantage* by Michael F. Holick, and *The Healing Sun* by Richard Hobday.

BIGGER AND BETTER

You could focus on Solar Energy or Global Warming since there is much research written on these subjects. Be sure to check these Web sites for background on both of those subjects: http://dsc.discovery.com/?clik=www_nav_dsc and http://www.windows.ucar.edu/tour/link=/sun/sun.html

A simple Google image keyword search using the terms "fiction books on the Sun" will yield some colorful works of fiction for a summer beach read theme. Call it Summer Sizzles and use titles such as *Under the Tuscan Sun*, *The Sun Also Rises*, *Rising Sun*, *Raisin in the Sun*, and *Empire of the Sun*. Be sure to add some sand, sunglasses and tanning lotion to this display.

Select the universe for your sun-centered display and have the Milky Way serve as background. Check this online site: http://www.nineplanets.org/

Myth and Culture or Solar Eclipses could also be themes. For information on these topics, visit http://www.windows.ucar.edu/tour/link=/mythology/planets/sun.html

A collection of sundials and/or thermometers would make an interesting display on the topic of the Sun.

IN THE GARDEN

If we love Flowers, are we not "born again" every Day...
—Emily Dickinson to Mrs. George S. Dickerman, 1886

For many of us gardening is simply a joy. This pastime fills spring and summer hours with rhythmic physical exercise and purposeful activity. Off season, gardening can consume many hours of strategic planning, research and thoughtful contemplation. The end result of this body and mind activity is a vibrant combination of beauty and color and much deserved personal satisfaction.

No matter what type of garden you prefer—a formal English courtyard neatly pruned, a plethora of perennials for cut flowers, or a touch of Provence, individuals bring their own particular style of horticulture to the design. You may decide to take elements of one style and combine them with compatible essentials of another. Once done, your personal imprint has been established.

Although usually quite passionate, gardeners have different levels of commitment. There are the diehard growers who plant gardens fully prepared to tackle all adversaries. They are primed to conquer wildlife, fungi, insects and weeds with nary a complaint and with gratifying results. Conversely, there are planters who sit back and trust that their newly planted garden will thrive with relatively little care and practically no attention.

The first step toward success in the garden is to assess the environment. Before selecting plants, determine if they will thrive in the existing conditions. Questions to be answered are

- How long does the sun shine each day and for what portion of the day?
- Will the garden be sheltered from the wind, or is it a factor?
- Is the earth acidic or sweet? Is the soil dense, sticky clay; coarse-textured, dryish sand; or decent loam?
- Will a dependable water supply be available?

Once those questions have been answered, an informed decision can be made as to which plants will thrive in your garden.

Many practiced gardeners vow to outdo their efforts of previous years. They

In the Garden—The branch of a lemon tree hovers over an array of potted plants. A trowel and spade sit atop a moss and ivy covered base.

challenge themselves by making new and different choices, creating fertilizer blends, studying catalogs, analyzing past results, and touring horticultural display gardens for inspiration.

Despite the fact that the evolution of gardening can be traced back over a period of hundreds of years worldwide, the creative process inherent in this activity is in constant transition. Perhaps that is the main attraction and challenge for those involved in this activity.

Knowledgeable gardeners are cognizant of the importance of luring birds into the planting area. They will rid your garden of unwanted pests and help maintain a healthy growing area. Planting seed-producing flowers, such as black-eyed Susans and coneflowers, will help in the effort to lure these feathered friends. Birdbaths and fountains are decorative water sources which are sure to attract many varieties of birds. Berry-bearing shrubs and fruit trees are guaranteed to entice insect-eating species to your garden.

Healthy plants need rich soil and sufficient moisture. They also require air circulation to permit the foliage to dry and sunlight to filter through. When plants are spaced too closely together, they will grow sparse and leggy and become vulnerable to disease. Sheltering trees that grow low and dense prohibit the flow of air through and around the understory plants.

The demands of tending a garden are what you make them. Your allotment of time and energy dedicated to this pastime is personal. So whether you decide to make this therapeutic hobby a full-time preoccupation or merely an occasional excuse to spend time outdoors, enjoy the fruits of your labor!

CREDITS

A visit to the Philadelphia Flower Show several years ago left a lasting impression on this author. The size, scope and originality of the displays were amazing. This historic flower show, soon to celebrate its 180th anniversary, has a loyal following and draws enormous crowds, including many international visitors.

My mother, Eleanor, had the "green thumb," which several of my siblings inherited. Indeed, they are gardeners of note. As is true in most families, there is a bit of competition to at least *meet* the gardening standard that has been established.

Although, on occasion, I have given this pastime a valiant effort, notable results elude me! Blame it on the feasting of the native wildlife with whom we co-exist, the occasional drought, or a simple lack of imagination ... the results do not impress.

If rabbits and deer feast in your garden as well, visit this Web site for suggestions as to alternative plant varieties they find less appealing: http://www.jaredsgarden. com/anmlres.html

Hopefully, this gardening display will provide helpful information, as well as design and feeding suggestions that will serve to inspire those of us born lacking the elusive "green thumb"!

ASSEMBLING THE DISPLAY

1. Portions of a silk ficus tree were attached to a background of blue felt. Artificial lemons were pinned among the leaves. A silk bird was placed on a branch among the foliage. The font Rage Italic was chosen for the display title. This was sized at 400 and printed on cardstock. The letters were filled in with black Magic Marker then cut out and attached with pins to the background.

This quotation was placed on the top left of the display:

> When we touch the earth and involve ourselves cooperatively with nature's
> cycles, we reaffirm our link with the living planet that sustains us [Lima 11].

The quote was printed on white cardstock and mounted on black poster board. A butterfly, found through a Google image search, was printed on white cardstock, and pinned to the upper left of the quote, then pulled forward on pins.

2. On the top left were guidelines for designing a low maintenance garden. This information was available in many gardening books and also at this site: http://hort. ufl.edu/gt/designing/designing.htm

Next was a document titled "Helpful Hints for Pesky Pests." It was compiled from information found in *Trowel and Error: Over 700 Shortcuts, Tips and Remedies for the Gardener*. Online hints can be found if you visit: http://www.pioneerthinking. com/garden-pests.html

Garden clip art was inserted on these documents, which were printed on white cardstock and mounted on green and blue poster board.

3. On the top right, two quotations flanked the information regarding the use of lures in attracting allies to your garden. The quotations were:

> Cultivators of the earth are the most valuable citizens.
>
> —Thomas Jefferson

> Love your garden, and work in it, and let it give you what it surely will of sweetness and health ... and let no one feel that the benefit is all on the side of the garden, for truly you will receive more than you give.
>
> —Louise B. Wilder,
> Gardener/Writer

The information on how to attract allies in the garden was obtained from *Trowel and Error*. Included in this book were excellent tips relevant to this topic. Clip art graphics were inserted to the left of the text.

All items on the right were printed on white cardstock and mounted on green and blue poster board.

4. On the base of the display Styrofoam was placed to create different elevations. Silk flowers of varying heights were inserted into this. Pots of tulips and mums were placed in the forefront. Sprigs of silk ivy were interspersed among the pots and over the Styrofoam. Sphagnum moss was placed over and around the ivy.

A silk bird, a spade and a trowel were placed in front of the pots.

Books featured in the display were *Trowel and Error: Over 700 Shortcuts, Tips and Remedies for the Gardener* by Sharon Lovejoy, *1,000 Gardening Questions and Answers* by Leslie Land, *The Gardens of Emily Dickinson* by Judith Farr, *Complete Guide to Gardening* by Marjorie P. Groves (ed.) and *100 Flowers and How They Got Their Names* by Diana Wells.

BIGGER AND BETTER

Your display would be very colorful if it included birds as well. Call it Flowers and Feathers! You could have as your focus particular types of gardens such as wildflowers, vegetable or organic gardening, exotic orchids, gardens in the shade or perennials. Add some fencing either in front of or behind your garden. Create an unconventional arrangement, using bold colors. Name it Flower Power or Gardens Galore.

Select a portion of the country with unique vegetation to highlight, such as the Southwest, and name it Scenic Southwest. Or, decide on a particular season and build your exhibit around it. How about urban gardens full of window boxes and flower pots? Call it Summer in the City or Pot Perfect.

The colors of autumn lend themselves to a brilliant display. Include pumpkins, mums, corn stalks, baskets of apples, haystacks, and goose neck squash and you could have a true Fallfest. Complete the tableau by including a scarecrow, if space allows. Larger exhibits could include rakes, shovels, a hoe or hand plough or even a small wheelbarrow.

JOHN MUIR

The Mountains are calling me, and I must go.

—John Muir

John Muir—farmer, inventor, sheepherder, naturalist, explorer, writer, and conservationist—was born in 1838 in Dunbar, Scotland. When he was 11, his family emigrated to the United States and settled in Wisconsin. Muir's father was a task master who demanded much from his family. Consequently, Muir and his brother would roam the countryside whenever the opportunity presented itself. His love of nature grew as his observational skills developed.

John Muir became an award winning inventor before enrolling in the University of Wisconsin. For specifics of his inventions, visit http://www.jmbt.org.uk/learn/fact sheets/inventor44.pdf

Although he did well academically at college, he did not earn a degree at that institution. He left after several years to travel the northern United States and Canada, taking odd jobs along the way.

John Muir—A hand carved walking stick creates the illusion of a mountain slope in this tribute to environmentalist John Muir. Lush natural materials provide texture and add dimension.

As a young man, Muir suffered a serious eye injury that changed the course of his life. About a month after the accident, he regained his sight and vowed to turn his eyes to the fields and woods. And so his wanderlust was born. He walked a thousand miles from the Midwest to the Gulf of Mexico. He then sailed to Cuba, onward through the Isthmus of Panama and up the Pacific Ocean to the West Coast, and ultimately reached San Francisco.

Although he spent years traveling around the world, Muir always thought of California as home. It was California's Sierra Nevada mountain range and the wilderness at Yosemite that won his heart. Muir would later write that these mountains were "the most divinely beautiful of all the mountain chains I have ever seen."

In 1874 he began his career as a writer. He retreated from the mountains and moved to Oakland, California, where he penned his *Studies in the Sierra* series. Several years later, he embarked on a trip to Alaska where he discovered Glacier Bay. In 1880, Muir married Louie Wanda Strentzel and went into partnership with his father-in-law on the family fruit ranch in Martinez, California.

Louie did not share her husband's thirst for nature, but she recognized his passion and permitted him the time necessary to pursue his adventures. A devoted husband and father, Muir wrote to his wife and daughters daily from the trail. He eagerly shared every detail of these journeys with his family.

Muir applied his interest in and love of plants to the specialized task of growing Bartlett pears and Tokay grapes. Although he amassed some personal wealth through this venture, he was increasingly discontented. Muir's passion for the preservation of the glorious wilderness was relentless and became his mission.

In 1892, John Muir and other supporters formed the Sierra Club "to make the mountains glad." Muir was the club's first president, an office he held until his death in 1914. This position provided the platform for educating a nation about the importance of preservation. Muir's words and deeds helped to inspire President Theodore Roosevelt's innovative conservation programs, including the first national monuments, established by presidential proclamation, and Yosemite National Park, voted by a congressional action.

Muir was honored by a stamp which was unveiled at the John Muir National Historic Site in Martinez, California, on January 7, 1998. Designed by Carl Herrman of Laguna Niguel, California, the tribute on the reverse side of the stamp reads:

> Often referred to as a father of National Parks,
> JOHN MUIR
> Was a naturalist who championed the wilderness and its
> preservation.

A second tribute occurred in January 2005 when California governor Arnold Schwarzenegger selected the John Muir–Yosemite design (crafted by artist Garrett Burke) for the state quarter. The executive director of the Sierra Club, Carl Pope, issued the following statement regarding this honor:

John Muir literally coined conservation as we know it and so it is particularly fitting that we have placed him on the California quarter. Muir's relationship with Yosemite reminds us of the powerful connections that people have to nature, and how beautiful places can inspire us to reach incredible heights. That was essentially Muir's dream when he founded the Sierra Club over a century ago.

Despite the fact that it has been almost a century since John Muir's death, it is generally acknowledged that his work is far from done. There remains spectacular coastline, cathedral forests, wild rivers and dazzling desert which still deserve to be preserved and protected for future generations.

CREDITS

Several years ago the American Library Association's annual meeting was held in San Francisco. While there my husband and I attended many informative sessions at the convention center. Later, we took advantage of some of the area attractions that this wonderful and energetic city has to offer.

Located north of the Golden Gate Bridge in posh Marin County, Muir Woods boasts the few remaining groves of virgin Coastal Redwoods in America. These redwoods are among the tallest (300 ft) and oldest (2,000 years) trees in existence. The Natural Trail at Muir Woods leads to the center of its cathedral-like grove. Many visitors have come away from this site feeling both spiritually uplifted and emotionally transformed.

After touring Muir Woods, I became curious about the man for whom it was named. Much has been written about America's most influential naturalist and conservationist, John Muir.

This display was the end result of the entire Muir experience.

ASSEMBLING THE DISPLAY

1. The quotation "The Mountains Are Calling Me, and I Must Go" conveys John Muir's dedication to the environment. The font type used was Arial black sized at 83. The phrase was enlarged and printed on cardstock then mounted on buff colored poster board. The background of the display case was black felt. Bright silk autumn leaves were positioned around Muir's large quote and sprinkled throughout the display.

The mountain scenes were calendar art and were mounted on buff poster board and hung in relief with long straight pins. Under the center photo was the quotation:

The clearest way into the Universe is through a forest wilderness.
—John Muir

The photographs were placed on the diagonal to represent the angle of a mountain. On the top right photo, this quotation was attached:

God has cared for these trees, saved them from drought, disease, avalanches, and a thousand tempests and floods. But he cannot save them from fools.
—John Muir

A hand carved walking stick by New York craftsman Joseph Scasny was positioned at a 45° angle and reinforced the angle of an incline.

2. On the top left was a biography of John Muir which was titled "A Journey from Yosemite to Love" and was taken from this Web site: http://www.ecotopia.org/ehi/muir/bio.html

Under that was this quote:

> As age comes on, one source of enjoyment after another is closed, but Nature's sources never fail. Like a generous host, she offers her brimming cups in endless variety, served in a grand hall, the sky its ceiling, the mountains its walls, decorated with glorious paintings and enlivened with bands of music ever playing.
>
> —John Muir

The items on the left were printed on cardstock and mounted on photos of Muir Woods taken by Dennis Phillips.

3. On the top right was a replica of the John Muir stamp. This image was easily found on a Google image search. Under that was a document that included information about the issuance of the stamp and some background facts about John Muir. This can be found if you visit www.nps.gov/jomu/stamp.htm

Next was this text, which appears on the reserve side of the stamp which is included in the introduction to the display: "Often referred to as a father of national parks, John Muir was a naturalist who championed the wilderness and its preservation."

All of these items were printed on cardstock and mounted on black and/or camel poster board.

There were many quotations by John Muir from which to choose. Excellent ones are available if you visit http://www.nps.gov/jomu/quotes.htm

4. The base of the display case was lined with pieces of firewood which were positioned so that books and artifacts could be inserted among them. Goldenrod flowering stems were placed on the left in a random fashion suggesting nature. On the right, the bottom stems of goldenrod were placed at varying heights among the logs. A vintage brass compass was tucked into the wood along with a pair of old binoculars.

The hand carved Muir Woods sign was surrounded by some rocks and river stones, twigs, pinecones and dried leaves. Finally, artificial moss was placed throughout the display, and several carved and silk birds were set atop the logs.

The books included in this display were *Discover America* by Charles Little, *John Muir: Life and Work* by Sally M. Miller and *Kindred and Related Spirits: The Letters of John Muir and Jeanne C. Carr* edited by Bonnie Johanna Grisel.

BIGGER AND BETTER

There are many other items that could be used to illustrate the life and work of this great American. His relationship with Jeanne C. Carr, a tremendous friend and supporter, could be further explored through the many letters they exchanged. Name it Dear Jeanne/Dear John.

Old hiking boots, a journal, a vintage hat, a period American flag, a lantern, and photos of western mountain wildlife are just some of the objects that could be incorporated into a larger display space.

FLOWERS IN BOOKS AND DRAWINGS

Flowers have spoken to me more than I can tell in written words. They are the hieroglyphics of angels, loved by all men for the beauty of the character, though few can decipher even fragments of their meaning.

—Lydia M. Child,
19th century American writer

Manhattan's Pierpont Morgan Library contains works spanning Western book production from the earliest printed matter to significant first editions of the twentieth century. Their holdings include medieval and Renaissance manuscripts portraying flowers and plants, both in herbals and in books of hours and breviaries, where they are often shown in decorative borders for the illuminations. Exquisite miniature painted flowers were artfully arranged on the page to complement the text or illustration. The tradition of the illuminated manuscript was to meld with that of the printed herbal in the seventeenth and eighteenth centuries, when flower painting was recognized as a true art form.

Books of hours, which originally served as personal prayer books, neatly divided the day into sections devoted to prayer or business. Later they were used by men and women living more secular lives. Owning a book of hours was regarded as a status symbol among bibliophiles. Despite losses over the years, thousands of these illuminated manuscripts have survived and remain highly desirable collectibles.

The evolution of flower painting in Europe parallels the development of the book itself. The earliest examples of flowers in art were found in 6th and 7th century copies of classical discourses on plants. The need for botanical illustration was particularly great in the scientific and medical communities because of the potential value for food and medicine. A floral portrait, however crudely drawn, can serve to identify a plant better than words. Early woodcuts of plants were the main source of illustration, and the floral pictures were hand-colored. Information that could not be passed along in person could be best conveyed with a detailed illustration. In the 1700s, the truly illustrated flower book was first developed. It was in the first half of the 19th century when flower books blossomed by the hundreds. The sentimental flower book became popular in France and later in Victorian England. Despite its superficial content, these books were frequently illustrated by notable illustrators. Artists, engravers and printers could now do full justice to the botanical image.

Floral imagery in literature is common and varied. Many authors and poets have chosen flowers with significant meaning to convey messages and suggest underlying

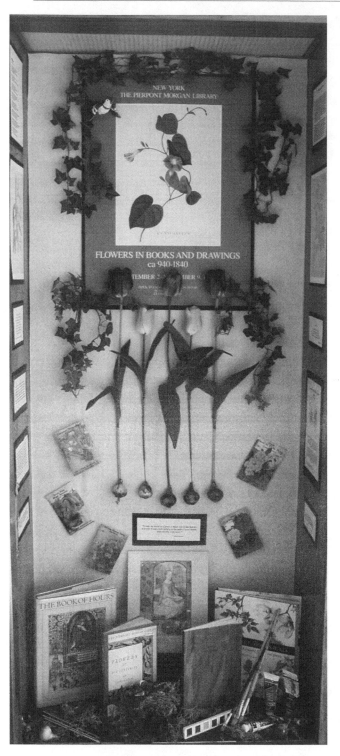

Flowers in Books and Drawings—Silk tulips with bulbs attached overlap the poster featuring an early botanical painting. Ivy adds warmth and texture.

tones. A dramatic example can be found in the works of William Shakespeare. Floral imagery is apparent in a number of his plays. In Ophelia's speech (*Hamlet*, act 4, scene 5), she distributes flowers to various characters. Rosemary symbolizes remembrance, rue means grace, pansies suggest luck, blue violets signify faithfulness while white violets represent modesty. Added associations can be made when the medicinal implications of these plants are considered.

A notable Flemish painter, Pierre Joseph Redoute, made significant contributions to the art of botanicals during the 18th and 19th centuries. Redoute was the official court artist for Queen Marie Antoinette, and later Empress Josephine. He was one of the most prolific botanical artists. His precise renderings have withstood the test of time. Should you want to learn more biographical information about Redoute, please visit http://www.globalgallery.com/artist.bio.asp?nm=pierre+joseph+redoute

Today there is a renaissance of floral art. Botanical gardens throughout the country offer a host of courses and the demand for botanical illustrations remains steady.

CREDITS

In the fall of 1980, the Pierpont Morgan Library mounted an exhibition titled Flowers in Books and Drawings. The accompanying text of the same name gave excellent background information for this display. Several years ago, during a renovation period, the museum offered free posters which had promoted this prior exhibit.

I have always loved botanicals, and have many of these prints hanging in my home. Researching this display was a labor of love and learning about the early artists who mastered this art of the natural world was very interesting.

Assembling the Display

1. The cream felt background proved a good contrast for the cerulean blue poster featuring the trailing plant convolvulus. The poster was mounted on black poster board and secured with straight pins.

Silk ivy was arranged to both frame the poster and provide some depth and texture. A dollar store bird is perched on the upper left portion of the ivy. Both of these were secured with straight pins.

The taller purple and shorter pink silk tulips were attached so that they overlapped the lower portion of the poster. Real spring bulbs were affixed to the bottom of the stems, which added some dimension to the display. These flowers were readily available at a local craft store in a variety of colors.

The antique reproduction seed packets can be found if you visit www.california history.net/8images/sedsB_lrg.jpg

These images were centered, then printed on off-white card stock. They were then folded to replicate a real seed packet. These envelopes were arranged in a manner that would complement and balance the tulips.

This quote by William Blake was printed on off-white cardstock, mounted on blue and black poster board and centered under the bulbs:

> To see the world in a grain of sand, and to see heaven in a wild flower, hold infinity in the palm of your hands, and eternity in an hour.

2. On the top left was a poem titled "Wildflower," by Stanley Plumly. This can be found if you visit http://www.poets.org/viewmedia.php/prmMID/15494

Below that was a botanical print from a calendar on that subject.

Under that was a poem by C. M. Badger titled "Who Does Not Love a Flower," which can be found at this site: http://web.naplesnews.com/ceandw/012006/feature_flowers.html Next is a passage taken from the introduction to the display which included the reference to floral imagery in literature. Under that was a paragraph, from the same introduction, about the need for botanical illustration. This information was found in *Flowers in Books and Drawings*, featured in the display.

Last was the following quote by artist Georgia O'Keefe:

> When you take a flower in your hand and really look at it, it's your world for the moment. I want to give that world to someone else. Most people in the city rush around so, they have no time to look at a flower. I want them to see it whether they want to or not.

A botanical image from a calendar was cut out and placed between the two bottom passages.

All items on the left were printed on off-white cardstock and mounted on blue and/or black poster board.

3. On the top right was a document titled "Flowers for Everyone." For information on the history of the art of botanicals, visit http://www.oppenheimereditions.com/00_botanicalhistory.asp

Below that was a botanical print from a calendar.

Under that was the following poem:

The Lily

The modest Rose puts forth a thorn,
The humble sheep a threat'ning horn:
While the Lily white shall in love delight,
Not a thorn nor a threat stain her beauty bright.

—William Blake

Next was a floral sketch of mums which can be found at this site: http://www.bersk.com/art/sketches/maybe_mums.jpg

A passage explaining the observation of flowers was found in *Beautiful Botanicals*, which is featured in the display. Within that was the following quotation:

You are looking, my dear Watson, but you do not observe.

—Sherlock Holmes

Next was a quotation from Williams Wordsworth:

So fair, so sweet, withal so sensitive. Would that the little flowers were born to live. Conscious of half the pleasure which they give.

All items on the right were printed on off-white cardstock and mounted on blue and/or black poster board.

4. On the base of the display case, a bird was placed in a nest filled with moss and elevated on a Styrofoam form covered with black fabric. Silk ivy surrounds the nest and camouflages the cube. Also displayed in this area was a tray of watercolor paints, several tubes of acrylic paints, three paint brushes, three drawing pencils, and assorted bulbs. Moss was interspersed throughout these items.

The books featured in the displayed were *Roses* by Diane Wakoski, *Flowers in Books and Drawings*, and *Flowers of Ten Centuries*, both by the Pierpont Morgan Library, *The Book of Hours* by John Harthan and *Beautiful Botanicals* by Bente S. King.

BIGGER AND BETTER

Other props which would expand this display could include some birdhouses, an artist's palette, gardening tools, the names of specific flowers and a glossary, an easel and a sketch pad with botanical drawings. Add some butterflies and a net and name it Flying Flowers.

Other information that could be included would be biographies of some of the notable botanical artists such as Pancrace Bessa and Maria Sibylla Merian.

Pastimes

Exposed

> When words become unclear, I shall focus with photographs. When images become inadequate, I shall be content with silence.
>
> —Ansel Adams

In 1840, a fuzzy image of a French barnyard marked the beginning of what would come to be known as the art of photography. Since that time, millions of would-be photographers have captured countless subjects as diverse as a birth of newborn baby and an unexpected terrorist attack that startled a nation and shook the world.

Photography officially dates back to 1839. It was in that year that the public became aware of a photographic process named the daguerreotype. Forty years later marked the advent of the Golden Age of Photography. The exploration of the American West was a major theme during these years. Major advancements in the technology of the camera and film took place during this time. The golden era continued until the 1920s. An excellent timeline tracing the history of photography can be found if you visit http://www.photo.net/history/timeline

The dry plate, rolled film and the hand held camera were some of the mechanical developments comprised by modern photography. During this period Alfred Stieglitz, Edward Steichen, Clarence White and others clearly demonstrated that photography was an art form. This medium of artistic expression was made available to the masses when George Eastman founded the Kodak company during the later part of the 19th century. A novelty no longer, photography could be viewed as both a professional undertaking and a rewarding pastime.

In reality, the camera creates magic. This pocket sized device can seize an instant that will endure a lifetime. Photography is an effective method of documenting social conditions, communicating information and traversing time and space. This method of creative expression knows no geographic boundaries, and speaks all languages.

The term photography originates from the Greek words *photos* (light) and *graphos* (drawing) and is usually defined as drawing with light. A photograph is made by using a camera to expose film to light. The camera collects light reflected by the subject in order to create a negative image on the film. The negative is then used in the darkroom to print a positive image on light sensitive paper.

Manipulating the angle of light can be a useful technique to add dramatic effects to an image. Back lighting may lead to a haloed effect surrounding the subject. Lighting overhead can produce shadows that give the image greater contrast.

Exposure is controlled by the aperture opening, which is a ring of overlapping leaves within the camera lens that can be adjusted to determine the amount of light which can pass through the camera to the film. Shutter speed also affects the exposure. The speed of the shutter determines how long the film is exposed to the amount of light let in by the aperture. It is important to ensure that an image is properly exposed. Underexposure can lead to an extremely light image with little or no contrast. Overexposure can result in a dark image with too much contrast. Correct exposure combined with an interesting subject should produce a quality photograph.

The digital camera has become the latest trend in photography. The images created by this device are made up of hundreds of thousands or millions of tiny squares called picture elements, or simply pixels. The computer separates the screen or printed page into a grid of pixels. It takes the values stored in the photograph and assigns a specific color and intensity to each pixel.

The clarity of a digital image, whether printed or displayed on a computer screen,

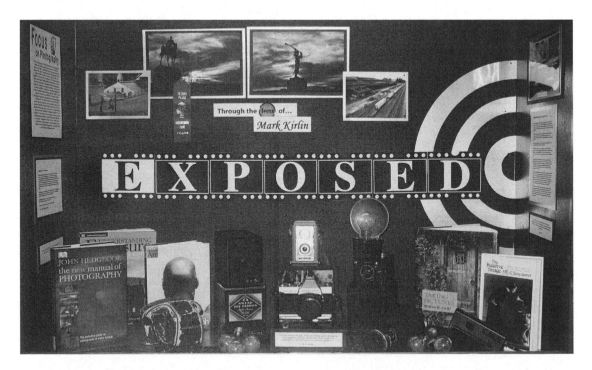

Exposed—A camera collection was the central focus of this display featuring the work of photographer Mark Kirlin. Colored lenses, bulbs and vintage cases provided a sense of authenticity.

depends in part on the number of pixels used to create the image or resolution. The more the pixels, the sharper the image.

Digital photographs are easy to distribute and share. They may be inserted into MS Word documents, attached to e-mails or posted to a Web site. Most digital cameras have small LCD screens that permit you to view the photos as you shoot them. Therefore, you know at a glance if you have captured the desired image.

For a comprehensive guide to using a digital camera, visit http://www.shortcourses. com/using/

Take a guided tour through the American Museum of Photography for a rich retrospective on the subject. They bill themselves as "A Museum Without Walls ... for an Art Without Boundaries." http://www.photographymuseum.com/main.html

CREDITS

The biggest challenge for the author in the process of creating this book was mastering the digital camera and the accompanying software. After signing the contract with the publisher, the phrase "I think I can, I know I can," became a haunting refrain. But, in truth, I have no eye for picture taking. All of my family members can testify to this fact. Each has missing body parts and severed limbs in the photos I've taken to chronicle their birth, growth and life achievements.

Lehigh Valley freelance photographer Mark Kirlin graciously agreed to provide some of his work for Exposed. Mark specializes in outdoor photography, and his photographs have been published in Lehigh Valley, Pennsylvania, newspapers since 2004. The award winning photo of Gettysburg was one of several that placed in recent photography competitions held at the Allentown Fair in Lehigh County, Pennsylvania.

ASSEMBLING THE DISPLAY

1. Concentric half circles were cut from silver poster board and pinned to the right side of the medium blue felt, which covered the background. This shape represented the chrome of the camera lens. The title Exposed was created using the font Movietime sized at 500 and printed on off-white cardstock. To obtain this font, visit http://www.1001freefonts.com

The Kirlin photographs were mounted on silver and black poster board, attached with pins and pulled forward. The phrase "Through the lens of" was created using Myriad Web Pro font sized at 59. Monotype Corsiva sized at 100 was used to create the photographer's name, which was printed on cardstock, attached with pins and pulled forward. An orange camera lens was pinned over the word "lens."

2. On the top left of the display "Focus on Photography" defined the terminology and provided a description of the process of creating a photograph. This document was created using Power Point. Clip art of a camera was inserted within the title area. This was printed on off-white cardstock and mounted on black poster board.

A biography of the photographer, Mark Kirlin, was printed on off-white cardstock and mounted on silver and black poster board.

The Ansel Adams quote introducing this chapter was next. It was printed and mounted as above.

3. On the top right was a black and white winter scene of a creek in Dedham, Massachusetts. This was double mounted on black and silver poster board.

The next document was titled "Composition and the Selective Eye." This was printed on off-white cardstock and mounted on silver poster board. For information on this topic, visit http://photographytips.com/page.cfm/6

A quote by Man Ray was printed on off-white cardstock and mounted on black poster board:

> Of course, there will always be those who look only at technique, who ask
> "how," while others of a more curious nature will ask "why." Personally, I have
> always preferred inspiration to information.
>
> —Man Ray

4. On the base of the display, vintage cameras were positioned on their original boxes or blocks of Plexiglas. An old camera case, flash bulbs, and various colored lenses were interspersed with a large zoom lens on the base of the case.

This quote was printed on off-white cardstock, mounted on black poster board and placed in the center front of the base:

> The ear tends to be lazy, craves the familiar and is shocked by the unexpected;
> the eye, on the other hand, tends to be impatient, craves the novel and is bored
> by repetition.
>
> —W. H. Auden

Above and behind the quote was a photograph of a hibiscus bloom taken by Laura Cole. This was mounted on black poster board.

Books featured in the display were *John Hedgecoe: The New Manual of Photography* by John Hedgecoe, *Understanding Exposure* by Bryan Peterson, *The Photograph* by Graham Clarke, *Taking Pictures* by William R. Zwikl, and *The Positive Image* by C. Jane Gover.

BIGGER AND BETTER

You may decide to narrow your display to specific topics such as Portraits, Sports Shots, Nature's Wonders, Seascapes, Scenes of Americana, Sight Seeing, Mothers and Children, Birthday Bashes, Sisters/Brothers/Siblings, Silhouettes, Till Death Us Do Part, Holidays, By the Beach, Capture the Landscape, Rally Round the Flag, Down the Open Road, etc.

Ask staff for photographic contributions and include books relevant to the theme. Chances are you have some skilled photographers in your workplace or community who would be happy to have their work on display.

Tracing the history of the development of the camera would be interesting and informative. Call it Daguerreotype to Digital. Consider creating a retrospective of the work of famous photographers, such as the ones quoted in Exposed.

SAILORS' TALES

The sail, the play of its pulse so like our own lives: so thin and yet so full of life, so noiseless when it labors hardest, so noisy and impatient when least effective.

—Henry David Thoreau

Covering over 140 million square miles, the sea represented an enormous challenge to the earliest of men. The need to confront this liquid barrier and master the art of sailing was apparent to those who were bent on exploration, trade, adventure and even war.

Although we typically think of the West as the "new frontier" in American history, overcoming the perils of a voyage across the Atlantic Ocean was the first challenge which the European immigrants had to face. Since overland travel was tedious and quite dangerous throughout the eighteenth century, many pioneers would bypass our nation's interior, and instead traverse the oceans to settle western shores.

The craft used for sailing have changed and evolved greatly over the centuries. The earliest vessels were simple rafts crafted from bundles of lightweight reeds which stayed afloat on the waves, permitting the sea's passage while keeping the passengers adrift. Subsequent materials, such as wood and canvas, have given way to the fiberglass, nylon and Dacron common on modern sailing craft.

Although true at one time, modern sailing is not just the means of transportation to a different destination. Rather, there is a state of mind and a transformation of heart that takes place within the sailor. Some of the mundane and routine technical preparations, such as hoisting the sails, can actually serve to change a mood and alter an outlook. Sailors are acutely in tune with their environment. They typically enjoy the beauty of nature and prefer working in the outdoors.

Weather is a challenge to seafaring folks. Too little wind is just as problematic as too much. The sea lies in wait for the innocent. Storms can terrorize and haunt the cocky or cavalier sailor who provokes its force. Add to this the possibility of fire, wreckage, misconduct and mayhem onboard a ship, and the scope of this menace becomes apparent. Waves can range from gentle swells providing a refreshing spritz, to towering walls of water intent on wreckage or termination. The lessons serious sailors need to glean are preparedness and respect for the power of nature.

Since the beginning of time, the sea has provided storytellers fodder for their craft. Sailors inevitably have appetites for reading about all things nautical. Whether it be a technical manual designed to increase skill and safety levels, true stories of the "perfect storm," or tall tales of adventures on the high seas, an audience can be found nestled in a berth, stretched out on a beach or perched atop a dock.

If you are looking to disappear into an exciting high-seas adventure, nautical novels will tell the tales. Some of the early maritime novels, such as *Treasure Island* by Robert Louis Stevenson, *Mutiny on the Bounty* by Charles Nordhoff and James

Norman Hall, *Kon Tiki* by Thor Heyerdahl and *Moby Dick* by Herman Melville, are true classics. Newer publications, such as *The Hunt for Red October* by Tom Clancy and *Captain Caution,* the final installment of the *Chronicles of Arundel* series by Kenneth Lewis Roberts, have found a wide audience.

For those interested in the unexplained and mysterious occurrences onboard ships, as well as collisions and disasters, look for *The Perfect Storm* by Sebastian Junger, or *Great Ship Disasters* by Kit and Carolyn Bonner. *The Lobster Chronicles: Life on a Very Small Island* was a worthwhile read authored by Linda Greenlaw, the captain of the sister ship of the *Andrea Gail* featured in Junger's best seller.

CREDITS

My children were born within sight of the Chesapeake Bay and grew up on the shores of the Severn River, near Annapolis, Maryland. Early on they developed a love and appreciation for the water. Our relocation to the state of Pennsylvania took us many miles from a sizeable body of water.

The large pond boat featured in this display sets the tone for Sailors' Tales. It sits aboard an antique trunk in the room in our home that is decorated in a nautical theme, reminiscent of our years by the bay.

Sailors' Tales—Pale blue sky meets the deep blue sea in this display on all things nautical. The title is spelled out in the international code of signals. A pond boat is surrounded by rocks and shells which are strewn throughout the books.

ASSEMBLING THE DISPLAY

1. The light blue felt background suggested the sky, and the white felt represented the clouds. Fiberfill was placed atop the clouds and tiny seagulls attached to it. The seagulls were found through a Google image search and darkened with a black permanent marker, then glued to the fiberfill. To the right of the boat ½" strips of red poster board were affixed to represent a large compass with east and westerly points that wrapped around the left and right sides of the display case, and vertically to suggest the north and south. The decorative font Caslon Initials, sized at 175, was used to create the directional points. These were printed on white cardstock and darkened with a black permanent marker.

Overlaying the compass is the title Sailors' Tales. The font selected was Antique sized at 300. These letters were printed on cardstock and traced onto black poster board. Nautical flags spelled out the title and were placed below the letters. The flags were 3½" square and cut out of red, white, yellow, black and white poster board. The flags were pinned to the background and pulled away from the corkboard for effect. To find the nautical flag alphabet, visit http://www.gma.org/Tidings/snailtale/flags.html

A 1" strip of green poster board was placed 12" above the base of the display case to represent the horizon. Below that, an 11" strip of blue poster board was attached to symbolize the ocean.

2. On the top left is the poem "Sea-Fever" by John Masefield. This can be found if you visit http://www.blupete.com/Literature/Poetry/MasefieldSeaFever.htm

Under that is an essay titled "On Sailing," which was composed after reading several introductions to technical books on sailing and collected short stories.

Both of these documents were printed on white cardstock with clip art inserted. They were mounted on red poster board.

3. On the top right was the following quote:

> It isn't that life ashore is distasteful to me. But life at sea is better.
> —Sir Francis Drake

Under that was a glossary of nautical terms that can be found if you visit http://www.marinewaypoints.com/learn/glossary/glossary.shtml

Below that was this quote:

> The pessimist complains about the wind; the optimist expects it to change; the realist adjusts the sails.
> —William A. Ward

Additional quotations on sailing can be found at this site: http://students.washington.edu/sailing/telltale/sum2003/Nautical %20Quotes.htm

All items on the right were printed on white cardstock with clip art inserted. They were mounted on blue and red poster board.

4. On the bottom left of the case was a 34" tall pond boat set at an angle. Sand, shells, rocks, starfish, and pebbles were strewn throughout the base of the case.

Books featured in the display were *The Greatest Sailing Stories Ever Told: Twenty-Seven Unforgettable Stories* edited by Christopher Caswell, *Sailing: A Celebration of the Sport and World's Best Places to Enjoy It* by Michael B. McPhee, *Billy Budd* by Herman Melville, *Desperate Voyage* by John Caldwell, *The Dictionary of Nautical Literacy* by Robert McKenna, *HMS Beagle: The Story of Darwin's Ship* by Keith S. Thompson, *Barrow's Boys: The Original Extreme Adventures* by Fergus Fleming, *Ahab's Wife: or, The Star Gazer* by Sena Jeter Naslund, *Great Ship Disasters* by Kit and Carolyn Bonner, *Atlantic High: A Celebration* by William F. Buckley, Jr., and *The Perfect Storm: A True Story of Men Against the Sea* by Sebastian Junger.

BIGGER AND BETTER

Your display could include the one of the palm trees originally created for Hot Nights, Cool Reads, which would create a tropical feel. You could add sand dollars on the base, shellfish and some beach toys. Or, you could hang a fishing net for a background, and attach shells to it. A life preserver, anchor, treasure chest, ship's wheel or bell, nautical rope or flags could be included. You could add some grasses and a heron, or seagulls perched on pilings crafted from three paper towel cylinders tied together.

Your display could feature passages from journals kept by crew members, such as *Our Ship's Diary "As Told by the Crew": USS Samuel N. Moore DD-747* by Bob Culver. Ship disasters could also be a theme, since there are numerous titles on that subject. *Lost at Sea: The Truth Behind Eight of History's Most Mysterious Ship Disasters* by A. A. Hoehling would be an excellent source to include. A model ship could anchor your display.

GAME, SET, MATCH!

It's difficult for most people to imagine the creative process in tennis. Seemingly it's just an athletic matter of hitting the ball consistently well within the boundaries of the court. That analysis is just as specious as thinking that the difficulty in portraying King Lear on stage is learning all the lines.

—Virginia Wade

In Great Britain it was known as real tennis, Australia referred to it as royal tennis, Americans coined the title court tennis, and the French named it *jeu de paume*, or the game of the palm. Call it what you may, this primitive form of indoor tennis was as much the result of evolution as invention. Court tennis, which is still played in countries such as England, France, Australia and the United States, was the precursor of the modern game of tennis.

Although there is some dispute regarding the origin of court tennis, it is generally agreed that the game started around the 11th or 12th century as handball enjoyed within the walls of monasteries in both Italy and France. Gradually, as the monks traveled

through Europe, the rules of the early game were changed to suit the whims of the competitors. The more enjoyable rules were adopted, and the less popular features eliminated. In fact, the game became so popular the reigning pope actually banned the monks from playing. However, by then the appeal of the game had spread well beyond the walls of the cloister—to the castle, where it ultimately became a favorite game among the royals.

In this early version of tennis, the ball was hit against courtyard walls. Initially propelled by the bare hand, the monks realized that they had more control of the ball when using a leather glove. Over time, the glove was supplemented with a wooden handle—and thus the invention of the first tennis racket.

Beginning in the 16th century and continuing until the mid 18th century, rackets of differing sizes and shapes were developed. The tennis racket as we know it today, but with a lopsided head, thick gut, and extended handle, was used until 1750. The size and shape of the racket enabled the player to retrieve balls out of the corners and to put a spin on the ball. The walls and floor of the facility were considered within bounds.

Over the years, the tennis ball has evolved as well. Some sources indicate that the balls were once carved from solid wood. Others claim that they were made from softer materials such as leather stuffed with bran, wool or hair. Despite the efforts to soften the balls,

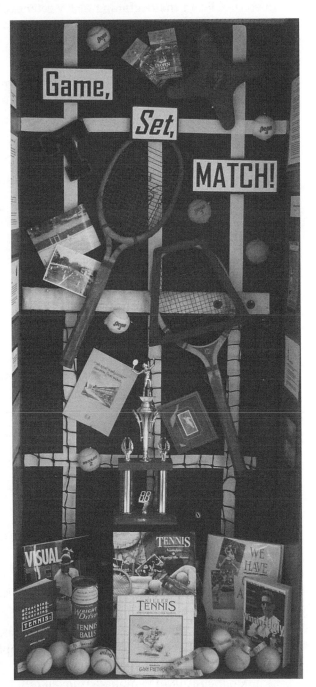

Game, Set, Match—Sports tape and netting transform the display case into a tennis court. Vintage rackets and tennis memorabilia provide a sense of the history of the sport.

they remained hard enough to cause serious injury, and were even known to result in death. The 18th century tennis ball contained strips of wool, string and a white cloth covering. From the beginning of lawn tennis in the 1870s, India rubber, made from a vulcanization process invented by Charles Goodyear in the 1850s, was used to manufacture lawn tennis balls.

According to some historians, the sport of tennis came to America in 1874 when New Yorker, Mary Outerbridge, returned from a Bermuda vacation full of passion for the game to which she had been recently introduced. In addition to this enthusiasm, Mary also brought with her all of the accoutrements needed for the game. The sport quickly gained popularity and made its way to key cities such as Boston, Newport, Philadelphia and New Orleans. The United States National Lawn Tennis Association was founded in 1881, and the first U.S. championship was played on the grass courts at Newport Casino in Rhode Island.

CREDITS

My husband, Dennis, is a player, teacher, coach and author of the sport of tennis. His total commitment and love of the game has permeated our family. Making a decision to do a display on this topic was rather simple, given the equipment, literature, and memorabilia present in our home.

Several items displayed in Game, Set, Match! represent milestones in my husband's tennis career. The letter "T" was earned during his years on the varsity team at Trenton High School in New Jersey. The photograph was taken of him during a USTA Junior Tennis Tournament in Princeton, New Jersey, in 1963. The trophy was won in 1988 when he coached the Cedar Crest College tennis team to the NAIA championships. His first book, *Teaching, Coaching, and Learning Tennis: An Annotated Bibliography*, was published the following year by Scarecrow Press, and is featured in the display.

ASSEMBLING THE DISPLAY

1. White adhesive sport tape was used to line the forest green felt to create the backdrop of a tennis court. A portion of nylon tennis netting was placed in the center and pinned to the background. The font for the title *Game, Set, Match!* was created using Agency FB bold, sized at 250. This was printed on white cardstock and glued to black poster board. The title was attached with straight pins and pulled forward for effect. At the top of the display was a vintage wooden tennis racket head protector which was nailed to the background and supported with pins. To the left of that were two ticket stubs to the 1997 U.S. Open.

A varsity tennis letter was attached under the title of this display. Next was a photo of the USTA Junior Tennis Tournament in 1963 in Princeton, New Jersey. Beneath that was a post card of an 1885 mixed doubles match held at the Staten Island Cricket and Tennis Club, photographed by Alice Austen.

The wooden tennis rackets were hung on nails and angled with pins. The racket on the right also had a wooden head protector attached. Tennis balls were cut in half and hung on pins, or reinforced with pins, as needed.

A pamphlet from the Royal Tennis Court at Hampton Court Palace was hung on the lower left. A vintage framed tobacco card of a German Davis Cup player, Dr. D. Penn, was attached on the lower right. Dr. Penn was depicted illustrating the correct position for a backhand drive. Both were attached with pins.

2. On the top left of the display was a quote by Pete Sampras:

> It's one-on-one out there, man. There ain't no hiding. I can't pass the ball.

Under that was a brief summary of tennis records and facts. This data can be obtained if you visit http://ourworld.cs.com/atomalt/

Next was information about the evolution of the tennis ball which was found at http://www.itftennis.com/technical/equipment/balls/history.asp

Under that was this quote by J. M. Barrie:

> What a polite game tennis is. The chief word in it seems to be "sorry" and admiration of each other's play crosses the net as frequently as the ball.

Other quotes on the game of tennis can be found at this site: http://ourworld.cs.com/atomalt

Last was an illustration of the proper dimension of a tennis court. This can be found if you visit http://www.easitennis.com/TennisCourt1.jpg

All of this information was printed on white cardstock and mounted on green and/or black poster board.

3. On the top right of the showcase was a list of tennis fundamentals found in *Tennis: Nostalgia [and] Playing the Game* by Christopher Dunkey. This can also be found online if you visit http://www.manteno5.org/webquest/UNwebquests/TennisFundamentals/tennis.htm

Under this was this quote:

> Love is nothing in tennis, but in life it is everything.
>
> —Author unknown

Next was a reproduction of *The Art of Tennis*. This can be found if you visit http://www.animationalley.com/images/re/30.jpg

Then came a passage titled "The Beginnings of Tennis," with clip art of a tennis player inserted on the upper left. For information on the origins of the game of tennis, visit http://www.cliffrichardtennis.org/planet_tennis/history.htm

Under that was a vintage photo of a group of tennis players from the turn of the century. You can find similar photos using the terms "vintage tennis photos" in an online image search.

All of this was printed on white cardstock and mounted on black and/or green poster board.

4. On the base of the display was a tennis trophy. Old tennis balls of varying colors

were placed at the front of the display case along with a vintage can of tennis balls. A tape measure (used to assure that the tennis net is always 36" at the center) was laced through the balls and over the center book.

Books featured in the display were *Tennis: Nostalgia [and] Playing the Game* by Christopher Dunkey, *Visual Tennis* by John Yandell, *Killer Tennis* by John R. Powers and Carol Kleiman, *Teaching, Coaching, and Learning Tennis: An Annotated Bibliography* by Dennis J. Phillips, *Winning Ugly* by Brad Gilbert, and *We Have Come a Long Way: The Story of Women's Tennis* by Billie Jean King.

BIGGER AND BETTER

Should your display space permit, you could feature a carrier of tennis balls, a selection of rackets from different periods, or articles of clothing such as a tennis visor, a sweatband, a tennis bracelet and sunglasses.

You could select a particular topic such as Tennis Venues, Ladies of the Game, Teaching Tips, Grand Slam Winners, Athletes of Color, or FUTURE STARS (of the circuit). You could install the display in conjunction with one of the Grand Slam events, such as Wimbledon or the U.S. Open. You could add touches of artificial strawberries, which are a popular staple on the menu at Wimbledon, the International Tennis Hall of Fame, in Newport, and other tennis events.

For information about the origin of the association between strawberries and tennis, visit http://www.wimbledonvisitor.com/tennis.html#strawberries

HOLD 'EM, FOLD 'EM

The poker player learns that sometimes both science and common sense are wrong; that the bumblebee can fly; perhaps, one should never trust an expert; that there are more things in heaven and earth than are dreamt by those with an academic bent.

—David Mamet, American playwright

The lure of poker is that it appears to be a game of sheer simplicity, yet the underlying layers are rich and subtle. Because the rules are fairly easy, beginners may think they have mastered the game after a relatively short period of time. Poker experts value this illusion of simplicity, which easily translates into a monetary gain for the veteran players. The newest players inevitably chalk up their losses to bad luck, as opposed to bad strategy. The loser's repeat return to the challenge of the gaming table is a sure bet!

There seems to be some dispute regarding the origin of the game of poker. It is likely that it is actually a derivative of many different games. Jonathan H. Green makes one of the oldest references to poker in the year 1834. He refers to it as the "cheating game," which was a popular diversion on the Mississippi riverboats. Green was unable to find it mentioned in the *American Hoyle, the Gentleman's Hand-Book of Games Containing All the Games Played in the United States*. Since his was the initial reference to the game, he assigned it the title *poker*.

Most of the dictionaries and historians of the game attribute the origin of the word *poker* to an 18th century French game called *poque*. The early French settlers living in New Orleans played that game, which involved both bluffing and betting. *Poque* was described as the first card game to use a deck consisting of spades, diamonds, clubs, and hearts. Some sources refer to the German game of *Pochspiel*, which includes an element of bluffing involving rapping on the table while saying "Ich Poche." There are those who think poker was a variation of the Hindu word *pukka*. Some see a correlation with the Chinese game of dominoes, and still others equate it to the Persian game referred to as *as nas*.

For more information regarding the history of the game of poker, visit http://www.pokerpages.com/poker info/history.htm or http://www.poker sourceonline.com/learn/history.asp

Poker is a term that encompasses hundreds of interrelated card games. There are the high games like Seven-Card Stud and Texas Hold 'Em, in which the highest hand in the showdown wins, and the low games, like Razz and Draw Lowball in which the player with the lowest hand wins. There are also high-low split games in which the winnings are divided between the best high-hand and the best low-hand. Among high, low, and high-low split games there are some, like Five-Card Draw, in which the

Hold 'Em, Fold 'Em—Cash in on the popularity of this card game. Poker chips, fake bills, and lots of playing cards morph the display case into a mini casino for a Texas Hold 'Em marathon.

hands are concealed, and those like Seven-Card Stud, in which some of the playing cards are visible to all players.

Texas Hold 'Em, better known as simply Hold 'Em, is far and away the most popular game of poker played in the world today. Learning the basics is easy, but the game is not without complexity, and there is a great deal of strategy involved. *Play Poker Like the Pros* by Phil Hellmuth, Jr., is an excellent source for learning all aspects of the game of Hold 'Em. The appendix contains a glossary of the colorful terms of the game such as *big blind*, *elephant*, *bubble*, *cowboys* and *mouse*. For an online glossary, visit http://conjelco.com/pokglossary.html

The psychology of poker is a critical aspect of the game. The savvy player thinks not only about what his opponents have, but about what they think he has, and about what they think he thinks they have. It is important to go through such analysis, especially against formidable players. The more skilled the player, the more difficult it will be to discern their strategy. These same thought processes can be costly against weak players, because they simply aren't capable of advanced level analysis.

The scoring of the game of poker can be a bit of a challenge. For information regarding this element of the game, visit http://www.compendia.co.uk/poker_scores. htm

Probability theory predicts that in the long run, every skilled player will hold the same amount of good, bad, and indifferent hands. That being said, the basic difference between the skilled and the unskilled player is that the former will have the patience to wait out a run of bad cards by placing cautious wagers. The latter will bet on all the indifferent, and some of the bad hands so recklessly, that by the time his luck turns, the possibility of recouping his losses is just about nil.

Good luck in developing the skills that will enhance your enjoyment of any of the variations of this game of cards!

CREDITS

It is hard to ignore the growing popularity of the game of poker. Cable television devotes many hours to gambling destinations and poker tournaments. Recent celebrity involvement has served to elevate the profile of the game.

Texas Hold 'Em, one of the simpler games of poker, is appealing to the novice. Our family and neighbors enjoy the challenge of the game of poker, especially over holidays and on those long winter nights. The newly acquired electronic version has provided many hours of entertainment for our family.

ASSEMBLING THE DISPLAY

1. A background of green felt was chosen to suggest a gaming tabletop. Pinned at the top center of the display was a casino sign which was created using WordArt. The font selected was Rockwell Extra Bold, sized at 250. The clip art diamond was inserted into a Word document, then transferred to Paint, where the colors were changed

to better blend with the hues used in the display. This was printed on white cardstock, then cut out and attached to the sides of the sign. This was then mounted on gold poster board, attached with pins, and pulled forward. A crown, located via a Google image search, was printed on white cardstock and enhanced with red magic marker, attached with pins and pulled forward.

Red patterned playing cards were fanned out and attached with pins around the casino sign. Gold confetti was glued in this area and throughout the arrangement. Red, yellow and white poker chips were attached with glue around the casino sign.

The map of the state of Texas was found on a Google image search. A grid was drawn to divide the map and make drawing it freehand, and to scale, a little easier. The map was drawn on red poster board and outlined with black permanent marker. Gold confetti was glued throughout most of the state. The title Hold 'Em, Fold 'Em was printed on white cardstock so that it could be cut and traced onto black poster board. The font chosen was Vanilla Whale sized at 320. To obtain this font, visit http://www.1001freefonts.com

The lettering was attached to a piece of white poster board that measured 15"h × 22"w. Imitation dollar bills, found through a Google image search, were printed on cardstock and fanned above the state of Texas. More playing cards were pinned to the right of the money.

Playing cards with the suits exposed were found through a Google image search, printed on cardstock, attached with pins, then pulled forward. Dollar signs were found and produced in the same manner, attached with pins and pulled forward throughout the lower half of the display. The sign "Poker Room," found via a Google image search, was printed on cardstock and flanked with imitation bills and confetti. Poker chips were glued throughout.

2. On the top left of the display was a synopsis of the game of Texas Hold 'Em. A border of black and red diamonds, found in MS Word clip art, was inserted at the bottom of the text.

For an introduction to this game of cards, visit http://www.texasholdem-poker.com/beginnersintro.php

Next was a document titled "Standard Five Card Scoring." An image of a playing card found in Word clip art inserted at the top. The scoring can be found in many of the books on this subject. To retrieve information on poker scoring online, visit http://www.munk.org/munkdotorg.php?p=poker&a=poker&game=rules

These two quotes were printed on white cardstock, mounted on red poster board, and hung above the information on scoring:

> Hold 'em—like life itself—has its defining moment. It's the flop. When you see the flop, you're looking at 71 percent of your hand, and the cost is only a single round of betting.
>
> —Lou Krieger

> Skill, courage and a little luck.
>
> —Well known poker phrase—anonymous

All items on the right were printed on cardstock and mounted on red poster board.

3. On the top right of the display was an overview of the History of Poker. For information, visit the previously mentioned history Web sites.

A red, black and gold poker graphic found in MS Word clip art was inserted at the bottom of this page. This was printed on white cardstock and mounted on red poster board.

Under that was a glossary of poker terms which was printed on white cardstock and mounted on red poster board. A playing card graphic was inserted at the top.

Above and below the glossary were several quotes. First was the quote introducing the display. Next was:

> Baseball is like a poker game. Nobody wants to quit when he's losing; nobody wants you to quit when you're ahead.
>
> —Jackie Robinson

The phrase "Place Your Bets" was created in MS Word, then transferred into Paint, where a gold background was chosen. The font selected was Gill Sans Ultra Bold sized at 72.

All items on the right were printed on cardstock and mounted on red poster board.

4. Styrofoam forms were placed at the base of the display to provide varying elevations. This was covered with green felt to represent a gaming table top. On the top of these forms, a was poker chip carrier filled with chips. Several cards were fanned and placed on either side of the carrier. Additional chips were strewn around the base. Ten cards were taped, then fanned and set on the level below.

Books featured in the display were *The Theory of Poker* by David Sklansky, *Play Poker Like the Pros* by Phil Hellmuth, Jr., *Doyle Brunson's Super System : A Course in Power Poker* by Doyle Brunson, *What Are the Odds: Chance in Everyday Life* by Mike Orkin, *Foster's Complete Hoyle: The Encyclopedia of All Indoor Games* by R. F. Foster, and *Magic Tricks, Card Shuffling and the Computer Memories* by Brent Morris.

Poker chips and additional imitation dollar bills were placed among the books.

BIGGER AND BETTER

Should space permit, your display area could include other dimensions of a casino, such as Black Jack, the roulette wheel, craps, or video poker games! If a poker table-top would fit in the space, you could use it as a backdrop. Your casino could be set in an exotic or tropical setting, or perhaps onboard a ship. You could use Las Vegas as the site and call it Viva Las Vegas! Use Atlantic City as a backdrop for your display on the gaming world and title the display Boardwalk & Black Jack.

The Mind

DREAMS

Dream no small dreams for they have no power to move the hearts of men.
—Goethe

What are dreams? There is no simple answer to that question. Because dreams are a universal human experience, men have pondered the subject throughout the ages. Dreams are a source of guidance, optimism, foretelling, and resolution. They have no boundaries with respect to age, class, nationality, faith or ethnicity.

Since approximately one-third of our lives are spent sleeping, it follows that a good percentage of that time is devoted to the process of dreaming.

Sleep and dreams are activities of our everyday life, yet they remain enigmas. Each generation has attempted to analyze the cause and decipher the meaning of this activity of the mind that occurs during slumber.

Throughout the past centuries, dreams were defined as "states of consciousness occurring during sleep" (Robinson 7). Historically, dreams were awarded much more significance and played a more vital role in human affairs. Ancient texts contain numerous accounts of the importance of dreams in daily life. Dreams provided contact with another world, or form of existence, vastly different from that with which they were familiar during waking hours.

Dreams were regarded as supernatural events that could sometimes predict future scenarios. Dream events made men aware of their connection to the paranormal and even their destiny during their lifetimes as well as the world beyond.

Dreams were the inspiration for many in the medieval period. Both Saint Francis of Assisi and Saint Dominic were inspired to vocations as a result of these nocturnal revelations. Later, during the 19th century, dreams gained an acceptance in the West and were the subject of great intellectual attention among scholars, mystics and poets.

The variety of dream experiences, both tantalizing and terrifying, generate speculation and analysis. The cast of characters encountered in dreams could include those who had passed on to another life, beings who possessed superhuman powers, and creatures who had morphed into monstrous forms. Many dream events could never occur in reality, and serve to challenge the mind to superhuman insights.

Every human emotion and event can be reflected in dreams. Dreams may be uplifting or maudlin, frightening or comforting, replete with love or loathing. They may

Dreams—A peach colored moon is perched in a starlit sky. The stainless steel clock ticks the minutes of dreams into hours of sleep. Fiberfill clouds cover the display base.

have either religious overtones or sacrilegious tendencies. Dreams inspire, depress, amuse and shock. In general, these nighttime fantasies far exceed the realities of our everyday existence.

Sigmund Freud published his influential study *The Interpretation of Dreams* in 1911. Almost one hundred years later, we are still attempting to unlock the mysteries associated with the dream process and to understand its meaning. According to Freud, all of our dreams are linked to sexuality. Since he wrote during the Victorian era, when talk of sexual matters was considered taboo, his revelations helped to free the citizens of the Western world from those repressive mores.

However, Freud's narrow view of the power of sex has been the subject of much speculation and criticism. It is now thought by some researchers that sex dreams may not actually have anything at all to do with sex.

Many of the books on the subject of dreams included glossaries of terms relevant to their interpretations. *The Everything Dreams Book* by Trish and Rob MacGregor includes a comprehensive dream symbol dictionary which is quite helpful for the layman interested in becoming more aware of the significance of themes and symbolism experienced in these events.

CREDITS

The design of the book cover for *Einstein's Dreams* by Alan Lightman, cover art by Marjorie Anderson, inspired this display. The clean lines and simplicity of design were a good basis which could be enhanced by shadowed lettering and the addition of some stars. The polyester fiberfill would serve to suggest clouds and also soften the starkness of the moon within the universe.

There were countless sites on the Internet covering the subject of sleep and dreams. One of the most helpful for this display was http://science.howstuffworks.com/sleep.htm/printable

ASSEMBLING THE DISPLAY

1. The black felt background suggests the dark and vast universe. The quarter oval section of peach poster board represents the moon present during our sleeping hours. Silver stars of varying sizes were found through MS Word clip art, sized and printed on cardstock. The stars were then traced on both silver and black poster board and affixed to the moon and felt. The font for *Dreams* was Perpetua Titlng MT sized at 500. The word was printed on cardstock and then traced on silver and black poster board. The modern stainless steel clock hangs on the top left and represents the time spent dreaming.

2. On the top left was the quote introducing the display. Next was a paragraph about the symbolism of horoscopes in dreams found in *The Everything Dreams Book* by Trish and Rob MacGregor. Clip art of a fortune teller was inserted into that document.

Under that was the following quote:

> Our truest life is when we are in dreams awake.
>
> —Henry David Thoreau

For more quotations on dreams visit http://www.bellaonline.com/articles/art10883.asp

Beneath that was a chart showing the brain activity during sleep. This was readily found through an online image search.

Both of the remaining documents on creativity and dreams were taken from information found at this site: http://www.apa.org/monitor/nov03/canvas.html

Items on the left were printed on white cardstock and mounted on peach and/or black poster board.

3. On the top right of the display was a image of the god Hypnos found through a Google image search. The text about this Greek god was found at http://messagenet.com/myths/bios/hypnos.html

Under that was a selected glossary of terms found in *The Everything Dreams Book*. A glossary can be found online if you visit http://www.dreammoods.com/reference/glossary.htm

Under that was this quote:

> Myths are public dreams, dreams are private myths.
>
> —Joseph Campbell

At the bottom right was an essay, "Man and Dreams" compiled from material found at http://www.urday.com/dreams4.html

Items on the right were printed and mounted as those on the left.

4. At the base of the display Styrofoam blocks were positioned to provide different elevations for the books. Fiberfill was placed in and around the books to suggest clouds. The letter "Z" was printed at different font sizes on cardstock and placed atop the clouds.

Books featured in the display were *Dreamscape: Voyage in an Alternate Reality* by Bruce A. Vance, *The Dreamer's Dictionary* by Lady Stearn Robinson and Tom Corbett, *The Scientific Study of Dreams* by William G. Domhoff, *The Complete Dream Book* by Gillian Holloway, *13 Dreams Freud Never Had* by Allan S. Hobson, and *Private Myths: Dreams and Dreaming* by Anthony Stevens.

BIGGER AND BETTER

Your design might include a pillow and headboard, a single large closed eye, a large replica of the Greek god Hypnos, or a doorway surrounded by butterflies and unicorns with a blue sky background with fiberfill clouds.

You might decide to focus on the experts in the field, for example Jung or Freud, or perhaps the concept of the interpretation of dreams. If you decide to do a display on dream interpretation, why not name it About Last Night... There are also many books dealing with trauma and dreams, nightmares, and the brain and dreams. Any of these could be made into an interesting and colorful display.

MOOD AND MADNESS

> I honestly believe that as a result of it I have felt more things, more deeply;
> had more experiences, more intensely; loved more, and have been more loved
> ... laughed more often for having cried more often; appreciated more the
> springs, for all the winters.
>
> —Kay Redfield Jamison,
> from *Touched with Fire: Manic Depressive Illness
> and the Artistic Temperament*

That manic and depressive symptoms are components of a single disorder was suspected by Hippocrates (460–377 BC) and has remained a consistent assertion within the psychiatric community. Formerly termed manic-depressive psychosis, bipolar disorder is diagnosed whenever manic features are present, regardless of the observance of depressive features.

Bipolar disorder is a brain anomaly that causes unusual shifts in a person's temperament, energy level, and basic ability to function. The symptoms of bipolar disorder are severe. Although all people experience normal ups and downs, those diagnosed with this condition frequently experience damaged relationships, poor job or school performance, and even contemplate thoughts of suicide. However, on the plus side, bipolar disorder does respond to treatment, and people with this illness can expect to lead full and productive lives.

About 5.7 million American adults have bipolar disorder. The onset typically occurs in late adolescence or early adulthood. However, there are case studies indicating that some people present their first symptoms during childhood. Still others develop this disorder at a much later stage of life.

Bipolar disorder is often not recognized as an illness, and people may be afflicted for years before a correct diagnosis is made and treatment begun. The disorder is a long-term illness, much like heart disease or diabetes, that must be carefully controlled throughout a person's life. Symptoms of the manic dimension of bipolar disorder are incoherent, rapid or disjointed thinking; impaired judgment; ever-changing plans and ideas; constant elation or euphoria; inappropriate optimism; grandiose delusions; sleeplessness; early waking; promiscuous behavior; and excess spending.

Depression manifests itself in these behaviors: feelings of worthlessness; loss of energy and motivation; inattention to personal cleanliness; pessimism; loss of concentration; self-doubt or self-blame; isolation; sleeplessness; inability to get out of bed until late morning or early afternoon; and thoughts of suicide.

Studies have tried to establish

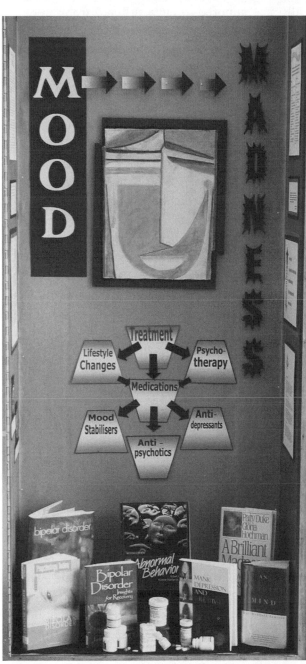

Mood and Madness—Bipolar disorder is explored in this display. The contrasting title fonts represents the manic and depressive elements inherent in this medical condition.

a connection between artistic ingenuity and mood disorders or other forms of psychosis. Many well known artists, writers and musicians suffered from some form of mental illness. Sadly, many of their lives ended in acts of suicide. Writers Sylvia Plath, Virginia Woolf, and Ernest Hemingway all were rumored to have suffered from bipolar disorder. William Blake, Samuel Taylor Coleridge, Percy Bysshe Shelley, and Lord Byron were just some of the poets who exhibited symptoms of this illness throughout their lives. Musicians afflicted ranged from Cole Porter, Charlie Parker and Irving Berlin to Nirvana's Kurt Cobain. Artists known to have suffered from bipolar disorder are Vincent Van Gogh, Frida Kahlo and Georgia O'Keeffe. Treatment of major depressive illness in artists has been a difficult task. There is a natural concern that creativity and the disorder are so interrelated that treatment might have a negative impact on the artists' unique talent and ability to continue to create.

Kay Redfield Jamison has written extensively on this topic. She is the co-author of the standard medical text on mood disorders, and has authored or co-authored numerous other books including *Touched with Fire: Manic-Depressive Illness and the Artistic Temperament, Unquiet Mind: A Memoir of Moods and Madness, Night Falls Fast: Understanding Suicide.* Dr. Jamison is considered an expert psychiatrist on mood disorders and has presented more than one hundred scientific papers about that topic, as well as creativity and psychopharmacology. She is currently on the faculty of Johns Hopkins University School of Medicine and is an honorary professor of English at the University of St. Andrews in Scotland.

For more information about bipolar disorder, visit this site: http://www.mdf.org.uk

There are many facets to bipolar disorder. The highs experienced by those affected are incredibly enticing. Their thoughts and ideas flow. Everything fascinates. It may be short lived, however, when feelings of emptiness and self-loathing appear and depression envelops. For a host of provocative personal accounts of those dealing with bipolar disorder, visit http://talentdevelop.com/bipolar.html

CREDITS

Although this illness has often been associated with highly creative or even brilliant people, many of those affected are ordinary people dealing with an extraordinary range of emotional extremes. Many of us have been personally touched by friends or family diagnosed with bipolar disorder. I have seen the destruction that this disorder causes within families, and the constant struggle to regulate medications and maintain normalcy within the family.

It has been encouraging to note the amount of recent research that has been devoted to this disorder, and the strides that have been made with various treatments and associated prescriptive drugs.

ASSEMBLING THE DISPLAY

1. The font Callistroke was used to create *Mood,* while Aftermath BRK was selected for the word *Madness. Mood* was printed on white cardstock and the font sized

at 370. It was mounted on black poster board with pins and pulled forward. *Madness* was printed on white cardstock and traced onto black poster board. It was attached with pins and pulled forward. Both of these fonts are available at this site and may be downloaded at no cost: http://www.1001freefonts.com

The arrows connecting the title were found through a Mamma image search and printed on white card stock. To retrieve this image, visit http://www.zb.edu.sh.cn/wuli-kg/g2/g2-15a/dzjc/jctp/images/arrow.jpg

The inspiration for the *Mood and Madness* graphic was found through an online image search. This graphic was created using chalks on white poster board. The image was framed in black poster board, attached with pins to a gray felt background, and pulled forward.

Below that was a diagram for the treatment of bipolar disorder which was created using PowerPoint. This was printed on white cardstock. The idea was adapted from a diagram found at this Web site: http://www.psychiatric-disorders.com/bipolar/treatment/php

2. On the top left of the display was information titled "Linking Creativity and Bipolar Disorder," which was printed on white cardstock and attached to silver poster board. Visit this site for relevant text: http://www.lorenbennett.org/creativity.htm#MADNESS

Below that was the quote by Kay Redfield Jamison which introduced this chapter. This was printed on white cardstock and mounted on black poster board.

Next came "Bipolar Disorder Revealed." This information was printed on white cardstock and double mounted on silver and black poster board. A graphic of the faces of comedy and tragedy, showing extreme moods, was found through a Google image search, and inserted at the top of the document. For information relevant to this topic, visit http://www.nimh.gov/publicat/bipolar.cfm

Images of a normal brain scan, and one of a person in a manic stage, were printed on white cardstock, cut and attached to black poster board. Comments on these scans were created, printed and attached in the same manner as the images. For all of this information, visit http://braininspect.com/spect_lib/spid.php?cat=bipolar&lang=EN&theme=MOK

3. On the top right was information titled "Symptoms of Bipolar Disorder." This was created in PowerPoint, printed on white cardstock and mounted on black poster board. This information can be found if you visit http://www.mdf.org.uk/?o=1617

Under that, a quote was printed on white cardstock and double mounted on silver and black poster board:

> Then Big Harry said to me, "You know, Bobby, I think old Suicides was crazy."
> He was right, too, because when his family sent for him the man who came
> explained to Commissioner old Suicides had suffered from a thing called
> Mechanic's Depressive. You never had that, did you, Roger?
> —Ernest Hemingway,
> *Islands in the Sun*

A graphic of a continuum showing the extremes between severe mania and severe depression was copied into PowerPoint, enlarged, printed on cardstock and double mounted on black and silver poster board and attached next. This graphic was available at the same Web site as "Bipolar Disorder Revealed" (above).

Lastly, information on the types of medications used to treat bipolar disorders was created using information found at this Web site: http://www.psychiatric-disorders.com/bipolar/treatment.php

Clip art of a medicine bottle and pills was inserted into the top of the document. This was printed on white cardstock and mounted on black poster board.

4. On the base of the display medicine bottles were arranged along with some pills. Styrofoam was used to create different elevations for the books on display.

Books featured in the display were *Taming Bipolar Disorder* by Lori Oliwenstein, *An Unquiet Mind: A Memoir of Moods and Madness* by Kay Redfield Jamison, *Manic Depression and Creativity* by D. Jablow Hershman and Julian Lieb, M.D., *Bipolar Disorder: A Cognitive Therapy Approach* by Cory F. Newman, et al., *Bipolar Disorder: Insights for Recovery* by Jane Mountain, M.D., *Case Studies in Abnormal Behavior* by Robert G. Meyer and Yvonne Hardaway Osborne and *A Brilliant Madness: Living with Manic Depressive Illness* by Patty Duke and Gloria Hochman.

BIGGER AND BETTER

You could feature famous literary figures who suffered from bipolar disorder. Call it Literary Madness. If you focus on musicians that have been afflicted, you could title your display Music Mania or Moods & Music. Artists such as Frida Kahlo, Vincent Van Gogh and Georgia O'Keeffe could be central figures in your display titled Artists and Angst.

You may choose to focus on other mental disorders such as schizophrenia, Munchausen syndrome or Munchausen syndrome by proxy, Anxiety Disorder, or Narcissistic Disorder for your display.

For information about an entire range of mental disorders, visit http://www.mic.ki.se/Diseases/F03.html

DYING TO BE THIN

Developing an eating disorder is no easy task. Becoming an anorexic, for example, requires months, even years, of obsessive, destructive tunnel vision. Anorexia demands absolute, single-minded dedication. It's exhausting—and it can be extraordinarily lonely.

—Jessica Reaves

Eating disorders produce the highest mortality rate of any mental illness. Once unrecognized by medical professionals, serious eating disorders affect over eight million Americans. Statistics indicate that 86 percent of victims report the onset of their illness by age twenty. Although the great majority of people suffering from body dysmorphic disorders are women, in general there are no boundaries with respect to gender, age or ethnicity.

Anorexia nervosa, bulimia nervosa, binge eating and related illnesses are complicated. There are varying theories regarding their cause. Some of the proposals include early trauma, low self-esteem, sexual abuse, body image distortion, impact of the media, striving to be perfect, family dysfunction and inability to cope. The physical consequences can involve a broad range of medical conditions including heart or kidney failure, osteoporosis, gastrointestinal problems, enamel erosion, and even death.

A diagnosis of anorexia nervosa is made when the patient is unable to obtain a body weight at or above a minimally normal level for height and weight. Usually the person has an intense fear of gaining weight, even though they are underweight. Patients suffering from anorexia are often disturbed by the way in which they experience their body weight or shape. As a result, their self-evaluation is measured primarily by their own perception of these physical characteristics.

Bulimia nervosa includes recurrent episodes of binge eating. A bulimic's out-of-control eating results in inappropriate compensatory behavior in order to prevent weight gain. These actions might include vomiting, misuse of laxatives, diuretics, enemas, fasting or excessive exercise. As with anorexics, a bulimic's self-evaluation is unduly influenced by body shape and weight.

Dying to Be Thin—The anorexic in the forefront sees a larger form of herself in the reflection in the mirror. Junk food and wrappers cover the base of the display.

Binge eating disorder is characterized by consuming, in a discreet period of time, an amount of food that is larger than most people would eat during a similar period of time, and under similar circumstances. It is sometimes referred to as compulsive overeating. The patient senses a lack of control over eating during the episode. Those suffering from binge eating disorder eat vast quantities of food while alone and report feelings of disgust following the event. Binge eating is diagnosed when this behavior occurs at least two days a week for a period of six months.

For information related to all of these disorders, visit http://www.edreferral.com/binge_eating_disorder.htm

Time is of the essence with respect to addressing the matter of diagnosing and treating eating disorders. The longer these harmful eating behaviors prevail, the more difficult it is to empower the patient to opt for reform. Ultimately, it must be the decision of the patient to alter the course of their eating, if there is to be significant, positive and enduring life change.

The cure rate for people with eating disorders varies from a low of 50 percent to a high of 75 percent, depending on the source. Partial recovery numbers are higher still. Comprehensive treatment centers, staffed by knowledgeable health professionals, are now available across the country. These experts are committed to providing proper diagnosis and ongoing treatment to the victims of a host of eating disorders.

The treatment, after all, is a matter of life and death.

CREDITS

As a staff member at a women's college for the past two decades, I have seen my fair share of anorexic and bulimic students within the community. These disorders have both troubled and puzzled me. How can vital, intelligent and beautiful women have such distorted self-images? What drives them to this point of self-destruction?

Researching the information included in the text for the display Dying to Be Thin has been an enlightening experience. Discovering that over 400 pro-anorexia web sites are available through the Internet was shocking! These sites attempt to provide emotional support and helpful tips to the new breed of emerging anorexics. Titillating images of waif thin starlets are interspersed among words of encouragement that challenge fragile readers to accept the dare, and achieve the quest for the "perfect body."

For information about anorexia going high tech, visit http://www.time.com/time/health/article/0,8599,169660,00.html

For other valuable sites housing information about this mental illness, visit http://www.nami.org/ http://www.something-fishy.org/whatarethey/anorexia.php

ASSEMBLING THE DISPLAY

1. The font Forte, sized at 375, was used to create the words *Dying to Be*. The word *thin* was created using Agency FB, sized at 450. The title was printed on cardstock in

black ink and traced onto cranberry poster board. Both color letters were aligned to create a shadow effect and pinned to the medium gray felt background, so that the letters became more prominent. The image of the anorexic girl in the mirror was found through an online image search. This interpretation was drawn freehand since the lines were quite simple. Cranberry, pink, tan, and ecru poster board was used to create the figures. Facial and body details were added with colored pencils, chalks and fine line markers. Silver poster board was used to create the mirror effect with black poster board cut to serve as a frame.

2. On the top left of the display was a diary entry written by a recovering anorexic found in the book *Hunger Pains.* Under that was information regarding the distorted perception people have who are dealing with anorexia and bulimia. An image of food with the caption "Is Food a Problem?" was found through an online image search, saved into a photo file, and inserted into the top of the document. Below that was a quote by a recovering bulimic named Barbara:

> I remember thinking, hey, other people lose weight this way and they lead good lives, like actresses and dancers and athletes. I figured if they can do it and look that good, so could I. Now I know that you don't hear the whole story when people put a good front on for the camera. The real story stays the way it was for me: behind closed doors. Until someone smart enough and strong enough helps you discover that you're killing yourself [Sacker 26].

All of these items were printed on white cardstock, mounted on cranberry and/or black poster board and affixed to the display case with double-sided tape.

3. The quote introducing this display was hung on the top right of the case. Below that were tips for women struggling with anorexia, which were available at this site: http://www.kzoo.edu/counsel/recovery.htm

The final document, "Overcoming barriers to treatment: the critical first steps to success," was compiled from information found in the book *Broken Mirror* (Phillips 206–210).

These were printed, mounted and hung as above.

4. The base of the unit was covered in black poster board. Blocks of Styrofoam were draped with black fabric and stacked to the right to give elevation and balance to the design. A basket of pretzels was set at an angle and taped to a small block of Styrofoam. A box of popcorn and an empty beer bottle were placed behind. A pink box of cookies was set to the right. Popcorn, pretzels, cookies and peppermints were strewn throughout the books and around the pretzel arrangement. Two empty soda cans were placed on their sides and taped together. Junk food wrappers were strewn throughout. Images of donuts, a hamburger, French fries, and cookies were found through a Goggle search and printed on cardstock and interspersed among the snack foods.

Books featured in the display were *The Broken Mirror: Understanding and Treating Body Dysmorphic Disorder* by Katherine A. Phillips, M.D., *Binge No More: Your Guide to Overcoming Disordered Eating* by Joyce D. Nash, Ph.D., *Wasted: A Memoir of Anorexia and Bulimia* by Marya Hornbacher, *Slim to None: A Journey Through the*

Wasteland of Anorexia Treatment by Jennifer Hendricks and Gordon Hendricks, *The Eating Disorder Sourcebook: A Comprehensive Guide to the Causes, Treatments, and Prevention of Eating Disorders* by Carolyn Costin, *Second Star to the Right* by Deborah Hautzig, *The Other America: Teens with Eating Disorder* by Gail B. Stewart, *Surviving an Eating Disorder: Strategies for Family and Friends* by Michele Siegel, Ph.D., and Margot Weinshel, MSW, *Stick Figure: A Diary of My Former Self* by Lori Gotlieb and *Hunger Pains: The Modern Woman's Tragic Quest for Thinness* by Mary Pipher, Ph.D.

BIGGER AND BETTER

If you are expanding the current display, include salt dough baked goods. Many candles are formed in the shape of food products and could be incorporated into the arrangement.

Your display on anorexia could be built around a bathroom scale. Place it upright, with bony or slippered feet attached, and have the weight read 100 lbs. You could hang a shower curtain for color and texture to create the look of a bathroom. Add a tape measure as well.

On the flip side of anorexia is obesity, which is also a huge and growing problem for our society. It is now recognized that obesity is a serious, chronic disease. The suggestions in the above paragraph would also work for a display on that subject. There are vast numbers of current books available on the subject of obesity. Obviously, this would be a relevant topic for your library staff and patrons.

ON SEEING

> The question is not what you look at, but what you see.
> —Henry David Thoreau

At first, it would seem that nothing could be easier than simply seeing. We merely turn our head and direct our eyes where we want them to go, and take in whatever there is to see. The world surrounds us, everything is visible. We view landscapes and people and buildings, etc. Science permits us to peer into distant galaxies and observe newly discovered viruses. We can even see into the workings of our own bodies! Seeing is rational. Our eyes obey our brain's commands.

However, those beliefs are not really true. The reality is that seeing is inconsistent and irrational, and not at all dependable. Seeing is arbitrary. It is intertwined in the unconscious. Our eyes roam at will and then falsely reassure us that they have only been where directed. No matter how intense our focus, we can see but a fraction.

In his comprehensive book *The Object Stares Back: On the Nature of Seeing*, James Elkins writes:

Seeing is like hunting and like dreaming, and even like falling in love. It is entangled in the passions—jealousy, violence, possessiveness; and it is soaked in affect—in pleasure and displeasure, and in pain. Ultimately, seeing alters the thing that is seen and transforms the seer. Seeing is metamorphosis, not mechanism [Elkins 11].

There are various aspects to how we look and what we see. But they all result in images that affect subsequent thinking. Sometimes, the simplest words and actions are the most challenging to interpret. The word *see* is chief among those words. Its meanings are many and varied, but at the very core the word is an awareness through sight.

Seeing cannot ensure understanding and can be perceived as strictly an instinctive function. However, essential perceptions are the result of purposeful looking.

Seeing establishes our place in the world. The correlation between that which we see and that which we know is unclear. An example is given in John Berger's *Ways of Seeing*:

> Each evening we *see* the sun set. We *know* that the earth is turning away from it. Yet the knowledge, the explanation, never quite fits the sight [Berger 8].

In Malcolm Godwin's *Who Are You?: 101 Ways of Seeing Yourself,* the differences experienced by the male and female with regard to color and peripheral vision are explored. It is interesting to note that the female sees a wider spectrum of colors and is better at viewing close up. This visual information is shared by both hemispheres of the brain in females. The male, however, discerns a narrower spectrum of colors. Links betweens hemispheres in the male brain are 30 percent fewer than in the female. The female has a wider peripheral and broader close-up vision, as well as a keener sense of hearing. The male has a tunnel vision which permits better distance viewing, but his hearing is not as acute.

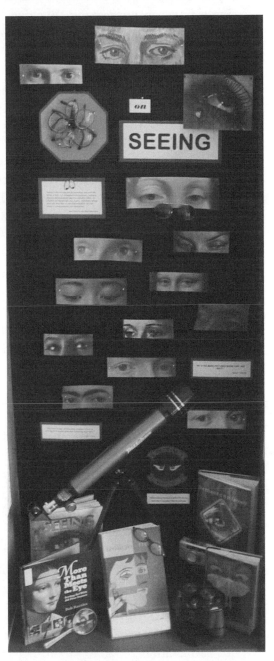

On Seeing—In addition to the many sets of eyes featured in the display, instruments used for seeing were also included. Binoculars, a telescope, a magnifying glass and eyeglasses provided some dimension.

In *Seeing What I Like and Liking What I See* by Charles Colbert, the author discusses the interpretation of photographs as one aspect of seeing. Every photograph captures a specific segment of time, place and life. This image can be compared to a single frame in filmmaking. Viewing these individual photographs, taken over various periods of time, allows us to make some predictions about activity and behavior that a single image would not reveal.

The 2005 best-selling book *Blink: The Power of Thinking Without Thinking*, by Malcolm Gladwell, offered some interesting perspectives on making quick judgments in the first two seconds of looking—the decisive glance that knows in an instant.

CREDITS

The inspiration for this display came from a March 2005 visit to the Jersey City Museum. It is located in the New Jersey's historic Von Vorst district, across the Hudson from lower Manhattan. *Jersey City Interprets* was part of a multi-year project titled Ways of Seeing, that seeks varying points of view about the content and installation of the permanent collection housed at the museum. Featured in the museum window's exhibit space was a series of eyes which became the core of this exhibit.

Much thought was given to the types of eyes chosen for the display. Some of those selected were recognizable, and others were chosen for their contour, size, or ethnicity. The Evil Eye added some contrast to the more stylized eyes which dominated the display. Some eyes were in color and others black and white. One of the sets of eyes was adorned with sun glasses, which provided some comic relief.

ASSEMBLING THE DISPLAY

1. Eye glasses were arranged in a circular fashion and affixed to gold poster board which was double mounted on royal blue poster board, both of which were cut into the shape of an octagon. This was attached to the top left of the black felt background.

The font used for the title *On Seeing* was Bodoni MT Black cursive bold, sized at 90 for the word *on,* and Arial Rounded MT Bold, sized at 165 for the word *Seeing.* These words were printed on off-white cardstock and mounted on royal blue poster board.

The Elkins quotation (see above) was placed under the eyeglasses. Comical eyes, found on a Google image search, were inserted at the top of the quote. Other quotations on the topic of seeing used in the display were found at http://www.quotations. about.com/cs/inspiration quotes/a/Seeing3_p.htm

I am part of all that I have seen.

—Alfred Lord Tennyson

My eyes make pictures when they are shut.

—Samuel T. Coleridge

Stop a moment, cease your work, and look around you.

—Thomas Carlyle

One does not see anything until one sees its beauty.

—Oscar Wilde

These quotations were printed on off-white cardstock, mounted on royal blue poster board and interspersed among the eyes.

3. Included on the left side of the display case are reproduction photographs of the Third Eye and pineal gland, along with a graphic illustration of gender differentiation in seeing. *Who Are You? 101 Ways of Seeing Yourself,* by Malcolm Godwin, was an excellent source for all of this information.

An informative source for background on the concept of the Third Eye can be found if you visit http://www.crystalinks.com/thirdeyepineal.html

An eye chart, easily located through a Google image search, was also included.

All of the above were printed on off-white cardstock and mounted on royal blue and black poster board.

4. On the right side of the display case was information about the "All Seeing Eye" taken from the Godwin text.

Additional data about the "All Seeing Eye" could be found at http://www.crystal links.com/allseeingeye.html

A synopsis of the concept explored in the Gladwell book was printed on off-white cardstock and placed on the right side of the display case. Also included was a passage from John Berger's visionary work titled *Ways of Seeing.*

5. The telescope, which provides another way of seeing, serves to anchor the display. This was placed at the base of the display case and angled to balance the "octagon of eyeglasses." A camera, binoculars and a magnifying glass were positioned among the featured books.

Books included in the display were *The Object Stares Back: On the Nature of Seeing* by James Elkins, *Visual Perception* by H. W. Leibowitz, *Seeing: Illusion, Brain and Mind* by John P. Frisby, *Image and Brain: The Resolution of the Imagery Debate* by Stephen M. Kosslyn, and *More Than Meets the Eye: Seeing Art with All Five Senses,* by Bob Raczka.

BIGGER AND BETTER

If your display space is larger, you could include some additional devices which change the way that we see. These objects could include a mirror, a microscope, a monocle, or a prism. Your display could include Braille material, optical illusions, information on color-blindness, seeing through paintings, image and mind. You could also explore vision as it exists through the sixth sense.

The eyes you feature could be those of your staff or patrons. You could have a contest to guess whose eyes are featured.

M. C. Escher's "eye" is available at http://www.printparade.com and would be a compelling graphic for this subject.

Month-by-Month Display Ideas

January

Sam Ellis's Island—Opened on January 1, 1892, it became the nation's premiere immigration station until its closing in 1954. Feature *Ellis Island Interviews: In Their Own Words* by Peter M. Coan. Include the personal accounts of some of the over 12 million people who landed there, seeking to pass through the gateway to a better future. Create a collage of photographs depicting the newest immigrants to our shores. Look for vintage hats, clothing or personal items to add some warmth and dimension to the display. Include immigrant numbers and patterns of emigration.

All Asimov!—Choose from the over 500 works he produced during his lifetime. Born January 2, 1920, Isaac Asimov wrote science fiction, textbooks for various scientific fields, and other works on subjects as diverse as the Bible and books for preschoolers.

Long Live the King!—Celebrating the birth of the official king of rock and roll, Elvis Presley, born January 8, 1935. Include a guitar, vinyl records, CDs and DVDs along with biographies of Elvis and books such as *All Shook Up: How Rock 'n' Roll Changed America* by Glenn C. Altschuler.

Gold Diggers—Design a display on the California Gold Rush. Feature letters and diaries of the frontiersmen who crossed the country in search of a better life. Gold was discovered on January 24, 1848. Use the cactus from Wild, Wild West and include some rocks and grasses. Spray paint some small stones gold for added effect. Add a wagon wheel if possible, a gold pan, and vintage maps of California.

Survivors' Stories—The anniversary of the liberation of the Nazi death camps on January 24, 1945, will be commemorated with accounts written by the survivors of this atrocity. Stretch barbed wire across the shelf or base of the display and stand a book between each coil. Feature *A Promise to Remember: The Holocaust in the Words and Voices of Its Survivors* by Michale Berenbaum, *Eyewitness Auschwitz: Three Years in the Gas Chambers* by Filip Muller and *Stolen Youth: Five Women's Survival in the Holocaust* by Isabelle Choko, et al. Enlarge some of the letters, frame them and place them in the background. Add stars of David and a copy of the Old Testament.

Mostly Mozart—Celebrate the prodigy Wolfgang Amadeus Mozart, born January 27, 1756.

Include biographies, classical recordings, CDs and DVDs, scores and librettos. Use musical graphics, such as a keyboard, musical cleft and notes.

Super Sunday—Mount a display around the upcoming Super Bowl, which is usually late in January. Create a goalpost and a scoreboard, include logos of the possible teams that could be paired in the competition between the NFL and the AFL. Add cleats, helmet, football, cheerleading pom-poms, and tickets. Include books about the Super Bowl and those who have participated. *Joe Montana: Comeback Quarterback* by Dan Jenkins and *Green Bay Replay: The Packers' Return to Glory* by Dick Schaap are some examples.

February

Black History Month—February is Black History Month. Create a collage of African Americans who have made a difference in their lifetimes. Include works by Maya Angelou and Nobel Prize winner Toni Morrison. Others you might include are Rosa Parks, Jackie Robinson, Ella Fitzgerald, Oprah Winfrey, Marian Anderson, Arthur Ashe, Althea Gibson, Shirley Chisholm, Frederick Douglass, Thurgood Marshall, Rita Dove and Colin Powell. Visit this site for additional suggestions: http://www.biography.com/black_history/bhm_barrier.jsp

Feature *100 African Americans Who Shaped American History* by Chrisanne Beckner and *From Slavery to Freedom: A History of African Americans* by John Hope Franklin.

The War Within—Mount this in commemoration of the birth of Abraham Lincoln on February 12, 1809. Focus on Lincoln and his role in the War of the States. Include a period American flag and a Confederate flag plus books on the Civil War and biographies of Lincoln, Grant and Lee.

Vintage Valentines—Display collections of old Valentine cards and candy boxes. Include books of romantic poems and holidays. Feature "How do I love thee? Let me count the ways..." by Elizabeth Barrett Browning. Add hearts and cupids.

Dynamic Duos—Lovers in history can be celebrated on February 14th. Include books on Georgia O'Keeffe and Alfred Stieglitz, Antony and Cleopatra, Robert and Elizabeth Browning, John Lennon and Yoko Ono, F. Scott and Zelda Fitzgerald, Grace Kelly and Prince Rainier, Arthur Miller and Marilyn Monroe, and James and Dolly Madison. Place the title in a large heart and have arrows pointing to each of the images of the couples.

Galileo Galilei—Born in Pisa, Italy, on February 15, 1564, this physicist and astronomer helped override the medieval concepts of the world at this time. Include a telescope and choose a background of midnight blue sky with stars attached. Include books such as *The Great Scientists* by A. J. Meadows, *Galileo: A Life* by James Reston, and *The Illustrated a Brief History of Time* by S. W. Hawking.

Big Boar!—Chinese New Year 2008—Incorporate graphics of a boar and other Asian artifacts to create a festive display. Add fireworks and confetti and include books on this holiday and the culture of the Far East. Visit this Web site for more information: http://www.nps.gov.edal

Portraits of a President—This display commemorates the first president of the United States, George Washington, born February 22, 1732. Include examples of the many portraits painted of this figure along with biographies of Washington and the artist Gilbert Stuart. Attach these portraits to a red, white and blue banner. Add the stars used in The Sage of Monticello.

In Praise of Books and Libraries—February is Library Lover's Month. Feature books on home libraries as well as academic and public libraries. Include books on Johannes Gutenberg and books such as *Illuminations* by Jonathan Hunt and a reproduction of *The Book of Kells*. Visit this Web site for graphics from the latter: http://www.snake.net/people/paul/kells/thumbnails

March

Go Fly a Kite!—March is National Kite Month. Hang colorful kites on a sky blue background. Include "how to" books on kite making such as *The Ultimate Kite Book* by Paul Morgan and Helene Morgan, *Making Kites* by David Michael and Jim Robins and *Kite Flying* by Grace Lin. Feature *The Kite Runner* by Khaled Hosseini.

Fabulous Festivals—These are held in February or March on the Tuesday before Lent. Carnival is celebrated in Brazil, Italy and other Latin countries. Mardi Gras is a familiar tradition in New Orleans. Use brilliant colors, lots of beads, masks, hats, crowns and confetti and include books and media on this subject.

Gutsy Girls—March is Women's History Month. Include heroines such as Susan B. Anthony, Edith Wharton (the first woman to win the Pulitzer), Harriet Tubman, Amelia Earhart, Eleanor Roosevelt, Dr. Sally Ride and Sandra Day O'Connor. Include books by and about women who made a difference. Choose an eye-catching font for the title.

Sam and Santa—Explore the rivalry of Sam Houston, born March 2, 1793, and General Antonio Lopez de Santa Anna, absolute ruler of Mexico, who met on April 21, 1836, for an 18 minute battle. The Mexican army was deterred and the general was captured. This significant Battle of San Jacinto ended the Texican struggle for civil rights and established the Republic of Texas. Houston and Santa Anna would also have an encounter at the Alamo. Include a map of Texas from this era and the seal of the state of Texas. Include *The Eagle and the Raven* by James Michener and *In the Shadow of the Alamo* by Sherry Garland.

Patrick of Ireland—Celebrated on March 17, St. Patrick's Day is observed in the Republic of Ireland as a legal national holiday. St. Patrick is credited with bringing Christianity to Ireland and instilling a sense of literacy and purposeful learning that would permit Ireland to become the "isle of saints and scholars." He was able to preserve Western culture while barbarians overran Europe. Include *How the Irish Saved Civilization: The Untold Story of Ireland's Heroic Role from the Fall of Rome to the Rise of Medieval Europe* by Thomas Cahill and *St Patrick of Ireland: A Biography* by Philip Freeman. Include the shamrocks from the C. S. Lewis: Into the Wardrobe display.

Blossom by Blossom—The Start of Spring—March 20th marks the beginning of spring. Create a festive and colorful display of silk flowers, butterflies and a net, birds and birds' nests. Feature the cherry blossoms which abound in the nation's capital. Use some of the items included in the display In the Garden. Include poetry books and poems about the spring by Algernon Swinburne, Emily Dickinson and Robert Herrick. For these writings and others, visit http://www.factmonster.com/spot/springquotes1.html

April

The Greatest Show on Earth—P. T. Barnum complained that the *New York Times* never said anything good about a person until they were dead. As a result, the paper ran his obituary several weeks prior to his death! This great showman, along with partner James A. Bailey, created the circus, one of the most famous forms of entertainment, which continues to this day. In 1882, these men were able to acquire the elephant Jumbo, dubbed "The Towering Monarch of His Mighty Race, Whose Like the World Will Never See Again." Jumbo arrived in New York on April 9, 1882, and attracted enormous crowds. Barnum died April 7, 1891. Feature vintage circus posters, clown hats or a top hat. Divide the display background into 3 rings signifying the circus arrangement. Oh, and include the Barnum obituary!

Cleansing Hands—Joseph Lister, born April 5, 1827, is known as the "Father of Antiseptic Surgery." Dr. Lister promoted the idea of sterile surgery after lamenting the death of large numbers of surgical patients. He introduced carbolic acid to sterilize surgical instruments and to clean wounds. Include the research done on this subject by Dr. Louis Pasteur, which led to Lister's discovery. Incorporate surgical tools, a doctor's bag, rolls of gauze, and medicine bottles. Feature *Einstein's Luck: The Truth Behind Some of the Greatest Scientific Discoveries* by John Waller and *Master Surgeon: A Biography of Joseph Lister* by Lawrence Farmer.

A Certainty of Life—Taxe$—Due April 15th of each year. Set this up as a hands-on display. Include federal and state income tax forms. Have guide books available, such as *The Ernst and Young Tax Guide 2008* by Ernst and Young LLP and *J. K. Lasser's Your Income Tax 2008: For Preparing Your 2007 Tax Return* by J. K. Lasser. Present a fact sheet indicating major changes for the upcoming tax year. Display an 800-number for tax questions and the IRS URL. Arrange an informative program with a speaker from an area tax preparation company.

Unsinkable!—The anniversary of the 1912 sinking of the *Titanic* is on April 15. Take advantage of the recent books and DVDs that chronicle the events leading to the sinking of this luxury liner. Feature *Inside the Titanic: A Giant Cut-away Book* by Ken Marschall and *Exploring the Titanic* by Robert D. Ballard. Include nautical artifacts from the display Sailors' Tales and survivors' accounts as found in *The Story of the Titanic as Told by Its Survivors*, edited by Jack Winocour. Use bold lettering for the title and angle it downward so that it appears to be sinking.

Art and the Royals: Fabergé Eggs—In conjunction with the celebration of Easter, feature the porcelain and crystal eggs commissioned by the czars of Russia. From the early 18th century until the Russian Revolution, that aristocracy enjoyed a lifestyle of unparalleled affluence. Focus on Peter Carl Fabergé (1846–1920) who was the creator of these works of art for royalty throughout Europe and Asia. Include *Masterpieces from the House of Fabergé* by A. Von Solodkoff and *Fabergé Eggs: Imperial Russian Fantasies* by Christopher Forbes.

Giving and Getting Back—National Volunteer Week (usually the third week in April) salutes the men, women, teens and children who have found the simple joy in giving of themselves. Include photographs of your library volunteers, as well as those serving in the community at schools, hospitals, nursing homes, boys' and girls' clubs, etc. Display books on the subject such as *Make a Difference: America's Guide to Volunteering and Community Service* by Arthur Blaustein and *Creating a Habitat for Humanity: No Hands but Yours* by Jonathan T. M. Reckford.

The simple cover illustration on *Giving from Your Heart: A Guide to Volunteering* by Dr. Bob Rosenberg and Guy Lampard should help you with a graphic for this display. Or, use the hands created for the One Thousand Cranes display.

William's World—Both the birth and death of William Shakespeare occurred on April 23rd (1564–1616). Celebrate the Elizabethan times in which he lived and worked. Include information on the Black Plague, which affected the masses during his lifetime. Feature the Globe Theatre and the plays and sonnets for which he became famous.

May

Well Bred—Mount a display on the subject of horseracing in conjunction with the Kentucky Derby, held on the first Saturday in May. Include equestrian articles and some information on the breeding of horses for racing. Include a list of past winners and notable champions. Line the case with grass and add a mint julep and a large floppy hat like those frequently worn by the women attending the race. A jockey's cap, silks and a crop would be great touches.

Cinco de Mayo—The 5th of May is significant to Mexicans as it marks the victory of the Mexican Army over the French at the Battle of Puebla. Although the Mexican army was eventually defeated, the *Batalla de Puebla* came to represent a symbol of Mexican patriotism. With this victory, Mexico demonstrated to the world that it, and all of Latin America, was willing to defend itself from any foreign intervention. Add a sarape and a sombrero. Put the title in a banner using the colors of the Mexican flag. Include the history of this event.

Mothers and Daughters: Loving and Letting Go—Explore the bond of this complicated relationship in conjunction with Mother's Day. Include different size framed photographs of mothers and daughters of various ages. Arrange the photographs at different heights and add hats, jewelry, and a pair of heels. Feature books such as *Like Mother, Like Daughter* by Debra Waterhouse, *She's Leaving Home* by Connie Jones, and *The Mother Daughter Connection* by Susie Shellenberger.

A Silent Spring—Centennial celebration of the birth of Rachel Carson on May 27, 1907, in Springdale, Pennsylvania. Feature her most famous book, *Silent Spring*, which she began writing in 1957. It was published in 1962, and influenced President Kennedy to call for testing of the chemicals mentioned in the book. Carson has been called the mother of the modern environmental movement. Include Carson's *The Edge of the Sea* and the biography *Rachel Carson: Witness for Nature* by Linda J. Lear. Add a microscope and binoculars and items found in nature, such as those used in the John Muir display.

Remember When? Welcome Back Class of ???? (fill in the year)—Following graduation, institutions typically welcome back classes of specific years hoping to maintain those connections. Scan photographs from yearbooks and newspapers housed in the archives to create a warm and welcoming reminder of the years spent at your institution. Include programs and other memorabilia from the classes being feted. Consult with your alumni office and establish a "wall of updates" with current information about the alums being welcomed back that year.

The Doctor Was a Lady—Celebrating the life of the first modern woman doctor, Elizabeth Blackwell. Born February 3, 1821, she died at the age of 89 on May 31, 1910. Feature works about her such as *Elizabeth Blackwell: First Woman Physician* by Tristan Boyer Binns and *Elizabeth Blackwell: First Woman Doctor of Modern Times* by Adele Glimm. The physician's symbol would be an easy graphic to create for the background. Add a mortar and pestle, some vintage medicine bottles, tongue depressors and an old stethoscope.

June

Losing Oneself—German neurologist Alois Alzheimer was born on June 6th, 1864. In 1907, at the age of 43, he used special techniques to uncover the cerebral abnormalities after the death of a 56 year old patient who felt that she was "losing herself." This breakthrough was critical in the diagnosis of patients with dementia, a chronic, progressive, presenile disorder. Provide an overview of the disease and the progress that has been made in recent years. Use a graphic of a brain and have the title of the display fade from black to gray.

Art or Mathematics?—M. C. Escher was born June 17, 1898, in the province of Friesland in Holland. Was it art he created or was it really mathematics? Raise the question in your display featuring the broad range of graphics he produced. Include *The Magic of M. C. Escher* and *M. C. Escher: Life and Complete Graphic Work*, both by J. L. Locker.

Sacred Places—Sacred or holy places are found in different cultures, past and present, all over the world. Such places are frequently marked by architectural structures, such as Stonehenge. Others, namely Walden Pond, are famous for the peace and serenity that they offer through nature. The writer, naturalist, and philosopher Henry David Thoreau lived on the shores of the pond for two years starting in the summer of 1845. Feature the various sacred places located around the world. For more information visit http://www.sacredsites.com/

Be sure to include *The Atlas of Holy Places and Sacred Sites* by Colin Wilson and the *Encyclopedia of Sacred Places* by Norbert C. Brockman.

Shore Summer Reads—Obviously, June through August would be appropriate months for this display, if you live in an area with changing seasons. Use books with a light theme for easy vacation reading. Draw a portion of a sun and place it on the top right of the display. Have rays emanate from it. Include books about the summer or the beach such as *Summer* by Edith Wharton, *Sandcastles* and *Summer of Roses* by Luanne Rice, *Farewell Summer* by Ray Bradbury, *One Special Summer* by Jacqueline and Lee Bouvier and *Prodigal Summer* by Barbara Kinsolver. Add sand, sunglasses and sun hat, bottle of water, sunscreen and other beach items featured in the display Hot Nights, Cool Reads.

The Championships—Wimbledon—Beginning in late June and running through early July, this event is the oldest and most prestigious of the sport of tennis. Located in London, the tournament is the third of the Grand Slam events and the only Grand Slam event held on grass. Include a history of the facility and the traditions peculiar to it. Feature *Wimbledon Facts, Figures and Fun* by Cameron Brown and *Visions of Wimbledon* edited by Allsport Photo as well as the recent DVD *Wimbledon*. Add tennis racquets, balls, photographs of champions, and the traditional dish of strawberries and some of the items used in Game, Set, Match! Use the current Wimbledon colors of navy and cream as your color theme.

Heads Up! The World of International Football—Known as soccer in the U.S., this international sport meets every four years in June and July for a world tournament. The 2006 competition in Germany was the most widely viewed sporting event in the world. The next World Cup will be held in 2010 in South Africa.

Attach the net of a goal to the back of your display and mount a soccer ball at the top right. Feature books on the phenomenon of this sport, such as *How Soccer Explains the World: An Unlikely Theory of Globalization* by Franklin Foer, *Soccer Against the Enemy: How the World's Most Popular Sport Starts and Fuels Revolutions and Keeps Dictators in Power* by Simon Kuper and *Soccer* by D. K. Publishing. Include cleats, shin guards and uniforms.

July

Get Lit at the Library—In conjunction with National Literacy Day, July 2nd, this display could feature the great works of literature. When creating the title signage, make the "i" in literature a candle with a flame. Choose your favorite literary works. Include a quill pen and an ink well and add a list of the best books of the 20th century. For this information visit http://www.randomhouse.com/modernlibrary/100bestnovels.html

Founding Fathers—A Nation Born—Celebrate the birth of our nation on July 4th. Feature images of the signers of the Declaration of Independence as well as the document itself. Use a red, white and blue theme and include lots of stars. Hang the flag from the display Jewish-American Authors. Include *Founding Fathers: Uncommon Heroes* by Steven W. Allen, *Not Your Usual Founding Father: Selected Readings from Benjamin Franklin* edited by Edmund S. Morgan, and *The Founding Fathers on Leadership: Classic Teamwork in Changing Times* by Donald T. Phillips.

Dear John—Feature letters exchanged between former presidents John Adams and Thomas Jefferson, both of whom died on the 50th anniversary of the signing of the Declaration of Independence, July 4, 1826. Enlarge copies of their correspondence. Include titles such as *Adams vs. Jefferson: The Tumultuous Election of 1800* by John Ferling and *Adams and Jefferson: A Revolutionary Dialogue* by Merrill D. Peterson.

The People Speak—July 14th marks the anniversary of Bastille Day, which took place in France in 1789. The storming of that prison by the French people became a symbol of historic proportions. It proved that power did not reside in the king or God, but rather with the people. This was the prevailing philosophy of that era. Use the French flag as a backdrop with fireworks on either side. Feature *The Days of the French Revolution* by Christopher Hibbert, *Memoirs of the Bastille* by Simon-Nicolas-Henn Linquet and other books related to the French Revolution. Include *Les Miserables*. To participate in Philadelphia's annual storming of a city prison, held each July in conjunction with Bastille Day, visit http://www.easternstate.org/events/bastille.php

Papa—Ernest Hemingway was born on July 21, 1899, in Oak Park, Illinois. At the age of 17, he published his first literary work. He wrote twelve novels, 10 works of non-fiction and 11 short story collections before his suicide at the age of 61. He blamed the effects of ECT (electroconvulsive therapy) for tampering with his memory and thus his ability to write and subsequent depression.

Hemingway married four times and fathered three sons. He and F. Scott Fitzgerald shared many of the same passions and were close friends and expatriates living in Europe for a period of time. Create an island setting for the years that Hemingway lived in Key West, Florida. Use the palm trees from the display Hot Nights, Cool Reads. Include as many of his publications as you have available. Enlarge some of the poignant letters found in *Ernest Hemingway Selected Letters: 1917–1961.*

Banned Books—In 2000 the U.S. Congress deemed July 2 National Literacy Day. Create a camp fire out of kindling and gold and orange cellophane. Include titles that have been banned through history such as *Tom Sawyer* and *Huckleberry Finn* by Mark Twain, *Catcher in the Rye* by J. D. Salinger, *Canterbury Tales* by Chaucer, *Black Beauty* by Anna Sewell, *Gone with the Wind* by Margaret Mitchell, *Call of the Wild* by Jack London, and a Harry Potter book. Place one or two of the books in the "fire." Draw lines through the word *Banned*.

August

First Voyage—August 3, 1492, was the start of the voyage of Italian Christopher Columbus from Palos, Spain, with three ships and a crew of 90. Although headed for India and hoping to accumulate a wealth of spices, he instead landed on the island of San Salvador in the Bahamas on October 12th of that year. Include his coat of arms, illustrations of his three ships and nautical accoutrements such as a compass and maps. Books of note: *In Their Own Words: Christopher Columbus* by Peter and Connie Roop, and *Ships of Christopher Columbus* by Xavier Pastor.

Hiroshima Remembered—August 6, 1945, was the day that nuclear power was used against the people of Japan. Feature photographs of the aftermath of the explosion and biographical information about the men who discovered the hydrogen bomb, Edward Teller and Stanislaw Ulam, and their link to Albert Einstein.

Include the controversy that surrounded this decision. Display *Hiroshima* by John Hersey, *Hiroshima and Nagasaki: Fire from the Sky* by Andrew Langley, and *Hiroshima: Why America Dropped the Atomic Bomb* by Ronald Takaki. Include photographs of the city today.

We Love Lucy—A tribute to television and movie actress Lucille Ball who was born August 6, 1911. Her sitcom, *I Love Lucy*, became a national pastime, and the innovative technology implemented by her husband and partner, Desi Arnaz, changed television forever. Recreate the famous red heart logo with white script used on the TV show. Include summaries of favorite episodes and feature the autobiography *Love, Lucy* and *Desilu: The Story of Lucille Ball and Desi Arnaz* by Coyne S. Sanders. Include videos and DVDs of the show.

Sultan of Swat—George Herman "Babe" Ruth was born on February 6, 1895, and died August 16, 1948. The 60th anniversary of his death will occur in 2008. Ruth achieved a record 714 homeruns in 22 major league series during his lifetime. Add images of Baltimore, Maryland, such as Fort McHenry and Camden Yards, and include Red Sox and Yankee memorabilia. Include *The Big Bam: the Life and Times of Babe Ruth,* by Leigh Montville, and other biographies of the Babe.

American Artists—August is American Artist Appreciation Month. Select a favorite and create a display celebrating his or her life and times. Include books about the artist and the style used in the art works. If you have a local artist, feature that person and be sure to have handouts such as postcards or pamphlets with information about purchasing specific works. Arrange a reception where people can meet the artist and have a verbal exchange. Include a palette, brushes, paints, chalks and preliminary sketches as well as biographical information.

Ruin and Recovery—Hurricane Katrina—August 29, 2005, was the date that the Gulf Coast sustained the costliest and one of the deadliest hurricanes in our nation's history. Cities in Louisiana, Mississippi and Alabama were the most affected. The strength of the storm caused the levees in New Orleans to fail and caused catastrophic damage to that city. At least 1836 people lost their lives to this hurricane and the subsequent floods.

Have a section "Then and Now" feature photographs of the original devastation and areas that have been successfully restored. Include *The Great Deluge: Hurricane Katrina, New Orleans,* and *The Mississippi Gulf Coast* by Douglas Brinkley, *Come Hell or High Water: Hurricane Katrina and the Color of Disaster* by Michael Eric Dyson and *Hurricane Katrina: Stories of Rescue, Recovery and Rebuilding in the Eye of the Storm* edited by Susan M. Moyer.

September

The Plain People—September is the perfect time for a visit to the Amish farms located in Lancaster County, Pennsylvania. These "plain people" have been employing horse-drawn power since their arrival in this country. The Amish trace their heritage back hundreds of years and continue to live and work in the manner of their forefathers. God and family are their primary values and they are kind and generous neighbors.

Make or hang a simple Amish quilt as a backdrop for your display. Include books about these devout people and include crafts that they have mastered, such as woodworking, doll making, leather crafts and items of wrought iron. Feature seed packets, faceless dolls, and quilting items such as hoop, needles, thread and quilt squares.

Master of Middle Earth—Tolkien's World of Fantasy —The anniversary of the 1973 death of English author J. R. R. Tolkien is September 2. Explore the trilogy of the *Lord of the Rings* as well as the many of works of fiction and non-fiction created by this prolific writer. Feature *The Letters of J. R. R. Tolkien* and *The Shaping of Middle Earth* along with his popular works of fantasy. Maps of Middle Earth can be found through an online image search. Use three rings to signify the trilogy.

Conflict and Compromise—Back to school advice for college students adjusting to dormitory living. Use the book *Getting to Yes: Negotiating Agreement Without Giving In* by Roger Fisher, or the sequel *Getting Together: Building Relationships as We Negotiate.* Base your illustration on an exasperated comic strip character, such as *Cathy*, created by Cathy Guisewite. Include other books on the art of negotiation, such as *Essentials of Negotiation* by Roy Lewicki.

Lamentation 9/11—Feature the book by that title, text by E. L. Doctorow, photographs by David Finn, a tribute to our fallen Americans. Include books on terrorism and 9/11, photographs from Ground Zero and newspaper headlines and articles. Feature NYPD and NYFD insignia and a flag of the U.S. Include the Twin Towers.

The Beautiful and the Damned—Written by F. Scott Fitzgerald, born September 24, 1896, the title of this book also summarizes his life with wife Zelda. Include letters from the text *Dear Scott, Dearest Zelda* by the Fitzgeralds along with Jackson Bryer, as well as the graphic from the Princeton University Triangle Club, for which he wrote comedy. Add mementos representing their life in Paris: martini glasses for their fondness of alcohol, a feather boa, and a flapper's hat to suggest the nightlife and fashion of their time. Line the base of the display case with velvet or brocade.

Feature F. Scott's writings and Zelda's book *The Collected Writings.*

Unlocking Autism—September means "back to school." But some children will not have this experience, since they are not capable of functioning within a classroom. Many of these are children with autism. Use the graphic associated with this disorder that can be found on the Autism Society of American Web page. Visit http://www.autism-society.org/site/PageServer

Include *Ten Things Every Child with Autism Wishes You Knew* by Ellen Notbolm and *1001 Great Ideas for Teaching and Raising Children with Autism Spectrum Disorders* by Veronica Zysk and Ellen Notbolm. Have the "o" in the title word *Unlocking* be an illustration of a real lock.

October

Gallery of Rogues—October is Crime Prevention Month. Create a background with vertical measurements suggesting a police lineup. Attach mug shots at varying heights depicting notorious crime figures such as Al Capone, the Son of Sam, Ted Bundy, and Bonnie and Clyde. Describe their crimes and attach this information under the photographs. Include artifacts such as a gavel, a bandana, a toy gun and handcuffs. Feature *America's Most Vicious Criminals* by Carl Sifakis.

Pretty in Pink—Use the pink ribbon symbol associated with breast cancer and place photographs of breast cancer survivors in the center of the loop. Include the signs of breast cancer, and some stories of women who have survived the disease. Use pink and white as the color theme. Add balloons. Include the lyrics to Melissa Etheridge's song *I Run for Life,* which can be found if you visit http://www.melissaetheridge.com/discography/lyrics/greatesthits. php# irunforlife

Man and the Machine—Upcoming centennial of the introduction of the Model T Ford on October 1, 1908. "You can paint it any color ... as long as it is black" was never actually attributed to founder Henry Ford, but it has a lot of merit. Feature the Ford founder and some interesting facts about the car's development and introduction and the phenomenal sales this model Ford accrued at $850 per vehicle. This invention made the U.S. a nation on wheels. Include photographs of the evolution of the Model T up to and including today's Ford vehicle. Add vintage automobile items such as old hubcaps. Drawings of the Model T can be found at this site: http://www.3dcenter.ru/blueprints/ford/ford-model-t.gif

Mystery and Madness—Tie this into a display around Halloween. Include tales by Edgar Allen Poe. Visit the National Historic site home page for suggestions: http://www.nps.gov/edal

Include *The Raven* and mystery novels with an eerie twist, such as those by Stephen King, *The Prestige* by Christopher Priest, and *Come Closer* by Sara Gran. Tap into items created for the displays Tales of Horror and The Life and Times of Bram Stoker.

Nobel Laureates—Celebrate the newest winners that will join the almost 800 previous notables to win the prize. For information visit http://nobelprize.org/. *100 Years of Nobel Prizes* by Baruch A. Shalev is an excellent print source. Include works of the winners as well. Images of the prize can be found through an online search.

A Wild Wilde Ride—Highlight the fascinating life and times of the Irish poet and dramatist Oscar Wilde, born October 16, 1854. Include a timeline of his life and his contributions to the theatre, such as *The Importance of Being Earnest* and *An Ideal Husband*, both of which have recently been made into films. Use items from the display C. S. Lewis: Into the Wardrobe.

And the Crowd Went Wild—Mount this display prior to the World Series of baseball. Feature events in the sports world that brought the crowd to their feet. Draw silhouettes of the back of the heads of fans of varying heights standing. Include events such as Lou Gehrig's farewell to baseball, and Ted Williams's career ending home run. Use the source *And the Crowd Goes Wild: Relive the Most Celebrated Sporting Events Ever Broadcast* by Joe Garner and Bob Costas. Add memorabilia used in the display Baseball as America. Place the title within a scoreboard.

November

Smoking 101—November is National Tobacco Awareness Month. Include books proposing the cessation of cigarette smoking, such as *The Price of Smoking* by Frank A. Sloan and *1,440 Reasons to Quit Smoking: One for Every Minute of the Day ... and Night* by Bill Dodds. Use the cover of *Thank You for Not Smoking* by Christopher Buckley as a guide to an easy graphic that you can create as a focal point for this display. Include cigarette butts, used packages of cigarettes and ashtrays.

Hairy Faces—November is National Beard Month. Celebrate the men in history who were known for their full facial hair. Provide information on the significance of beards in many religions. Provide a glossary of the different types of beards such as the goatee or the Van Dyke. Include the bearded gods Zeus or Poseidon, also Abraham Lincoln, John Muir, St. Nicholas, Jesus Christ, William Shakespeare, Galileo, Moses and U. S. Grant. Include old razors, shaving mugs and graphic of a barber pole.

Teen Queen—Maria Antonia Josefa Johanna von Habsburg-Lothringen was born on November 2, 1755. Better known historically as Marie Antoinette, she was born an archduchess of Austria and later became queen of France. She married Louis XVI of France at age 15. Marie Antoinette is perhaps best remembered for her lust for the good life. She was beheaded in 1793 at the height of the French Revolution for treasonous crimes.

Include the recent DVD titled *Marie Antoinette,* along with the books *Marie Antoinette: The Journey* by Antonia Fraser and *Marie Antoinette: The Last Queen of France* by Evelyne Lever.

Presidency 2008—Celebrate the road to the White House. The national presidential election is on November 4, 2008. Feature books on past elections and political strategy and trends. Add the heads of a donkey and an elephant facing each other. Include lots of stars, campaign hats, buttons, flags and banners. Use appropriate items previously included in the display Citizen Ben. Feature titles such as *Perspectives on Election: Five Views* by Jack W. Cottrel and *Winning Elections: Political Campaign Management, Strategy and Tactics* by Ronald A. Faucheux.

Now You're Cooking—4th Thursday of November. Create a Thanksgiving display featuring a large cornucopia with fruit and vegetables. Place cookbooks and cooking accoutrements throughout the display. Add an imitation turkey or fruit pie. Include a recipe for cooking turkey.

Tutankamun—Boy King—The tomb of this king was discovered November 26, 1922, by Howard Carter, who made archaeological history by unearthing the Egyptian pharaonic tomb that housed priceless treasures. The map of the chambers within the tomb would be an interesting feature of this display and can be retrieved through an image search online.

Print large pages of hieroglyphics and run them across the back of the display. Draw two silhouettes of pharaohs and have them flank the title signage. Check the book *The Egyptian Book of the Dead,* edited by Eva Von Dassow, for excellent graphics. This Web site will translate text into hieroglyphics: http://www.isidore-of-seville.com/hieroglyphs/5.html

Include *The Complete Tutankhamun: The King, the Tomb, the Royal Treasure* by Nicholas Reeves and *Tutankhamun and the Golden Age of the Pharaohs: Official Companion Book to the Exhibition sponsored by National Geographic* by Zahi Hawass.

December

A Day That Will Live in Infamy—December 7, 1941, was the Japanese attack on Pearl Harbor. In addition to the huge loss of battleships, warships and aircraft, 2403 servicemen and 68 civilians perished. For an overview of this historic day, http://www.archives.gov/education/lessons/day-of-infamy/

Include maps of the area, and books on the attack, such as *At Dawn We Slept* by Gordon W. Prange, *Pearl Harbor: America's Darkest Day* by Susan Wels and the recent DVD titled *Pearl Harbor.* Include a photograph of the Arizona Memorial. Use some of the graphics from the display D-Day Remembered.

First Flight—On December 17, 1903, Orville and Wilbur Wright launched the Wright Flyer, which became the first powered, heavier-than-air machine to achieve controlled, sustained flight with a pilot on board. Pay homage to this event which took place in Kitty Hawk, North Carolina. Provide information that explains how two small town businessmen invented a technology that marked the dawn of the aerial age.

An online image search will provide photographs of the brothers, illustrations of the plane, and maps of the area. Include books such as *The Wright Brothers: How They Invented the Airplane* by Russell Freedman and the Wright Brothers, *The Wright Brothers: A Biography* by Fred C. Kelly and *Wright Brothers and the Invention of the Aerial Age* by Peter L. Jakab. If possible, suspend a bi-plane plane from the top of the display.

Season's Readings—Create a rectangular shape wrapped in seasonal paper with a bow on top and place the title signage in the box. Substitute a Christmas ball for the "o" in *Season.* Choose seasonal titles such as: *Skipping Christmas* by John Grisham, *A Christmas Carol* by Charles Dickens, *A Christmas Guest* by Anne Perry, *A Stranger for Christmas* by Carol Pearson, *Tidings of Comfort and Joy* by Davis Bunn, and *A Redbird Christmas* by Fannie Flagg. Add balls, a miniature fir tree, ornaments and holiday greens. Line the case with festive fabric.

Sacagawea—On December 20, 1812, Sacagawea, the daughter of a Shoshone chief and the wife of Toussaint Charbonneau, died of putrid fever. At twenty-five years of age, she had made her mark on American history by serving as a guide to Meriweather Lewis and William Clark as they made their expedition westward. Use a map of the Northwest Territory as a backdrop for your display. Enlarge a photograph of the coin depicting her likeness. Feature *Sacagawea: Guide for the Lewis and Clark Expedition* by Hal Marcovitz and *Lewis and Clark: An Illus-*

trated History by Dayton Duncan. Add Native American artifacts along with items previously featured in the display Wild, Wild West.

Surviving the Holidays... — Who can endure the demands of the holiday season without some stress and even a little depression? Make a checklist containing ideas that will make the holidays more enjoyable. Use these sources as guides: *The Don't Sweat Guide to Holidays: Enjoying the Festivities and Letting Go of the Tension* from the Don't Sweat Press and *The Worst-Case Scenario Survival Handbook: Holidays* by Joshua Piven and David Borgenicht. Use the tips provided by the Mayo Clinic as well. Simplify. http://www.mayoclinic.com/health/stress/MH00030

Heroes and Icons — As the end of the year approaches, we look to *Time* magazine and their annual selection of "Man of the Year." Look at their Web site and see the men and women that they have included in the category of heroes and icons: http://www.time.com/time/time100/leaders/index.html

For your display, choose people who have articulated the journey of the last 100 years displaying courage, selflessness and humility. Suggestions: Mother Teresa, the American GI, Bill Gates, and the Dalai Lama. Include biographies of those you select.

Some Construction Techniques

Hot Nights, Cool Reads

Making 3D palm trees for display: see page 58.

Trunk

1. Using the brown poster board, cut out a flat trunk for the palm tree (about 28" high, and 8" wide at the base). It will look more realistic if it is slightly bowed along its length and tapers slightly at the top.

Example:

2. Cut about 10 long strips of the brown construction paper. These should be from 3" to 6" in height, and 14" to 16" in length.

3. Cut an irregular zigzag pattern across the length of these strips.

Example:

4. Take one of the strips, and fold it near one of the ends (leave an inch or two of slack beyond the fold). Starting at the top of the trunk you cut out, place the strip so that the bend is right up against the side edge of the trunk. Staple or tape this piece in place. Flex the rest of the strip across the trunk piece so that when you look at it from the bottom there is a "D" shaped hollow. Bend the strip and staple or tape in place as you did on the other side (you may have to trim some length off the strip so it doesn't peek out the back).

Attach the rest of the strips in the same fashion, overlapping each other, so that there are no gaps, with the zigzag always facing up, until the trunk is completely covered and 3-D from top to bottom.

Leaves

1. Cut out 3 or 4 pieces of green tag board, about 12" by 12."

2. Taking each of these 12" by 12" pieces, cut out a palm frond, leaving enough of a "stem" to attach to the trunk.

 Example:

3. To give the frond a more realistic appearance, fold the frond along the center line and also fold each "leaf" along the center.

4. Tape or staple the "stem" of the frond into the top hollow of the trunk.

Whodunit

See page 65.

Profile of Sherlock Holmes

1. Go to http://www.sherlock-holmes.co.uk.
2. Find the image on the top of the page.
3. Right click on the image and select "save picture as."
4. Save the picture and print from the saved location.
5. To enlarge the image, use the photocopy machines set at +200%.
6. Cut out and trace the image on the black poster board.
7. Mount the image on another piece of red poster board to form the oval around the head.

Image of a Dagger

1. Go online to www.google.com.
2. Choose "Images" then type in "daggers."
3. Find an image you prefer.
4. Copy and paste into a Word document or photo editor.
5. Right-click on the image in the new document.

6. Select "format picture."

7. Then select "size" and enlarge to your specifications.

Poison Label

1. Go online to Google.

2. Choose "Images" then type in poison label.

3. Proceed as above.

4. Make a 2" high paper strip of this graphic and put it around the jar or bottle that you have selected.

If you would like to give a more finished look to the content material, you can select "Borders & Shading" under "Format" in MS Word, click on the tab for "Page Border," select from the drop down menu labeled "Art" and click on "o.k."

Chinese Calligraphy

See page 128.

Bamboo Image

This image was scanned using HP precision LTX software. The Help screens in this program will easily take you through the process of reproducing your image. One could also photocopy this if the copier is capable of providing good results. (See Chinese Calligraphy Scan on thumb drive.)

City of Lights

Creating the Eiffel Tower: see page 131.

A PC was attached to the data projector, which illuminated a replica of the structure of the Eiffel Tower onto silver poster board which was taped to the wall. The lines of the tower were filled in using a black marker. This image was cut and pinned to the cobalt blue felt background and pulled forward.

Formatting Pictures

1. Open Microsoft Word.

2. Select "Insert from Menu Bar."

3. Choose "Picture from File."

4. Select the picture you wish to format.

5. Once you've inserted it into MS Word, right-click on the image.

6. Choose "Format Picture."

7. Select size from the tabs.

8. Adjust to desired height or width.

You want to only adjust one; the other will adjust automatically and the picture will not look pixilated.

Free Fonts for Downloading

http://www.typenow.net

http://www.grsites.com

http://simplythebest.net

http://www.1001fonts.com

http://www.highfonts.com

http://www.1001freefonts.com

http://www.fontfreak.com

Bibliography

Adler, Alan, ed. *Science-Fiction and Horror Movie Posters in Full Color*. New York: Dover, 1977.

Andrade, Mary J. *Dia de Meurtos en Mexico*. San Jose: La Oferta Review Newspaper, Inc., 1996.

Angell, Carole A. *Celebrations Around the World*. Golden: Fulcrum, 1996.

Arnett, Robert. *India Unveiled*. Columbus: Atman Press, 2002.

Asselin, Giles, and Ruth Mastron. *Au Contraire! Figuring Out the French*. Yarmouth: Intercultural Press, 2001.

Augenti, Andrea. *Art and Archaeology of Rome*. New York: Riverside Book Company, 2000.

Bacquart, Jean-Baptiste. *The Tribal Arts of Africa*. New York: Thames and Hudson, Inc., 1998.

Barber, David W., ed. *Quotable Alice: From the Works of Lewis Carroll*. Toronto: Quotable Books, 2001.

Baron, Joseph L. *Treasury of Jewish Quotations*. New York: Jason Aronson, 1996.

Barrett, Jalma. *Feral Cat*. Woodbridge: Blackbirch Press, Inc., 1999.

Barteluk, Wendy D. M. *Library Displays on a Shoestring: 3-Dimensional*. Metuchen: Scarecrow Press, Inc., 1993.

Baxter, Nicola. *Tales of Terror*. New York: Barnes and Noble, 2003.

Beimler, Rosalind Rosoff, and John Greenleigh. *The Days of the Dead*. San Francisco: Collins, 1991.

Belford, Barbara. *Bram Stoker: A Biography of the Author of Dracula*. Cambridge: Da Capo Press, 1996.

Berger, John. *Ways of Seeing*. London: British Broadcasting Corporation, 1977.

Berman, Daniel M., and John T. O'Connor. *Who Owns the Sun? People, Politics, and the Struggle for a Solar Economy*. White River Junction: Chelsea Green, 1996.

Bernstein, R. B. *Thomas Jefferson*. New York: Oxford University Press, 2003.

Bethards, Betty. *The Dream Book: Symbols for Self-Understanding*. Petaluma: New Century, 1983.

Bishop, Robert. *Folk Art in American Life*. New York: Viking, 1995.

_____. *Folk Painters of America*. New York: E. P. Dutton, 1979.

Blake, Quentin. *Magic Pencil: Children's Book Illustration Today*. London: The British Library, 2002.

Bloch, Abraham P. *Day by Day in Jewish History: A Chronology and Calendar of Historic Events*. New York: Ktav, 1983.

Bonner, Kit, and Carolyn Bonner. *Great Ship Disasters*. St. Paul: MBI, 2003.

Bowen, Laurel G., and Peter J. Roberts. "Exhibits: Illegitimate Children of Academic Libraries?" *College and Research Libraries News* 54 (1993): 407–415.

Bronfeld, Stewart. *Writing for Film and Television*. Englewood Cliffs: Prentice Hall, 1981.

Bunson, Doyle. *Doyle Brunson's Super System:*

A Course in Power Poker. New York: Cardoza, 2002.

Bussagli, Mario. *5,000 Years of the Art of India.* New York: Harry N. Abrams, 1971.

Calcagno, Anne, ed. *Italy: True Stories of Life on the Road.* San Francisco: Travelers' Tales, 2001.

Carmichael, Elizabeth, and Chloe Sayer. *The Skeleton at the Feast: The Day of the Dead in Mexico.* Austin: University of Texas Press, 1991.

Carus, Louise, ed. *The Real St. Nicholas: Tales of Generosity and Hope from Around the World.* Wheaton: Quest Books, 2002.

Case, Brian, and Stan Britt. *The Illustrated Encyclopedia of Jazz.* New York: Harmony Book, 1978.

Caswell, Christopher, ed. *The Greatest Sailing Stories Ever Told.* Guilford: The Lyons Press. 2004.

Caswell, Lucy S. "Building a strategy for academic library exhibits." *College and Research Libraries News* 46 (1985): 165.

Cavendish, Richard, ed. *Man, Myth and Magic: The Illustrated Encyclopedia of Mythology, Religion and the Unknown.* 12 vols. New York: Marshall Cavendish, 1983.

Chase's Calendar of Events: 2001. Lincolnwood: Contemporary Books, 2001.

Clayton, Virginia T., Elizabeth Stillinger, Erika Doss, and Deborah Chotner. *Drawing on America's Past: Folk Art, Modernism, and the Index of American Design.* Chapel Hill: University of North Carolina Press, 2003.

Coerr, Eleanor. *Sadako and the Thousand Paper Cranes.* New York: Dell, 1977.

Cohen, Hennig, and Tristram Potter Coffin, eds. *The Folklore of American Holidays.* Detroit: Gale Research Company, 1987.

Colbert, Charles. *Seeing What I Like and Liking What I See.* Metairie: Pendaya, 1991.

Complete Garden Guide. Alexandria: Time Life Books, 2000.

Coppola, Francis Ford, and James V. Hart. *Bram Stoker's Dracula: The Film and the Legend.* New York: Newmarket Press, 1992.

Costin, Carolyn. *The Eating Disorder Sourcebook: A Comprehensive Guide to the Causes, Treatment, and Prevention of Eating Disorders.* Los Angeles: Lowell House, 1999.

Cramer, Harriet. *Great Gardens in the Shade.* New York: Friedman/Fairfax Publishers, 1997.

D-Day: The 60th Anniversary. New York: History Channel Television Network, 2004.

Day, Jean. *Blackbeard, Terror of the Seas.* Newport: Golden Age Press, 1997.

Demi. *The Legend of St. Nicholas.* New York: Margaret K. McElderry Books, 2003.

Dimont, Max I. *The Jews in America: The Roots, History, and Destiny of American Jews.* New York: Simon and Shuster, 1978.

Ditzhazy, H. E. R. "Reading for Pleasure ... It's OK!" *The Delta Kappa Gamma Society* 70.3 (2004): 54–57.

D'Orazio, Federica. *Rome, Then and Now.* San Diego: Thunder Bay Press, 2004.

Draper, James P, ed. *World Literature Criticism: 1500 to the Present.* Vol. 1. Detroit: Gale Research, 1992.

Drew, Ned, and Paul Sternberger. *By Its Cover: Modern American Book Cover Design.* New York: Princeton Architectural Press, 2005.

Dunkley, Christopher. *Tennis: Nostalgia [and] Playing the Game.* Colsterworth: Open Door, 1998.

Dupre, Judith. *Skyscrapers.* New York: Black Dog and Leventhal, 1996.

Edwards, Betty. *Drawing on the Artist Within.* New York: Simon and Schuster, 1986.

Elkins, James. *The Object Stares Back: On the Nature of Seeing.* New York: Simon and Schuster, 1996.

Ellington, Darcy, ed. *America's New Year Celebration: The Rose Parade and Rose Bowl Game.* Santa Barbara: Albion Publishing Group, 1999.

Ellis, Joseph J. *American Sphinx: The Character of Thomas Jefferson.* New York: Alfred A. Knopf, 1997.

Epstein, Dan. *20th Century Pop Culture: The 80s.* Philadelphia: Chelsea House, 2001.

Ercoli, Olivia. *Rome.* London: D.K. Publishing, 1999.

Everhart, Nancy, Claire Hartz, and William Kreiger. *Library Displays.* Metuchen: Scarecrow Press, 1989.

Evory, Ann, ed. *Contemporary Authors: A Bio-bibliographical Guide to Current Writers in Fiction, General Nonfiction, Poetry, Journalism, Drama, Motion Pictures, Television and Other Fields.* Vol. 1. Detroit: Gale Research, 1982.

Ewing, Rex A. and Doug Pratt. *Got Sun? Go Solar: Get Free Renewable Energy to Power Your Grid-Tied Home.* Masonville, CO: PixyJack Press, 2005.

Farr, Judith. *The Gardens of Emily Dickinson.* Cambridge: Harvard University Press, 2004.

Fast, Julie A. *Loving Someone with Bipolar Disorder: Understanding and Helping Your Partner*. Oakland: New Harbinger Publications, Inc., 2004.

Finn, David. *How to Visit a Museum*. New York: Harry N. Abrams, Inc., 1985.

Fisher, Angela. "Africa Adorned." *National Geographic* 166.5 (November 1984): 602.

Foster, Jack. *How to Get Ideas*. San Francisco: Berrett-Koehler, 1996.

_____. *Ideaship: How to Get Ideas Flowing in Your Workplace*. San Francisco: Berrett-Koehler, 2001.

Fox, Sandi. *Cats on Quilts*. New York: Harry N. Abrams, 2000.

Franklin, Linda Campbell. *Publicity and Display Ideas for Libraries*. Jefferson: McFarland, 1985.

Fraser, James. *The American Billboard: 100 Years*. New York: Harry N. Abrams, 1991.

Frew, Andrew W. *Frew's Daily Archive: A Calendar of Commemorations*. Jefferson: McFarland, 1984.

Frizot, Michel, ed. *A New History of Photography*. Köln: Könemann, 1998.

Froncek, Thomas. *The Horizon Book of the Arts of China*. New York: American Heritage, 1969.

Gangi, Giuseppe. *Rome: Then and Now*. Roma: G and G Editrice, 1985.

Gardner, Martin. *The Annotated Alice*. New York: W. W. Norton, 2000.

Giddings, Robert, and Erica Sheen, eds. *The Classic Novel: From Page to Screen*. Manchester: Manchester University Press, 2000.

Gillon, Steven M. *10 Days That Unexpectedly Changed America*. New York: Three Rivers Press, 2006.

Gilreath, James, and Douglas L. Wilson, eds. *Thomas Jefferson's Library*. Washington: Library of Congress, 1989.

Ginzberg, Marc. *African Forms*. Milano, Italy: Skira, 2000.

Godwin, Malcolm. *Who Are You? 101 Ways of Seeing Yourself*. New York: Penguin Putnam, 2000.

Gover, C. Jane. *The Positive Image: Women Photographers in Turn of the Century America*. Albany: State University of New York Press, 1988.

Gowdey, David. *Before the Wind*. Camden: International Marine, 1994.

Grafton, Sue, ed. *Writing Mysteries: A Handbook by the Mystery Writers of America*. Cincinnati: Writer's Digest Books, 1992.

Grobel, Lawrence. *Talking with Michener*. Jackson: University Press of Mississippi, 1999.

Groves, Margaret, ed. *Complete Guide to Gardening*. Des Moines: Meredith Corporation, 1979.

Hahner-Herzog, Iris. *African Masks from the Barbier-Mueller Collection, Geneva*. Munich: Prestel Verlag, 2004.

Haim, Alexander. *Marketing for Dummies*. Hoboken: Wiley, 2004.

Halliday, E. M. *Understanding Thomas Jefferson*. New York: Perennial, 2002.

Hamanaka, Sheila. *Peace Crane*. New York: Morrow Junior Books, 1995.

Harrist, Robert E. *The Embodied Image: Chinese Calligraphy from the John B. Elliot Collection*. Princeton: Princeton University Art Museum in association with Harry N. Abrams, 1999.

Harter, Jim, ed. *Animals: 1419 Copyright-Free Illustrations of Mammals, Birds, Fish, Insects, etc*. New York: Dover Publications, 1979.

_____. *Harter's Picture Archive for Collage and Illustration*. New York: Dover, 1978.

_____. *Men: A Pictorial Archive from Nineteenth-Century Sources*. New York: Dover, 1980.

_____. *Women: A Pictorial Archive from Nineteenth-Century Sources: 488 Copyright-Free Illustrations for Artists and Designers*. New York: Dover, 1982.

Hausman, Gerald, and Loretta Hausman. *The Mythology of Cats: Feline Legends and Lore Through the Ages*. New York: Berkley Books, 1998.

Heath, Alan. *Off the Wall: The Art of Book Display*. Littleton: Libraries Unlimited, 1987.

Heath, Robin. *Sun, Moon, and Earth*. New York: Walker and Company, 1999.

Hedgecoe, John. *John Hedgecoe: The New Manual of Photography*. New York: Dorling Kindersley, 2003.

Hellmuth, Phil. *Play Poker Like the Pros*. New York: Quill, 2003.

Henderson, Sally, and Robert Landau. *Billboard Art*. San Francisco: Chronicle Books, 1980.

Hendricks, Jennifer, and Gordon Hendricks. *Slim to None: A Journey Through the Wasteland of Anorexia Treatment*. Chicago: Contemporary Books, 2003.

Hiam, Alexander. *Marketing for Dummies*. Foster City: IDG Books Worldwide, 1997.

Hobday, Richard. *The Healing Sun: Sunlight and Health in the 21st Century*. Findhorn: Findhorn Press, 1999.

Hoffman, Margaret. *Blackbeard: A Tale of Villainy and Murder in Colonial America.* Columbia: Summerhouse Press, 1998.

Holmes, Richard. *The D-Day Experience: From the Invasion to the Liberation of Paris.* Kansas City: Carlton, 2004.

Hornbacher, Marya. *Wasted: A Memoir of Anorexia and Bulimia.* New York: Harper Perennial, 1998.

Howard, Hugh. *Thomas Jefferson: The Built Legacy of Our Third President.* New York: Rizzoli International, 2003.

Howard, Rob. *The Illustrators Bible.* New York: Watson-Guptill, 1992.

Howeler, Eric. *Skyscraper.* New York: Universe, 2003.

Hughes, William. *Beyond Dracula: Bram Stoker's Fiction and Its Cultural Context.* New York: St. Martin's Press, 2000.

Ions, Veronica. *Indian Mythology.* London: Paul Hamlyn, 1967.

Isaacson, Walter. *Benjamin Franklin: An American Life.* New York: Simon and Schuster, 2003.

Ishii, Takayuki. *One Thousand Paper Cranes.* New York: Dell Laurel-Leaf Books, 2001.

Jamison, Kay Redfield. *Touched with Fire: Manic-Depressive Illness and the Artistic Temperament.* New York: The Free Press, 1993.

Johnson, Barbara. *Humor Me: The Geranium Lady's Funny Little Book of Big Laughs.* Nashville: W Publishing Group, 2003.

Johnson, David E. *From Day to Day: A Calendar of Notable Birthdays and Events.* Lanham: Scarecrow Press, 2001.

Johnson, Lady Bird, and Carlton B. Lees. *Wildflowers Across America.* New York: Abbeville Press, 1988.

Jones, John Philip. *The Ultimate Secrets of Advertising.* Thousand Oaks: Sage, 2002.

Jones, Stephen, and Kim Newman, eds. *Horror: The 100 Best Books.* New York: Carroll and Graf, 1998.

Josephy, Alvin M., ed. *Indian Resistance: The Patriot Chiefs.* Jackdaw Series A2. New York: Grossman Publishers, 1972.

Ketchum, William C. *American Folk Art.* New York: Todtri, 1995.

Kirk, Connie Ann. *Sky Dancers.* New York: Lee and Low Books, 2004.

Kirk, Gwyn, and Margo Okazawa-Rey. *Women's Lives: Multicultural Perspectives.* New York: McGraw-Hill, 2004.

Krenz, Carol. *100 Years of Hollywood: A Century of Movie Magic.* New York: Barnes and Noble, 1999.

Kumin, Maxine. *Looking for Luck.* New York: W. W. Norton, 1992.

Lach, William. *Curious Cats in Art and Poetry.* New York: Metropolitan Museum of Art: Atheneum Books for Young Readers, 1999.

Lallemand, Henri. *Manet: A Visionary Impressionist.* New York: Todtri, 1994.

L'Amour, Louis. *Education of a Wandering Man.* New York: Bantam Books, 1989.

Land, Leslie. *The New York Times 1000 Gardening Questions and Answers.* New York: Workman, 2003.

Lasky, Kathryn. *Days of the Dead.* New York: Hyperion Books for Children, 1994.

Lawrence, Richard W. "In Search of Blackbeard: Historical and Archeological Research at Shipwreck Site 0003BUI." *Southeastern Geology* 40.1 (February 2001): 1–9.

Leatherdale, Clive. *The Origins of Dracula: The Background to Bram Stoker's Gothic Masterpiece.* Essex: Desert Island Books, 1995.

Lee, Robert E. *Blackbeard the Pirate: A Reappraisal of His Life and Times.* Winston-Salem: John F. Blair, 1974.

Lepik, Andres. *Sky Scrapers.* Munich: New York: Prestel, 2004.

Lima, Patrick. *Perennial Garden.* Buffalo: Firefly Books, 1996.

Lipman, Jean, Elizabeth V. Warren, and Robert Bishop. *Young America: A Folk Art History.* New York: Hudson Hills Press, 1986.

Lovejoy, Sharon. *Trowel and Error: Over 700 Shortcuts, Tips and Remedies for the Gardener.* New York: Workman Publishing, 2003.

Loxton, Howard. *99 Lives: Cats in History, Legend and Literature.* San Francisco: Chronicle Books, 1998.

MacGregor, Trish, and Rob MacGregor. *The Everything Dreams Book.* Avon: Adams Media, 1997.

Maksic, Sava, and Paul Meskil. *Primitive Art of New Guinea: Sepik River Basin.* Worcester: Davis, 1973.

Markoff, Marjorie. "More than innovation: A popular exhibit shows the personal side of books and information." *College and Research Libraries News* 49 (1988): 367.

McPhee, Michael B. *Sailing: A Celebration of the Sport and the World's Best Places to Enjoy It.* New York: Fodor's Sports, 1992.

Mery, Fernand. *The Life, History and Magic of the Cat.* New York: Grosset and Dunlap, 1975.

Meyer, Robert G., and Yvonne Hardaway Osborne. *Case Studies in Abnormal Behavior.* Boston: Allyn and Bacon, 1987.

Morgan, Edmund Sears. *Benjamin Franklin.* New Haven: Yale University Press, 2002.

Morreall, John. *Humor Works.* Amherst: HRD Press, 1997.

_____. *Taking Laughter Seriously.* Albany: State University of New York Press, 1983.

Nash, Eric P. *Manhattan Skyscrapers.* New York: Princeton Architectural Press, 1999.

Nash, Joyce D. *Binge No More: Your Guide to Overcoming Disordered Eating.* Oakland: New Harbinger, 1999.

Neal, Arminta. *Exhibits for the Small Museum: A Handbook.* Nashville: American Association for State and Local History, 1976.

Neill, Peter, ed. *American Sea Writing.* New York: Library of America, 2000.

Nell, Victor. *Lost in a Book: The Psychology of Reading for Pleasure.* New Haven: Yale University Press, 1988.

Nicholson, Catherine. "What Exhibits Can Do to Your Collection." *Restaurator* 13.3 (1992): 95–113.

Nourmand, Tony, and Graham Marsh, eds. *Horror Poster Art.* London: Aurum Press, 2004.

Oates, Joyce Carol, and Daniel Halpern. *The Sophisticated Cat.* New York: Dutton, 1992.

Peters, Tom, and Robert Waterman. *In Search of Excellence.* New York: Vintage, 1994.

Peterson, Bryan. *Learning to See Creatively: Design, Color and Composition in Photography.* New York: Amphoto Books, 2003.

Petras, Ross, and Kathryn Petras. *The 776 Stupidest Things Ever Said.* New York: Doubleday, 1993.

Phillips, Katherine A. *The Broken Mirror: Understanding and Treating Body Dysmorphic Disorder.* Oxford: Oxford University Press, 2005.

Photographs by Man Ray: 105 Works, 1920–1934. New York: Dover, 1979.

Pictorial Encyclopedia of Japanese Culture. Tokyo: Gakken, 1987.

Pipher, Mary. *Hunger Pains: The Modern Woman's Tragic Quest for Thinness.* New York: Ballantine Books, 1995.

Polley, Robert L. *Treasures of American Folk Arts and Crafts in Distinguished Museums and Collections.* Wisconsin: Country Beautiful Corporation, 1971.

Porter, Darwin, and Danforth Prince. *Frommer's Paris, 2001.* Foster City: IDG Books Worldwide, 2001.

Pride and Prosperity: The 80s. Alexandria: Time-Life Books, 1999.

Read, Kay Almere. *Mesoamerican Mythology: A Guide to the Gods, Heroes, Rituals and Beliefs of Mexico and Central America.* Oxford: Oxford University Press, 2000.

Reynolds, Renny. *The Art of the Party: Design Ideas for Successful Entertaining.* Salt Lake City: Gibbs Smith, 1992.

Riquelme, John Paul, ed. *Bram Stoker: Dracula: Complete Authoritative Text with Biographical, Historical, and Cultural Contexts, Critical History, and Essays from Contemporary Critical Perspectives.* Bedford: St. Martin's Press, 2002.

Robinson, Lady Stern. *The Dreamer's Dictionary.* New York: Warner Books, 1974.

Roman, Kenneth, and Jane Maas. *How to Advertise: Building Brands and Businesses in the New Marketing World.* New York: St. Martin's Press, 2003.

Rosenak, Chuck, and Jan Rosenak. *Contemporary American Folk Art: A Collector's Guide.* New York: Abbeville Press, 1996.

Sabbagh, Karl. *Skyscraper: The Making of a Building.* New York: Penguin Books, 1989.

Sacker, Ira M., and Marc A. Zimmer. *Dying to Be Thin.* New York: Warner Books, 1987.

Salisbury, Martin. *Illustrated Children's Books: Creating Pictures for Publication.* New York: Barron's, 2004.

Schaeffer, Mark. *The Library Displays Handbook.* New York: H. W. Wilson, 1991.

Schneider, Pierre. *The World of Manet.* New York: Time-Life Books, 1968.

Shepherd, Roger, ed. *Skyscraper: The Search for an American Style 1891–1941.* New York: McGraw Hill, 2003.

Shulevitz, Uri. *Writing with Pictures.* New York: Watson-Guptill, 1985.

Silverman, Herman. *Michener and Me: A Memoir.* Philadelphia: Running Press, 1999.

Simon, Seymour. *The Sun.* New York: Morrow Junior Books, 1996.

Skaggs, Gayle. *On Display.* Jefferson: McFarland, 1999.

Sklansky, David. *Theory of Poker.* Las Vegas: Two Plus Two, 1999.

Smiley, Robin H. *Books into Films: The Stuff That Dreams Are Made Of.* Santa Barbara: Capra Press, 1969.

Smith and Hawken. *The Book of Outdoor Gardening.* New York: Workman, 1996.

Stoker, Bram. *Dracula.* New York: Penguin Books, 2003.

Stone, Gregory P. *Games, Sport and Power.* New Brunswick: Transaction Books, 1972.

Tedeschi, Anne C. *Book Displays: A Library Exhibits Handbook.* Fort Atkinson: Highsmith Press, 1997.

Temko, Florence. *Origami Favorite Series: A Thousand Cranes.* Torrance: Heian International, 1998.

_____. *A Thousand Cranes.* Torrance: Heian International, 1998.

Tharp, Twyla. *The Creative Habit: Learn It and Use It for Life.* New York: Simon and Schuster, 2003.

Thompson, Sue Ellen. *Holidays, Symbols, and Customs.* Detroit: Omnigraphics, 2003.

Time-Life Books, ed. *The Camera by the Editors of Time-Life Books.* New York: Time-Life Books, 1970.

_____. *The Great Themes by the Editors of Time-Life Books.* New York: Time-Life Books, 1970.

Ting, Hsing-Wu. *Treasures of China.* Taipei: International Culture, 1970.

Torr, James D., ed. *The 1980s.* San Diego: Greenhaven Press, 2000.

Towey, Cathleen A. "Flow: The Benefits of Pleasure Reading and Tapping Readers' Interests." *Acquisitions Librarian* 25 (2001): 131–140.

Trachtenberg, Alan. *Reading American Photographs: Images as History, Mathew Brady to Walker Evans.* New York: Hill and Wang, 1989.

Vogel, Dan. *Emma Lazarus.* Boston: Twayne, 1980.

Ward, Geoffrey C., and Dayton Duncan. *The West: An Illustrated History.* Boston: Little, Brown, 1996.

_____, and Ken Burns. *Jazz: A History of America's Music.* New York: Alfred A. Knopf, 2000.

Weng, Wan-go. *Chinese Painting and Calligraphy: A Pictorial Survey.* New York: Dover, 1978.

West, John O. *Cowboy Folk Humor: Life and Laughter in the American West.* Little Rock: August House, 1990.

Williams, Robin. *The Non-Designer's Design Book: Design and Typographic Principles for the Visual Novice.* Second edition. Berkeley: Peachpit Press, 2004.

Wilson-Bareau, Juliet, and David Degener. *Manet and the Sea.* Philadelphia: Philadelphia Museum of Art, 2003.

Wingert, Paul S. *Art of the South Pacific Islands.* New York: Beechhurst Press, 1953.

Woeller, Waltraud. *The Literature of Crime and Detection.* New York: Ungar, 1998.

_____, and Bruce Cassiday. *The Literature of Crime and Detection.* New York: Ungar, 1988.

Woolmer, J. Howard, ed. *The Leonard L. Milberg Collection of Jewish American Writers.* Princeton: Princeton University Press, 2001.

Yamauchi, Yoichi "Yami." *Yami's Origami: First Steps to a Thousand Paper Cranes.* Haworth: Woodbridge, 1998.

Index